DOLCI TOSCANI

Also by Anne Bianchi

From the Tables of Tuscan Women:
Recipes and Traditions

Zuppa! Soups from the Italian Countryside

Solo Verdura: The Complete Guide to
Cooking Tuscan Vegetables

Dolci Toscani

THE BOOK OF TUSCAN DESSERTS

Anne Bianchi and Sandra Lotti

THE ECCO PRESS

THE ECCO PRESS

100 West Broad Street

Hopewell, New Jersey 08525

Published simultaneously in Canada by

Publishers Group West, Inc., Toronto, Ontario

Printed in the United States of America

Library of Congress Cataloging-in-Publication Data

Bianchi, Anne, 1948–

Dolci toscani : the book of Tuscan desserts / by Anne Bianchi &
Sandra Lotti.

p.   cm.

Includes index.

ISBN 0-88001-587-X

1. Desserts—Italy—Tuscany.   2. Cookery, Italian—Tuscan style.
3. Food habits—Italy—Tuscany.   I. Lotti, Sandra.   II. Title.

TX773.B497   1998

641.8'6'09455—dc21   98-8312

CIP

9 8 7 6 5 4 3 2 1

FIRST EDITION 1998

To Alessio

Contents

Acknowledgments

Sandra Lotti would like to thank the following for their much-appreciated help: Italo Marchetti, the fabulous pastry chef who has been my teacher for the past eight years, Anna Bianchi for her great support and generous help as I struggled through my first English-language book; Douglas Hatscheck, who helped me develop enough self esteem to face the American market; my mother, who stopped just short of putting the food in my mouth as I sat for days on end in front of a computer screen; my grandmother, Angelina, an expert chronicler of Tuscan festivals and traditions; Tom Gelinne, for his masterful recipe checking and also for verifying my conversions (a bottle of '65 Tignanello awaits you), the students of Toscana Saporita cooking school, especially Joy and Bob Heiman, Ian Koeppel, Paula Roy, Chris Walters and David Boccutti, all of whom supported me with loving e-mails and practical suggestions as to which desserts they would like to see reproduced.

A special thanks also to the American friends whose ears I bent with angst-filled writing-related chronicles: Linda, Claude, Jeff, Aline, Lucy, Barbara, David, Rian, Russ and Alicia. Thanks to my friend, Cinzia Spini, and her father Silvano, for their cultural expertise; to Marzia for her continued inspiration (*cara,* you are my eternal muse), and to Michele and Bianca Aniello from Saturnia, for sharing with me their world-famous recipes. Thanks to Rita and Sandro Elmi who supported me during my research forays to the province of Prato, to Giancarlo Cannas, who was as always ready to wade through ancient Latin texts for the original meaning of words as well as for the precise nature of historic religious celebrations; to Judy Capodanno, my wonderful editor, Carol Munson, and all the people at The Ecco Press, especially Dan Halpern, for reaching out across the ocean and giving me this opportunity to speak to Americans. And finally, thanks to all the men and women who generously shared with me their traditional recipes.

Anne Bianchi would like to add a special note of thanks to the staff of her local Chinese restaurant, who nourished her with nutritious food and speedy delivery in the last frenzied weeks associated with the writing of this book.

Introduction

Anyone familiar with my previous books will note that there is always an acknowledgment credit for "Sandra Lotti," or simply "Sandra." *"Grazie bellezza, che avrei fatto senza di te?"* I say of her and to her in *From the Tables of Tuscan Women.* ("Thank you beautiful one, what would I have done without you?") The dedication in *Zuppa!* was "To Sandra, colleague and friend, *grazie.*" In *Solo Verdura,* I was both more effusive and more specific: "To Sandra Lotti, writer-researcher extraordinaire and one of only two people I know who has, at her fingertips, the answers to every conceivable question."

At times, it seems as though I've spent a good part of the past seven years thanking this amazing woman, who also happens to be my cousin. At first, she provided the technical support I needed to get my books done: setting up the necessary contacts, foraging for traditional recipes, arranging for transportation and communications capability, helping with recipe testing and conversion, and if necessary, actually ferrying me from place to place.

Later, she began helping with recipe development. By then, she had become a cookbook author in her own right, one known throughout Italy for her chatty manner, accessible recipes and scrupulous research. By then, she and I had also opened the Toscana Saporita Cooking School, located about a mile between our respective homes in the province of Lucca; students who came to the school (mainly American and Canadians) were always saddened by the knowledge that her books had no English-language translation.

In 1997, I began pressing her to write a book for the American audience. "Make it a dessert book," I told her. "Our students already think of you as the cooking school's dessert maven—why not broaden your audience?"

She always demurred, citing language problems (Sandra is one hair's breath away from English mastery) and what she refers to as "the great cultural divide" that, in her mind, would hamper her ability to know which recipes work internationally and which ingredients are readily available to

American cooks. The answer, obviously, lay in a collaboration between us, but there simply was never enough time.

Two years ago, I finally offered to do for her what she'd long done for me—bridge the gap between the two countries. "I'll check the conversions and help with the testing," I told her—an easy promise to make since we spend an endless number of hours side by side cooking at our school. "I'll also fix any language problems that come up and present your stories in a way that makes sense to Americans."

The agreement served to reverse our roles. Now, she was the chief and I was the grunt, and the arrangement worked just as wonderfully in that particular manifestation as it had always worked the other way around.

You, the readers, have been with me through three books now, which is why I feel completely comfortable and inordinately proud to introduce you to this luminous Tuscan jewel. What follows are Sandra's stories and Sandra's recipes, many developed at our cooking school and tested by our students, some tweaked by me (see Chapter 10, Low-Fat Desserts). I have no doubt that you will fall completely in love with her. Just, please, don't forget about me, *d'accordo*?

Anne Bianchi
New York City

DOLCI TOSCANI

CHAPTER ONE

Ingredients and How to Use Them

Are You Ready to Start?

Before you start baking, you should read this chapter to become acquainted with your ingredients and how to use them. A few tips before you begin:

- Read over the entire recipe to make sure you have the proper ingredients.
- Bring to room temperature whatever ingredients are required by the recipe: Frozen butter will not cream and icy cold milk added to a warm batter will harden the blended butter.
- Sift all the dry ingredients, and chop, grate and otherwise prepare anything requiring advance attention.
- Check to make sure you have all the tools and pans needed.
- Preheat the oven 15 minutes before using it.
- Breathe deeply and whenever you feel ready, start!

Recipe Guidelines

There are certain assumptions underlying the recipes in this book that are important to note before starting:

- All eggs are Grade A large.
- Butter is unsalted unless stated.
- All measurements are level.
- Flour is unsifted unless specified; sifted flour is sifted before measuring.
- Pre-sifted flour should also be sifted if specified by the recipe—shipping, handling and sitting on the shelf causes it to settle.
- Dry ingredients are measured without tapping or shaking the measuring instrument.
- Confectioner's sugar is always sifted; granulated is not.

- Nuts, herbs and zest are chopped or grated before measuring.
- Milk is homogenized whole milk unless otherwise stated.
- Skillets and baking pans are measured across the top, not the bottom.
- Recipe times are calculated from starting time to completion except where separate refrigeration or rising times are noted.
- Oil for frying is heated to 375°F. In lieu of using a thermometer, immerse a small cube of bread in the oil. If the oil is hot enough to fry, the bread will sizzle around the edges and turn golden within 5 seconds.
- Juice is fresh squeezed. Commercially squeezed juice can be substituted.

Ingredients

FLOURS

Wheat Flour

Wheat flour comes in two basic types, hard and soft, both containing less than 15 percent moisture. High in protein, hard flour is perfect for bread baking because, when mixed with liquids, the proteins form gluten, whose strength and flexibility are necessary for rising. Soft wheat, which is low in protein but high in starch, gives cakes and baked goods a tender, flaky texture.

Since flour loses moisture the longer it is stored, the flour you use today may have either more or less moisture than yesterday. Also, different brands have different moisture levels of moisture as specified on the package, and flour picks up additional moisture if used on humid days. For these reasons, you must sometimes make adjustments in the amount of flour used in order to keep the dry-to-liquid ratio in proper balance. If the flour has more than an average amount of moisture or the day on which you use it is excessively humid, add more flour. If it is on the dry side or older than four months, use less flour.

Flour contains about 10 to 15 percent vitamins, 65 to 73 percent starch, mineral salts and various proteins including gluten, which is activated by both adding liquids and kneading. Breads are made with high-gluten flour because they require a strong elastic structure to tolerate the gases given off by the expanding yeast. Kneading makes that structure even more elastic at the same time as it helps incorporate air and, hence, creates additional lift. Cakes on the other hand, require only the small amount of gluten necessary to support the carbon dioxide given off by the baking powder or soda.

Besides "hard" and "soft," flours are further broken down according to the type of processing they undergo:

Bread Flour
Bread flour (sometimes called baker's flour) is milled from hard wheat and has a very high gluten content (about 13 to 14 percent).

All-Purpose Flour
All-purpose flour is a mix of hard and soft flours that have been blended to create a medium strength product with about 12 percent gluten. Used on their own, hard and soft flours are each ideal for specific tasks. Hard flour is ideal for bread baking because of its high gluten content which makes bread rise. Soft flour works perfectly for baked goods which do not require gluten-rising. But, when you use the blend of hard and soft flours that make up "all-purpose," your bread doesn't really get enough gluten; when you use it for pastries, the texture is too tough because of the gluten. Although you can substitute unbleached all-purpose flour for the pastry or bread flour called for in the following recipes, you are better off using pastry (sometimes called cake) flour for pastries and bread (sometimes called baker's) flour for bread.

Bleached All-Purpose Flour
Bleached all-purpose flour has been bleached with chemicals and is much whiter than the pale wheat color of its unbleached counterpart. There is no discernible difference between bleached and unbleached when it comes to performance.

Cake Flour
Cake flour (often referred to as pastry flour) is a very finely ground flour milled from soft wheat with about six to 10 percent gluten.

Self-Rising Flour
Self-rising flour is all-purpose flour with baking powder and salt already added. I do not recommend this product since bakers should be in control of the amounts of each ingredient as determined by individual

recipes. Also, baking powder loses its strength after about four or five months, and there is no way of knowing how long self-rising flour has been sitting on the shelf.

LEAVENING AGENTS

Yeast

Yeast is one of this planet's most ubiquitous living organisms, and is considerably older than almost any other form of life. History teaches us that it was discovered accidentally by ancient Egyptians who, one day, left a piece of bread dough in a warm humid place, and, before long, yeasts from the air mixed with natural yeasts in the dough and began doing what yeasts routinely do: growing and multiplying. The enzymes in the flour converted starch into sugar—yeast's favorite food—and the dough began miraculously to rise.

Once the strange thing was cooked, the Egyptians realized how much better it tasted than the common flat bread they were used to, and, from that day on, they made beautifully puffy breads. Their discovery eventually spread to the Greeks and Etruscans and consequentially to the Romans, who went the Egyptians one step further by applying the magic powers of yeast to the making of beer.

Yeast is made up of microscopic one-cell fungi that multiply rapidly if given sugar or starch in a moist environment. The ideal temperature for growing yeast is 110 to 115 degrees Fahrenheit, although for bread purposes, 70 to 95 degrees Fahrenheit yields the best results. When the yeast feeds on the sugar (or starch that the yeast enzyme converts to sugar) a chemical reaction takes place: the sugar ferments and is converted into alcohol and carbon dioxide. As with other leavening agents (baking powder, baking soda), the carbon dioxide joins with the trapped expanding air or steam and leavens the food or causes it to rise.

Modern-day Tuscan bakers always make their own yeast, which they call *levame* or *seme* (seed). A natural by-product resulting from the acidification of a warm water and flour mixture, the yeast sits for two or three days before being added to sweet breads such as panettone and *buccelloto* as well as everyday bread and focaccia mixtures.

My baker in Tuscany, Italo Marchetti, inherited his yeast from his father and last year celebrated its 65th birthday. Twenty kilometers away, in Santa Anna, Bianca Pierini, an extraordinary baker who makes daily batches of focaccia and potato bread, uses yeast that is over 200 years old. According to Italo, bread and pastries made with natural yeast have a sturdier texture and more complex flavor than those made with commercial yeast.

The next best leavening agent after homemade sour dough starter is called, appropriately, "fresh yeast" and comes in one-inch cubes, which can be found in the dairy section of supermarkets. In Tuscany, fresh yeast is simply called *lievito di birra* (beer yeast), because, in the old days, people who needed yeast for baking simply rubbed their hands along the sides of old beer barrels or scraped it off beer sediment.

Fresh yeast comes in two-thirds-ounce cubes, contains 70 percent moisture (as opposed to 8 percent for dry yeast) and must be stored in the refrigerator where it will last for up to two weeks. Moist to the point of being somewhat sticky, fresh (or compressed) yeast is ivory-colored and its flavor vaguely resembles that of beer. It is the fastest acting of the commercial varieties and bubbles almost immediately upon being dissolved in a mixture of ½ cup warm water and 1 tablespoon flour. In fact, if nothing happens after two or three minutes, the yeast is dead; discard it and begin again. Also discard it if the yeast is old, in which case it has turned brown around the edges. One standard cake of fresh yeast has the leavening power of one packet of active dry yeast (about one tablespoon).

A good Tuscan suggestion when baking with fresh yeast is *avere le mani in pasta* (have your hands in the dough instead of using forks or spoons or mixing tools). The warmth of your hands will activate the yeast immediately and, furthermore, you will interact with your ingredients on a more visceral level and thus have more fun.

To otherwise activate a cake of fresh yeast, add one cup warm water and one tablespoon of flour (the flour is the food which kick-starts the eating process—aka multiplication). After the dough has been formed and kneaded, place it in a warm location so that the yeast can begin growing and rising. The best temperatures are between 70 and 85 degrees Fahrenheit (average home temperatures); yeast goes into hibernation at 45 degrees Fahrenheit on one end and 100 degrees Fahrenheit on the other although it will return to activity upon returning to its preferred climate. At 130 degrees Fahrenheit it dies.

Some people have been known to try to speed the process of rising by adding greater quantities of yeast. This is a big mistake. The dough develops an overly acidic flavor and an extremely porous texture because quickly multiplying yeast organisms struggle for a rapidly diminishing source of food. Time is very important when working with fresh yeast. Slow rising produces better flavor and texture, and multiple risings produce more even consistency.

Salt kills yeast; never use salted warm water to dissolve it. If the weather is extremely hot, however, a very small quantity of salt will help stop overly rapid fermentation. But whether used for flavor or to slow fermentation, salt should be added only after the dough ball has formed.

In addition to fresh, or compressed varieties, commercial yeast is also available in instant, active dry and rapid-rise. Instant yeast—not to be confused with rapid-rise yeast—is a recent French discovery that can be used without first being dissolved in water (proofing). It has a great tolerance to variations in temperatures and rises even when refrigerated.

Active-dry yeast is a dormant yeast that can be activated by adding warm or lukewarm liquids. It is available in small sealed packets, which can be found in the dairy section of supermarkets. The most popular brands are Fleishmann's and Red Star. Look for freshness dates on the package and be sure the yeast has not passed the expiration date. If too old, it will probably be dead, in which case no foam will form on top after the yeast has been dissolved in warm water. Active dry yeast can also be purchased in bulk in health food stores.

Rapid-rise yeast is a dream-come-true for frenetic bakers because it cuts in half the amount of time required for dough to rise. My suggestion is, however, to choose the old method: a slow rise, which gives the best results.

Baking Powder

Baking powder is another type of leavening agent, this one relies on a mixture of acid (cream of tartar) and alkaline (baking soda or ammonium bicarbonate), which react with each other in the presence of moisture to create carbon-dioxide bubbles for rising. There are three basic types of baking powder: single acting, slow acting and double acting. Single acting is the fastest of the three and releases carbon dioxide immediately upon contact with liquid. Batters mixed with single acting must be baked immediately. Slow acting releases very little carbon dioxide unless placed in the oven, so batters can be held for a very long time. Many commercial bakeries choose slow acting. The third type is double acting, which means it produces two separate reactions: The first occurs when the batter is initially mixed, and the baking powder releases a small amount of gas to start the rising. The second occurs when the batter comes in contact with oven heat, and rising reaches its climax. Double acting is most commonly used in home kitchens.

To use baking powder effectively, sift before using and then blend well with the rest of the ingredients. Failure on either score will result in a cake that rises unevenly and has a slightly acidic flavor in places where the powder has concentrated. To check whether baking powder is active, add one teaspoon to one-third cup hot water. If it bubbles vigorously, go ahead and use it.

What if you realize you are out of baking powder? Fear not. For every cup of flour called for in the recipe, add two teaspoons of cream of tartar, one-half teaspoon salt and one teaspoon of bicarbonate of soda (baking soda). Another way to calculate the amount is to use one-half teaspoon cream of tartar and one-quarter teaspoon baking soda for every one teaspoon baking powder called for in the recipe. This homemade mixture stores poorly, however, and should be made fresh.

Italian baking powder (*lievito in polvere*) is sold under two labels: Bertolini or Pane degli Angeli. Both have *vanillin* (vanilla) added to weaken the acidic flavor.

Baking Soda

Baking soda (bicarbonate of soda) is the alkaline component of baking powder and often used in its place, especially when working with recipes involving acidified (sour) milk or yogurt or acidic sweeteners, such as molasses or honey. The reaction of the soda with the acids in the recipe is essentially the same as when the two ingredients in baking powder come into contact with moisture. Recipes with acidic ingredients often call for both baking powder (which serves as the main leavening agent) and baking soda (which is required to neutralize the acidity). In addition to its use as a leavening agent, baking soda (because it is an alkali) also darkens the color of chocolate or cocoa.

EGGS

Whole Eggs, Egg Yolks and Egg Whites

Tuscans have a saying that serves to underscore the importance of eggs in the culture at large, but most importantly, in baking: *"Meglio un uovo oggi che una gallina domani"* ("Better an egg today than a hen tomorrow").

Most Tuscan desserts use eggs, both for flavor and volume. When confronted with the American aversion to the fat and cholesterol content of eggs, Tuscans merely shrug and declare that an occasional slice of cake never killed anyone. In fact, they maintain, egg yolks are a good source of vitamins (A; B_1; B_2; B_{12}; B_6; D), calcium, potassium and iron. More than their nutritive value, however, eggs contribute to the structure, flavor and color of baked goods as well as serving as yet another leavening agent.

In the United States, egg size is standardized by federal regulation. All the recipes in this book use large eggs, which weigh about two ounces each. Extra large eggs weigh about two and one-quarter ounces, mediums about one and three-quarter ounces and smalls about one and one-half ounces, although smalls are rarely sold anymore. To halve an egg, break it into a cup, beat with a fork and measure off half—about one and one-half tablespoons.

When cooking with eggs, avoid high temperatures and long cooking times because they result in the separation of egg solids and egg liquid—in other words, curdling. Most recipes in this book that call for cooking eggs in liquid form use a double boiler, which prevents direct contact with heat. When using a double boiler (or a pan suspended over hot water), do not allow the water to touch the bottom of the boiler, or pan.

Only use the freshest eggs. How can you determine when an egg is fresh or beyond the pale? Here are a few Tuscan tips:

- A fresh egg should be heavy and the color of the shell should be uniform.
- Fresh eggs sink to the bottom when immersed in a bowl of water. Eggs that are five to seven days old will sometimes stand in a vertical position. Older eggs will float horizontally; these should be discarded.
- The freshness of an egg can also be determined by shaking it (a fresh egg will not "thump") or viewing it against the light of a candle or light bulb (the yolk should be firmly centered; the white, clear and the air sac, small).
- Never use an egg with a cracked shell or a shiny surface. Egg shells are porous and should be stored in the refrigerator away from foods with strong odors, such as onions or fish. Alternately, the best way to create truffled eggs is by nestling a truffle in a bowl of fresh eggs.

- Eggs should be stored with the "point" toward the bottom of the container or refrigerator compartment. The ideal storage temperature is 35 to 37 degrees Fahrenheit.
- For best baking results, use eggs that have first been returned to room temperature by placing whole in a bowl of very warm water for 10 to 15 minutes.
- Leftover whites can be frozen in a sealed container. Thaw before using. Whites can also be refrigerated in a sealed container for up to four days.
- Leftover yolks can be placed in a container, covered with one-half inch water and refrigerated for two or three days. To freeze, they must first be stabilized, or they will become dense and hard to mix after thawing. To stabilize, sprinkle with salt (one-quarter teaspoon per three yolks) or sugar (one-half teaspoon per three yolks) depending on the recipe they will eventually be used for and then freeze in a sealed container (be sure to label whether you used salt or sugar).

Separating eggs

There are several ways to separate eggs but all work best when the eggs are cold which reduces the chance of breaking the yolk. The easiest method of all is, of course, to use a commercial egg separator. Of the two manual methods, the least messy is to gently break the egg in half and carefully pass the yolk from shell to shell like a circus juggler, letting the white dribble into a bowl. Be sure to scrape the last bit of white from the inside of the halves; more than 10 percent of the white can be lost if not done.

If you are not squeamish about having raw eggs in your hands, gently break the egg in half and pour it into the palm of your hand. By slightly separating your fingers, the white will ooze into a bowl as the yolk continues to sit comfortably in your palm.

Beating egg whites

Beaten egg whites incorporate air into certain preparations, such as sponge cakes and meringues, and thus give the light, fluffy consistency for which they are known and loved. Beat the whites just before using, however, so they do not deflate.

Egg whites can be beaten with a portable beater, a heavy-duty electric mixer or a large whisk, but, in all cases, they should be absolutely and pristinely white; even a speck of yolk will prevent the formation of stiff peaks. Bowls should be pristinely clean; the tiniest dot of fat will cut volume, so be sure utensils aren't greasy.

To beat by hand, place the whites in a large bowl (copper, glass or stainless but not aluminum because it can discolor the whites) with salt, which helps them foam. Too much salt cuts volume, however, so stick to one-quarter teaspoon salt for one cup of egg whites.

The mixing bowl should be large enough to accommodate the expansion of the whites; beaten egg whites can grow to eight times their original volume. Hold the bowl in the crook of your arm or place it on a wet towel to keep it from moving around as you beat the eggs. Always start beating slowly, with a clockwise motion, and increase the speed as the whites start foaming. At this point, add one-eighth teaspoon cream of tartar for each egg white. Cream of tartar is a stabilizing agent that helps keep egg whites firm. It is almost impossible to beat egg whites uniformly so although the entire mass won't be beaten stiff, none of it will be overbeaten to the "dry" stage. Cream of tartar also helps keep the beaten mass soft, which helps with the folding.

Continue to beat until the peaks become a mass of large and small bubbles. A little more beating, and the whites will begin to hold their shape but still feel wet and fragile and slide around in the bowl. At this point, watch closely to avoid overbeating.

Continue to beat until the peaks are snowy, firm and do not slide when the bowl is tilted. The original volume will have increased five or six times and the whisk can be lifted in and out easily. If the peaks feel dry and the mixture starts to separate into clumps, you have gone too far and the whites will deflate when other ingredients are folded in. Don't despair: simply add another unbeaten white to the bowl and begin again.

When using a hand or heavy-duty mixer, start on slow and, after about a minute when the whites are foamy and covered with bubbles, add the cream of tartar, increase to fast and beat until the peaks are stiff but moist.

Egg safety
While salmonella-free eggs can now be found in more and more markets, an alternative method for assuring safety is to pasteurize your eggs by breaking them into a double boiler with milk (two teaspoons milk for every two eggs) and cooking over hot water, stirring gently, until the tem-

perature of the egg mixture reaches 160 degrees Fahrenheit. While this temperature would be too high for eggs on their own (eggs curdle at between 144 and 150 degrees Fahrenheit), eggs mixed with other ingredients, especially fats, can be cooked to higher temperatures without worry.

Another way to insure safety when dealing with eggs is to look for pasteurized, liquid eggs, which are still very hard to find but becoming less so with time. Pasteurized eggs are available whole and separated into yolks and whites.

FATS

Butter

Butter provides flavor and texture and is all but irreplaceable in that no other fat used for baking performs in quite the same way. It gives baked goods a fluffy, moist texture and superb flavor. Oil, on the other hand, is largely useless in that it collects instead of diffusing throughout the dough, causing baked goods to be too grainy.

Despite the large use of salted butter in the home kitchen, good pastry chefs almost always prefer unsalted varieties because the flavor is neutral, allowing them to add as much salt as is called for in the recipe. When in Tuscany, I either use a locally made butter or make it myself; in the States I use Plugrá because of its high butterfat content (82 percent as opposed to 80 percent for most commercial butters) and low moisture. Increasingly found in gourmet and specialty food stores, Plugrá is ideal for making puff pastry and gives a fresh butter flavor and flaky texture. To make your own butter, simply place cold heavy cream in a food processor, process until the liquid separates from the fat and remove the soft butter using a slotted spoon.

Some recipes require butter that has been softened to room temperature; others, butter that is ice cold. The difference has to do with whether the butter is to be absorbed by the starch, as in a cake batter, or layered on top of it, as in flaky pie crusts. As a rule, the harder and colder the butter, the less it is absorbed.

Refrigerated butter will keep for up to two weeks if placed in sealed containers which prevent the absorption of other flavors and odors. Butter can also be frozen, in which case it should be used within two days of thawing to preserve maximum flavor.

In general, butter comes in sticks weighing four ounces each, four to a one-pound package. One four-ounce stick equals eight tablespoons or one-half cup.

Clarified butter has had the milk solids removed so it can be heated to a higher temperature (the smoking point of common butter is from 260 to 265 degrees Fahrenheit). To clarify butter, cut into small chunks and slowly bring to a boil, skimming the froth from the surface at intervals. As the evaporating milk solids pop and crackle up from the surface, the pure butter that remains will look increasingly clear. Strain it through cheesecloth into a clean container. One and a quarter pounds of raw butter will make one pound clarified butter.

Lard

Lard (pork fatback) is another type of fat commonly used by Tuscans in everything from soups to stews to sauces. In olden days, when few people could afford butter, it was also widely used in baking, especially in the winter after the killing of the pigs.

I sometimes use it still, albeit in small quantities, to give a flaky texture to pie crusts and cookies. In fact, my old friend Roberto Martinelli, a butcher, brings me some every year right before Christmas because he knows I like to use it when I make *Befanini* (Epiphany Cookies) or *Buccellato con le mele* (Christmas Apple Cake).

MILK

Milk and Milk Products

Milk comes in many forms, depending on method of processing and butterfat content. Pasteurizing (required by Federal law for all milks crossing state lines) is a carefully controlled heating process that effectively halts many milk borne diseases. Homogenizing blends the fat, or cream with the milk or milk liquids. Whole milk has approximately four percent butterfat milk after homogenization. Skim milk is milk from which the fat has been removed. Low-fat milk is skim milk with one or two percent of the fat remaining. Buttermilk is what remains after milk has been churned into butter. Cultured buttermilk is milk treated with an acidic bacterial culture. Evaporated milk is whole milk with most of the water removed. Sweetened condensed milk is made by evaporating half the water from whole milk, sweetening it with cane or corn sugar, and then heating, cooling and canning it.

Creams

Creams are available in three main types, and butterfat content determines which type to use for any recipe. Heavy cream, also called heavy whipping cream, is the clotted layer that rises to the top of unhomogenized milk; its butterfat content ranges from 36 to 40 percent. Light whipping cream has from 30 to 34 percent butterfat and will whip, but not well and not for very long. Used mainly in coffees or hot chocolates, light cream has about 20 percent butterfat and half-and-half about 11 percent. Both are inappropriate for whipping.

Sour cream is processed by means of specifically added lactic cultures and is useful in both cutting the development of gluten and helping to produce short or flaky baked goods and tender cakes.

To whip heavy cream, chill both whisk and bowl. As with egg whites, start whipping slowly and increase the speed as thickening begins.

Mascarpone

Mascarpone is an ultrarich (86 percent butterfat) double-cream cow's milk cheese native to Northern Italy. Its buttery flavor and binding ability make it a perfect choice for pasta sauces, cakes and custards. Mascarpone is generally available in gourmet and cheese shops; if you cannot find it, substitute a mix of half cream cheese and half ricotta, or one-quarter crème fraîche mixed with three-quarters whipped cream.

SWEETENERS

Sugars

Sarkara means sugar in Sanskrit—an etymological fact that dates the process of boiling sugar cane sap to produce sugar. That beets could produce the same kind of sweetener—and at a much cheaper price—was discovered in the eighteenth century by a German chemist. His findings thrilled the frugal Napoleon whose empire consumed more sugar than the West Indian market could supply—at any price.

In baking, the uses of sugar range from sweetening the taste to tenderizing and aerating the dough to adding texture to giving color to preserving shelf life to (when used in small quantities) hastening the growth of yeast.

There are many types of sugar, each with its own advantages and dis-advantages:

White Sugar

White sugar comes in regular granulated and superfine varieties. The size of the crystals directly effect the texture and workability of doughs and batters. Granulated works best when the sugar is slated to be creamed or whipped with a fat. The sharp edges of the crystals rip into the fat and create air pockets that lift the volume of the baked good. Superfine is useful in situations where the sugar needs to dissolve quickly, as in drinks or un-baked meringues.

Confectioners' Sugar

Confectioners' sugar is powdered granulated sugar with a small amount of cornstarch added to prevent caking. It comes in 4, 6 and 10X, 10X being the finest, and should always be either cooked or mixed with flavorings to disguise the taste of the cornstarch. Because it dissolves almost instantly, it is most often used in icings and meringues (in equal combination with granulated or superfine, the mixture produces a light, fluffy texture) and should always be sifted before using. Confectioners' sugar should never be substituted for granulated.

Brown Sugars

Brown sugar, including light brown and dark brown varieties, is white sugar that has been sprayed with molasses. The darker the sugar, the greater the amount of molasses that has been used.

Because it contains molasses, brown sugar is moister than white and tends to clump with time, often turning into a rock hard ball. To store, place in a tightly sealed glass jar or plastic bag in a cool, dry location. If it still clumps, sprinkle with a few drops of water and return to its sealed container.

Sugar Syrups

Sugar syrups are used for poaching fruit, making icings and fudges, blending with creams, or, in caramelized form, forming threads, cages or candy. When sugar is dissolved in water, it forms a solution with a water to sugar ratio that varies according to the temperature of the water. Cold water holds twice its weight of sugar; warm water, almost twice as much as cold. The greater the heat, the greater the amount of sugar that can be dissolved.

To make a sugar syrup, heat one or more cups of sugar in a heavy pan over very low heat with a few tablespoons water. Stir constantly with a wooden spoon (metal spoons will absorb heat and cool the sugar) for eight to 10 minutes or until the sugar melts and begins to turn color.

Sugar syrups form in different stages, each stage with its own particular temperature, color, consistency and texture. There are two ways to determine the appropriate stage for a specific recipe: use a candy thermometer or use the finger pinching method. The finger pinching method can strike fear into the heart of a novice in that it involves plunging your fingers into boiling syrup. But done correctly, it serves as a very useful method for ascertaining the consistency of the sugar.

Simply dip your thumb and index finger simultaneously into a cup of ice water and then immediately into and out of the syrup. Rub the two fingers together until the syrup coating crystallizes. Check the following table to determine the stage of the crystals.

Stages of Sugar Cooking

STAGE	DESCRIPTION	TEMP. (°F)	USES
Thin thread	When you pull your fingers apart, a thin thread forms.	215 to 219	soaking cake layers
Thread	When you pull your fingers apart, the thread is similar to the above stage but thicker and more solid.	230 to 234	some types of soft candy
Soft ball	The coating on your fingers crystallizes into a soft, gummy mass.	235 to 240	fudge and some buttercreams
Firm ball	The syrup crystallizes into a firm but flexible mass.	244 to 248	caramels, nougats and toffees
Hard ball	The syrup forms a hard ball between your fingers.	250 to 266	many types of hard candy

Soft crack	The syrup is pale yellow and forms a slightly pliable but firm string.	270 to 290	many candies
Hard crack	The syrup is pale amber and forms a completely brittle string.	295 to 310	nut brittles and glazed fruits
Caramel	The color changes quickly from amber to brown. If not watched, it can quickly blacken and burn.	320 to 355	caramel cages and strings

Honey

Honey was known in Greek mythology as "ambrosia" and referred to as "the food of the Gods." Prized by ancient cultures as both a sweetener and a medical remedy, it was also thought to have religious powers. Both Greeks and Egyptians buried their beloved with honeyed breads that were to be used as offerings to the gods met in the afterlife.

Because honey is made from flower pollen borne on the bodies of bees, its flavor and texture is determined by the type of flower visited by the bees. The flavor can be what is called "single blend," which means it is the product of one or more hives feeding on the same flowers, or "blended," which means the hives fed in dispersed areas. In Tuscany, honey varieties range from chestnut to acacia, to thousand flowers and includes honeys made from the flowers of the various herbs: thyme, sage, and rosemary. Clover honey is the most common American variety; orange blossom is also easy to find.

Besides sweetness, honey adds moistness and chewiness to baked goods. Although its ability to sweeten is roughly equal to that of sugar, the two cannot be used interchangeably because they work in different ways. Honey caramelizes quickly at lower temperatures than sugar and imparts a distinct flavor; its degree of acidity varies; hence, it is always used in conjunction with baking soda which acts as a neutralizer.

Honey should be stored in a cool, dry and dark place. Its color and flavor changes if kept too long as does its texture which tends to become hard and crystallized. To soften honey that has crystallized, place the jar in a saucepan filled with water and heat until melted.

FLAVORINGS

Extracts, Herbs and Other Flavorings

While all aspects of food preparation require a certain level of creativity, desserts bring out the consummate artistry in a cook. A high degree of experimentation is involved in determining shape, size, technique and, of course, ingredients. And no category of ingredients offers more room for personal expression than extracts, herbs and other flavorings. The various combinations can completely alter a dessert's flavor from nutty to lemony, from rum soaked to vanilla infused.

In Tuscany, when somebody gives us a new recipe, we add a little something just to be able to say *"Come la mia, non ce n'e!"* ("There is not another one anywhere like mine!") Similarly, when we give recipes, we are sly enough to never reveal that particular ingredient that makes a good cake sublime. Of course, I will break that rule here. You are, after all, not Tuscans!

The following extracts, herbs and other flavorings are commonly used in Tuscan desserts:

Vanilla

Vanilla is probably the world's most popular flavoring. Its name derives from the Spanish *vainilla,* a diminutive of *vaina,* meaning "pod." The plant, *Vanilla planifolia fragrans,* belongs to the Orchidaceae family, which grows mainly in Central America, the Seychelles, Tahiti and other tropical regions. Native to Mexico, the vanilla plant has pale yellow flowers, which bloom one at a time for one day each over a two-month period. After the flowers, come long, yellow-green pods that mature in about nine months and are picked unripe. From history, we learn that the Aztec king, Montezuma, loved to drink chocolate blended with *tlilxochitl* (the Aztec name for vanilla) and powdered chilies and that vanilla (along with the cocoa bean) was introduced to Europe by Hernando Cortez in the sixteenth century.

Vanilla's incomparable flavor and aroma is due to vanillin, a chemical that is bound to a sugar molecule and only released through curing, the original process for which was developed by the Aztecs. When freshly picked, the odorless green beans, or pods, look like common string beans. But the appearance changes during processing, which goes like this: The pods are boiled for several minutes in water, then the softened pods are piled into wooden boxes and steamed in intervals over several days. It is during this process, called fermentation, that the vanillin separates in the form of a white crystalline compound that settles on the pod's dark brown surface like a frosting. The actual vanillin content in the seeds is very small, however—only about two or three percent of their weight.

The pods are then sun-dried for six months, and finally can be graded for quality, length and aroma, and tied into bundles; then sealed in containers to keep their fragrance intact. Vanilla usually comes in two versions:

- Vanilla extract: Obtained from crushed vanilla beans macerated in alcohol for several weeks, a few drops of this highly concentrated extract will impart a noticeably distinct flavor.
- Vanilla beans, or pods: Placed in airtight jars filled with sugar, vanilla beans will scent and flavor the sugar; they can also be infused in milk or cream and then washed, dried and reused. Vanilla beans should be stored in an airtight container to avoid loss of aroma and flavor.

Lemons

Lemons are second only to vanilla as Tuscany's favorite flavoring. In many recipes, the two are added together for what I would describe as a match made in heaven! Recipes using lemon almost always stipulate "zest" instead of "peel." Zest (procured using a specialized hand-held tool that strips the rind into thin wisps) is purely the yellow part of the lemon—the outside rind which contains all the essential oils—as opposed to peel, which comes with some of the bitter white part attached. For baking, I prefer grating the rind directly into the mixture because a grate is finer than the strips produced by zesting and does not interfere with the smooth texture of a batter or sauce. Another way to use grated zest is to add it to an egg batter to weaken the strong flavor of the eggs. A julienne of zest makes a bright garnish for desserts.

Orange grate or zest can be substituted for lemon in many recipes (*Castagnaccio* or *Schiacciata fiorentina*, for example). Orange liqueur such as Cointreau or Grand Marnier, can be added to further enhance the citrus flavor.

Only organic lemons and oranges should be used for zest; chemicals sprayed on citrus concentrate in the rind and have been known to cause severe allergic reactions.

Mint and Spearmint

Mint and spearmint (*Mentha spicata*) are perennial wild herbs native to southern Europe and the Mediterranean area. Peppermint belongs to the same family, although it is mainly a cross between various wild species.

In Greek mythology, Menthe was a nymph of the underworld who was turned into a scented plant by the jealous Persephone as soon as he found out that Hades, king of the dead, had fallen in love with her. From that day on, the inconsolable Hades could only smell the pungent, inebriating scent of his ill-fated lover.

The Greek father of medicine, Hippocrates (460–337 B.C.) frequently prescribed mint as a digestive; in fact, dried mint is nowadays largely used to make tea. It was previously thought that mint's sweetish-sharp flavor overpowered most foods, but dessert chefs have apparently now changed their minds and begun pairing it with fresh fruits, chocolates and sorbets.

Bay, Laurel or Sweet Laurel

Bay, Laurel or Sweet Laurel *(Lauraceae)* is native to the Mediterranean region and is used by Tuscans as border trees around fields and cemeteries. Immortalized by poets, such as Giosue Carducci, bays have a history dating back to the ancient Greeks and Romans who wove them into crowns, which were worn by victorious warriors or athletes.

Tuscan bakers use bay leaves primarily when boiling chestnuts; their pungent aroma penetrates the skins and imparts a distinct flavor. Their strong, beautifully veined surface also works very well when making chocolate leaves (see page 28).

Vin Santo

Vin Santo (Holy Wine), also called *vino passito* or dried wine, is an aged marsala-like dessert wine used as a flavoring in a wide range of cookies and cakes. As a liqueur, it is traditionally paired with *cantucci*, hard almond biscotti made throughout Tuscany. Several Italian wines are called

Vin Santo, but only Tuscan *Vin Santos* have the prestigious *denominazione origine controllata* (DOC), which means that the grapes and the processing methodology have been certified to be of the finest caliber.

Generally made with white Malvasia or Trebbiano grapes left to dry for weeks and sometimes months, *Vin Santo* has a warm amber color and a smoky-scented fragrance with hints of dried fruits and spices. Its production begins in early winter when the grapes are pressed, the must poured into small wooden casks called *caratelli*. A thick residue of leftover wine is added to aid fermentation, which begins immediately. The fermentation goes through cycles of productivity, ceasing in winter, resuming in spring, when the temperature returns to 60 degrees Fahrenheit and halting again in summer when the temperature rises above 104 degrees Fahrenheit. The *caratelli* are sealed throughout the multiyear fermentation to create an oxygen-free environment. When *Vin Santo* is ready, it is bottled and left to refine for a few months before using.

Grappa

Grappa is a distilled brandy used throughout Tuscany as an after-dinner drink (often added to coffee, the resulting beverage referred to as *caffè corretto* [corrective coffee]) and in a wide variety of cookies, cakes and spoon desserts.

Grappa is made by distilling the residue (or marc) of grapes after pressing into a clear, colorless liquid whose alcoholic content hovers in the 42 percent range. Italians alternately refer to it as *acquavite* (waters of life), a term that adequately conveys its cultural significance. Because of the explosive dangers associated with distillation, home production has long been outlawed in Italy—a reality that deters all but the numerous diehards.

When I was a young girl, I remember my grandfather making grappa after the wine harvest and I also remember the confusion that attended his frequent nervous outbursts. "Go and see if someone is coming and stay there until I call you back," this otherwise gentle man would scream when the steam began rising through the distillation tubes. But a few weeks later, he would enter the dining room proudly holding a bottle of grappa scented with lemon verbena or juniper berries, and the smiling side of him would have thankfully returned. His pronouncement was always the same: *"Quest'anno è meglio degli altri anni"* ("This year's is better than last").

Currently, the best producer of grappa is Nonnino; the Nonninos were the first to make grappa from grapes fermented specifically for that purpose as opposed to those left over from making wine. They were also the first to bottle grappa in expensive Venetian glass, permanently raising grappa's marketing profile.

NUTS

Almonds and Almond Extract

Almonds and almond extract are quintessential ingredients in Tuscan desserts along with *Amaretto di Saronno*, the famous Italian almond liqueur. There are two types of almonds, sweet and bitter although only sweet almonds are used in this book. Almonds *(Prunus amygdalus dulcis and amara)*, belong to the Rosacee family and grow mainly in the Mediterranean basin and Asia Minor. In Italy, almonds come almost exclusively from Sicily and Puglia, where the landscapes are blanketed with thousands of trees.

Almonds must be shelled and generally peeled before using. To peel almonds, pour boiling water over them, then transfer immediately to a cold water bath. Rub the drained nuts between the palms of your hands, and the peel will come off. Almonds can be stored in an airtight container placed in a dark, cool place. They should be used as soon as possible; shelled nuts can easily turn stale and rancid.

When adding nuts (and dried fruits) to cake batters or doughs, coat first with flour to prevent them from settling to the bottom during baking. The coating absorbs some of the surface oil and water that exudes during baking, and therefore, reduces the tendency to slip downward.

Almond paste is very similar in both flavor and texture to marzipan, and the two are interchangeable in most recipes. Marzipan is somewhat less malleable, however, and may not work as well for some types of cake decorating. Almond paste is readily available in specialty stores. Unused portions should always be wrapped tightly and refrigerated to prevent drying.

Chestnuts

Chestnuts and chestnut flour are used in many of Tuscany's most popular winter desserts. In olden days, chestnuts often served as the main ingredient for an entire meal—the people of the Garfagnana (Tuscany's mountain region) literally lived on them in more ways than one. They used chestnut wood for building and warming their houses as well as for making furniture. Chestnut leaves were used to make bed mattresses. Bad chestnuts were fed to pigs and good ones used to make chestnut soups, chestnut polenta and chestnut cakes. An old proverb from those days maintains that *"nella selva ci si va solo per prendere!"* ("We only go into the woods to gather!").

Chestnuts *(Castanea sativa)*, belong to the Fagaceae family and grow mainly in the Mediterranean. These long-lived trees were venerated by the ancient Greeks and later by the Etruscans, who compared the three parts of the fruit (the spiny protective casing, the brown outer shell and the sweet fruit) to the Holy Trinity.

To make boiled chestnuts (a dessert referred to by Tuscans as *ballotte* or *ballocciori*), place the nuts in a stock pot along with enough water to cover by two inches, a pinch of salt, a few bay leaves and some dried dill. Cook until tender, about 45 minutes, peel and eat. To roast chestnuts, make a slit in the flat side of each fruit, and cook over medium flame in a tightly covered skillet, shaking the pan every 5 minutes. When the shells are burnt, douse the nuts with white wine, and cook until the liquid has evaporated. Transfer the chestnuts to a kitchen towel. Roll the towel back and forth until the shells are crushed. Peel the chestnuts and serve with *vino novello. Marron glacé* are large chestnuts *(marrone)* that have been boiled, peeled and poached in syrup.

Dried chestnuts can be substituted for fresh in many recipes requiring cooked chestnuts. To reconstitute dried chestnuts, soak in water for four hours, then boil for 20 to 45 minutes (depending on type and age).

Pine Nuts

Pine nuts (also called pignoli) grow in a huge Tuscan pine forest that stretches from Torre del Lago in the province of Lucca all the way to Livorno. In fall, the woods are filled with people foraging for pine nuts *(pinoli)* whose sweet buttery flavor makes them a highly-prized delicacy. While their use is mainly tied to cookies and cakes, they are also an ingredient in that famous Ligurian specialty: pesto. Like every other nut, *pinoli* should be stored in a dry, airtight container.

Aniseed

Aniseed (aka anise seed) is one of the oldest cultivated spices; history records its use by such diverse cultures as the peoples of the Mediterranean basin, India and Mexico. A member of the Umbelliferae family along with dill, fennel, cumin and caraway, *Pimpinella anisum* has a fennel-like aroma that makes it appropriate in both sweet and savory dishes. The Egyptians, Greeks and Etruscans used it largely to flavor meats and poultry. It was also prized as a digestive by the ancient Romans who routinely ended the first meal of the evening with aniseed cakes before moving to meal number two.

Today, aniseed is most widely recognized as the main ingredient in a variety of liqueurs ranging from anisette or sambuca to the French *Pastis* and the Greek *Ouzo*. In Tuscany, it is widely used in baking, especially at Easter, when it takes center stage in sweet breads, such as *schiacciate* or *Pasimata* (see page 265). A good way to release the flavor of the seeds is to place them between two sheets of paper and smash with a rolling pin or to put them in a mortar and crush with a pestle.

Cinnamon

Cinnamon *(Cinnamomum zeylanicum)* is a native of Ceylon and the Malabar Coast and belongs to the same botanical family as Laurel. Frequently cited throughout medical history for its benefits as a carminative and a fungicide, its presence has also been said to kill *Clostridium botulinum* that causes botulism. It is nevertheless, extremely mild, whether in quill form or ground into powder. Its essential, highly aromatic oils pair especially well with apples, custards and heavy cream as well as with savory dishes. Use the quill or stick form in hot chocolate, mulled wine or fruit compotes. When buying, check the botanical name; most of the cinnamon on the market today is really cassia *(Cinnamomum cassia)*, a similar spice with slightly bitter overtones.

Nutmeg

Nutmeg is the hard, woody, brown kernel of an evergreen tree native to the Spice Islands. The recorded use of nutmeg dates back to the first century A.D. when the Roman scholar Pliny first described his experience with "this aphrodisiacal nut whose flavor matches its aroma." In pre-

Christian Asia, courtesans carried little boxes of this ground spice—known for its euphoric and hallucinogenic properties—to sprinkle on wine.

Nutmeg comes in two versions: whole and ground. For freshest flavor, buy whole nuts and grate directly into the batter when needed. Since nutmeg quickly loses its aroma once scored, store in an airtight container.

CHOCOLATE
Chocolate and Cocoa

According to Tuscan legend, there once was a princess whose jewels were hidden in a secret place known only to her. One day looters arrived and demanded to know the location of the treasures. But the princess refused and was brutally murdered. On the spot where her blood was shed grew a beautiful tree with fruits as bitter as pain, as red as blood, and as strong as virtue—the cocoa tree!

History tells us that when the Spanish conqueror Hernando Cortez, landed on the shores of Mexico in 1519, the Aztecs believed he was the reincarnation of one of their gods. Their king, Montezuma, honored Cortez with a fabulous banquet that included hot *chocoatl,* an unusual black drink scented with spices and served in pure gold cups. Cocoa's botanical name *Theobroma cacao* was, in fact, an effort on the part of Swedish botanist Carl von Linne to blend the original Aztec name, *cacahuatl,* with *theobroma,* which in Greek means "food for the gods."

Apparently, the gods were not the only ones addicted to cocoa; as soon as it was introduced into Spain, chocolate became so popular and expensive that only rich and privileged people could afford it. Spain spread the word to France by way of a royal marriage between Louis XIII of France and the Spanish King's daughter, who brought with her a personal choclatier. Before long, the French Cardinals Mazzarino and Richelieu also had personal chocolatiers who worked from morning till night to satisfy the royal court's never-ending desire for the hot drink. From France, the love of chocolate spread to England, where it was made into bars, and then to Switzerland, where milk solids were added and chocolate turned into a household word.

Chocolate is produced from the pods of cocoa trees. The pods are slit open, the beans scooped out, air dried, fermented and cured to remove the bitter taste. During the curing process, the beans change in color from white to purple to brown. The cured beans are roasted to develop their chocolaty taste and hulled. The remaining nibs, which contain 50 to 54 percent butterfat, are then crushed and heated to separate out the cocoa fat, most of which is removed. What remains is called chocolate liquor, which is prepared for different uses:

Unsweetened, Bitter or Baker's Chocolate

Unsweetened, bitter or baker's chocolate is chocolate liquor that has been solidified and molded into cakes. About 45 percent butterfat, this form is used by a great many bakers both for its purity and as a way to control the addition of sugars and fats.

Bittersweet, Semisweet and Sweet Chocolate

Bittersweet, semisweet and sweet chocolate are made the same way as unsweetened but have sugar added. Of the three, bittersweet is the most bitter.

Milk Chocolate

Milk chocolate is the same as sweet chocolate but has milk solids added.

White Chocolate

White chocolate is not really chocolate in that it contains no chocolate liquor. Made with cocoa butter, sugar, milk and flavorings, it is rarely used in baking.

Cocoa

Cocoa is made by the same process as unsweetened chocolate, but even more of the cocoa butter is removed during the final extraction. "Dutch" cocoa means—not that the cocoa comes from Holland as is popularly believed—but that the cocoa has been treated with an alkali to lessen the bitter acid taste. Three tablespoons unsweetened cocoa plus one tablespoon butter or shortening can be substituted for a one-ounce cake of unsweetened chocolate.

Gianduia

Gianduia is an Italian mainstay consisting of chocolate (any type), blended with hazelnuts. Used in a wide variety of desserts from cakes to pastries to ice creams to candies, *gianduia* is largely unavailable in the U.S. To make *gianduia* at home, simply blend hazelnut butter (or paste) with chocolate. Nutella is a commercially made hazelnut spread that can be substituted for real *gianduia* although it lacks its precise flavor.

All chocolate scorches easily and should be melted in a double boiler set over hot water. Furthermore, it should be melted over very low heat and slowly to avoid having the fat separate out. Melt only half the chocolate at a time, remove the pan from the heat and then add the remaining amount. The heat of the already melted chocolate will be more than enough to finish the job. Water must never touch melting chocolate or it will become stiff and unworkable. If this happens, stir in a tablespoon of butter or shortening, and fluidity will be restored. Cool to about 80 degrees Fahrenheit before adding to cookies or cakes.

To grate chocolate, wrap it in aluminum foil and chill thoroughly. Keeping it wrapped on one side and using a grater or a vegetable peeler, grate or shave it.

Chocolate should be stored in a cool, dry place at about 60 degrees Fahrenheit. At warmer temperatures, a grayish layer called "bloom" develops on the surface as the cocoa butter separates out. The color returns to normal when the chocolate is heated.

To make chocolate leaves for decoration, choose smooth nonpoisonous leaves such as bay or camelia. Dip one side of the leaf into melted chocolate and place on a greased tray to dry. Gently peel the cooled chocolate off the leaf and use for garnishing.

There are many brands of chocolate but the best on the market are currently Callebaut, Lindt and Valrhona.

To amplify the flavor of chocolate, add fragrant cocoa powder such as Valrhona, VanHouton or Pernigotti or flavorings such as cognac, vanilla beans and espresso powder.

COFFEE

Arabica and Robusta Coffee
"*Spaghetti, pollo, insalatina e una tazzina di caffè. . .*" (Spaghetti, chicken, salad and a tiny cup of coffee. . .) This famous song by Fred Buongusto is essentially a list of life's important pleasures as viewed by Italians. Tus-

cans take the love affair to another level of definition with a proverb that states: "Coffee should be as hot as hell, black as ink and sweet as love."

Coffee's widespread use dates back to the seventeenth century when it was smuggled into Europe by Dutch traders who subsequently took it to Sri Lanka and the East Indies. Until then the Arabs of Mocha had completely monopolized the coffee trade, exporting only sterile beans to avoid the possibility of theft. But at the beginning of the nineteenth century, Brazil began producing coffee and eventually became the world's leading exporter.

Arabica is the most prized of coffee beans and can be identified by the S-shaped line that divides the bean in half. The most popular coffee varieties all use various types of arabica beans although they take their individual name from the country of origin: Blue Mountain, the most expensive and prized variety comes from Jamaica; Mocha, from the Southern part of the present-day Yemen; Santos, from Brazil; and Sumatra, from Sumatra.

Less prized than arabica, robusta beans are distinguished by a straight line across the middle. Widely used in coffee blends and instant coffee, robusta varieties are more resistant to deadly plant diseases. In fact, robusta got its start, so to speak, when a mysterious nineteenth century fungus destroyed most of the arabica species planted in present-day Sri Lanka.

In Italy coffee is widely used as a dessert ingredient and incorporated into everything from the famous *tiramisù* to the more esoteric espresso flan. When they're not getting their fix vis-à-vis food, Italians drink coffee every chance they get—eight cups per average Italian every day of the year. Throughout Italy, coffee comes in six versions: *macchiato con latte* (coffee "spotted" with milk), *cappuccino* (blended with steamed milk), *latte macchiato* (milk spotted with coffee), *alto* or *lungo* (high or long, meaning weaker and more of it), *basso* or *ristretto* (low or shortened, meaning concentrated) and *corretto* (spiked with liqueurs).

Coffee beans are roasted to develop their flavor. The degree of roasting—light, medium, dark—affects the flavor. Americans generally prefer medium roast, while Italians and other Europeans gravitate toward dark. Recipes in this book require dark, or espresso coffee. Decaffeinated espresso works just as well as its caffeinated counterpart—at least for baking purposes.

Coffee beans should always be ground at the last moment to insure the freshest and most concentrated flavor. If you must use already ground coffee, be sure to seal it tightly and store in a cool, dark place. But even with the best storage, ground coffee that is more than a week old has lost its aroma. Vacuum packed coffee lasts longer, but it, too, deteriorates as soon as it is opened.

Use fresh water when making coffee. Fresh cold water brought to a boil contains some dissolved air. Water that has been kept hot for a long time does not, so it tastes flat and makes a flat-tasting coffee.

SALT

Sea Salt

In Italy, which is surrounded on three sides by water, all salt is sea salt. The best Italian sea salt comes from Sicily, from the natural salt beds of Trapani. Sea salt is highly preferable to common table or kosher varieties because it contains minerals and trace elements that accentuate its flavor.

Baking Equipment

PANS

Baking Pans

Baking pans can be either round or square, with or without removable bottoms and made from various alloys. Because they are designed for oven use and not for placing on a source of direct heat (stovetop), their heat conducting properties are not important. Oven heat is general and even, and the pan simply transfers the heat to the batter from all sides. The most common type of baking pan for cakes is the round type with a removable bottom (springform). Size ranges from eight or nine inches in diameter and one to three inches high with straight sides.

Black baking pans cook foods more quickly than shiny varieties because a dull dark surface absorbs more of the oven's radiant energy. Glass pans bake foods more quickly than metal because that same radiant energy passes through the transparent glass surface.

Baking Sheets

Baking sheets or cookie sheets are flat metal boards with approximately one-half-inch-high edges. Baking sheets come in many sizes but the size you choose should fit your oven without touching the sides. Every kitchen should have two so that a second batch of cookies can be prepared while the first one bakes. Dough or batter can be placed directly on the sheets, especially if they have first been buttered, or greased and dusted with flour.

You can also line baking sheets with parchment paper (also known as baking parchment) or reusable baking sheets that prevent sticking. Both are available in kitchen supply stores.

Biscuit or Cookie Cutter

Biscuit or cookie cutters are open cylinders made of plastic or metal and come in various sizes and shapes. To use, simply press into rolled dough and lift out the shape.

Loaf Pan

Loaf pan or bread pans are rectangular pans usually measuring about eight or 10 inches long by four or five inches wide and three inches high. As their name implies, they are commonly used to bake bread or bread-like cakes. Loaf pans are available in a wide range of materials, such as aluminum, baker's steel, terra-cotta and glass.

Muffin Pans

Muffin pans are also known as muffin trays or cupcake pans and consist of rectangular metal trays with six or 12 cups molded in place. Cup sizes may be small, medium or large. Miniature muffin pans have a greater number of cups of smaller capacities and are frequently used to make *marzipan mignons*.

Pizelle Irons

Pizelle irons are perfect substitutes for the ancient iron tools called *testi* that we use in Tuscany to make pancakes and waffles either on the stove-top or over an open hearth. Made of two hinged cast aluminum disks about five inches in diameter, they have long handles and are held over an open burner until the waffles are baked on one side, then are flipped to complete the baking.

Tart Pans with Removable Bottoms

Tart pans with removable bottoms are used to make numerous Tuscan desserts. The term "tart" (in Italian, *torta*) comes from the past participle of the Latin verb *torquere*, which means to twist or torture. And so, a tart became a pastry whose edges had been twisted or, in the case of these flute-sided pans, pressed into the flutes to create ridged edges. Black steel tart pans are generally considered superior to ones made of tin because crusts bake more uniformly in steel. Tart pans come in diameters of eight to 12 inches and are generally about one inch deep. To remove the tart, simply place your hand under the cooled pan and push up on the bottom, allowing the outside ring to fall away.

OTHER ITEMS

Cooling Racks

Cooling Racks are square or round wire racks with feet that keep the metal surface about 1 inch off the countertop. Essential for cooling cakes, cookies and breads.

Custard Cups

Custard cups are precious items that come in porcelain, glazed earthenware or heat-proof glass and can be used either as serving or baking cups for custards, such as crème brûlée or baked cream tarts. There are cups for individual custards (capacity: four to six ounces) and ones as large as two-quart capacity, often referred to as soufflé bowls. Ramekins can be substituted.

Dough Blender

Dough blenders are U-shaped, thin-bladed items (also called pastry blenders) about four inches wide at the opening which allow you to easily incorporate solid fats, such as butter into pastry dough. In lieu of these precise tools, use two knives, with blades held parallel. Pass the knives over each other closely and repetitively until the mixture looks like coarse crumbs. Blending can also be done with the fingers, by flaking fat and flour together very quickly so the heat of the hands doesn't melt the fat.

Ice-Cream Scoop

Ice-cream scoops are commonly used to serve ice creams and *sorbettos* and are small, stainless steel or cast-aluminum, hand-sized shovels that come in different designs. The most common are the dipper (with a deep, crescent-shaped bowl and a thick round handle) and the half-sphere ice-cream scoop, which is the classic model found in every *gelateria*.

Pastry Bag

Pastry bags are cone-shaped cylinders made of plastic-lined cotton or polyester. Available in lengths ranging from eight to 21 inches, pastry bags come with tips of different shapes and sizes for applying icing. Piping is the term for the process of hand-squeezing a mixture from the pastry bag to decorate cakes, to form biscuits or to fill pastries, such as eclairs.

Pie Weights

Pie weights or baking beans are flat ceramic or aluminum bean-shaped pieces available in bags of about two pounds. They are useful to weigh down pie crusts during prebaking. Dried beans can be substituted.

Pizella Cone Roller

Pizelle cone rollers are wooden cones with short handles around which warm waffles are placed to shape them into cones. A good substitute is the cannoli form, a tin plated steel tube one inch in diameter and six inches long around which cannoli shells are placed for frying.

Pudding Mold

Pudding molds are deep containers with fluted sides and scalloped tops. Some molds come with a tube in the center or a lid that clamps onto the base. Frequently used to cook puddings or custards, the capacity of pudding molds ranges from one to two quarts.

Basic Custard

YIELDS ABOUT
2 CUPS

TIME:
40 MINUTES

LEVEL:
MODERATE

4 egg yolks, at room temperature
½ cup sugar
1 tablespoon cake flour
2 cups milk, warmed
1 teaspoon grated lemon zest

1. Using an electric mixer or a hand whisk, beat the yolks and the sugar in a large bowl until smooth, fluffy, pale and tripled in volume, about 5 minutes with a mixer (15 minutes by hand). Sift in the flour and blend well.
2. Transfer to a medium-size, heavy-gauge saucepan and stir in the milk. Cook over very low heat, stirring constantly and gently with a heat-proof rubber spatula or wooden spoon until slightly thickened, about 20 minutes. Do not boil. Remove from heat and stir in the lemon zest.
3. Pour into a medium-size bowl and let cool for 15 minutes.

MAKE AHEAD: This custard can be made up to 2 days in advance. Store it refrigerated in a sealed container.

Basic Pasta Frolla

MAKES
ENOUGH FOR
TWO 9-INCH
CRUSTS

TIME: 10
MINUTES PLUS 1
HOUR
REFRIGERATION

LEVEL:
MODERATE

2¾ cups cake flour
¼ cup sugar
½ teaspoon baking powder
½ teaspoon salt
1 cup unsalted butter
1 teaspoon grated lemon zest
½ teaspoon vanilla extract
2 eggs plus 1 egg yolk

1. Place the flour, sugar, baking powder, salt in a food processor and pulse for 30 seconds.
2. Cut the butter into small chunks and add to the dry ingredients. Process with 4 or 5 pulses until the mixture resembles coarse crumbs.

3. Mix the zest, vanilla, eggs and egg yolk in a cup, and pour through the feed tube with the motor running. Process just until the mixture comes together and before it forms a ball.

4. Transfer the *pasta frolla* (dough) to a lightly floured working surface and press into a flat disk. Wrap in plastic and refrigerate for 1 hour before using.

MAKE AHEAD: This dough can be made 3 days in advance. Store it wrapped in plastic and refrigerated. It can also be frozen for up to 3 weeks. Thaw before using.

Basic Zabaione

4 egg yolks, at room temperature
¼ cup sugar
½ teaspoon vanilla extract
½ cup *Vin Santo* or marsala

YIELDS ABOUT
1 CUP

TIME:
45 MINUTES

LEVEL:
MODERATE

1. Using an electric mixer or a hand whisk, beat the yolks and the sugar in a large bowl until smooth, fluffy, pale and tripled in volume, about 5 minutes with a mixer (15 minutes by hand).

2. Beat in the vanilla and *Vin Santo*.

3. Transfer the mixture to a double boiler and cook over gently simmering water, stirring constantly until thickened, about 10 minutes. The temperature should have reached 160°F. To tell if the *zabaione* is ready, lift the spoon and watch the mixture fall back into the pan. It should form a dense ribbon.

VARIATIONS: Dessert wine can be substituted for the *Vin Santo*.

Pasta Genovese
Basic Sponge Cake

MAKES ONE
9-INCH-
DIAMETER CAKE

TIME: 1 HOUR

LEVEL:
MODERATE

Unsalted butter or cooking spray, for greasing
3 eggs, separated, at room temperature
½ cup sugar
1 teaspoon grated lemon zest
¼ teaspoon salt
¼ teaspoon cream of tartar
¾ cup cake flour, sifted

1. Preheat the oven to 350°F. Grease the bottom of a 9-inch-round baking pan. Line the bottom with waxed paper cut to fit. Grease the paper, dust with flour and tap out the excess.
2. Using an electric mixer or a hand whisk, beat the egg yolks and the sugar until fluffy, pale and tripled in volume, about 5 minutes with the mixer (15 minutes by hand). Stir in the zest.
3. Using an electric mixer or hand whisk, beat the egg whites and the salt in a large bowl until foamy. Add the cream of tartar and beat until stiff peaks form.
4. Gently fold the whites into the yolks until just blended. Sift the flour over the top and fold.
5. Pour the batter into the prepared pan, tap against a counter to level and bake until golden, about 20 minutes. Cool for 2 minutes then invert onto a cooling rack, peel off the paper and cool completely.

MAKE AHEAD: Keeps for up to 3 days when wrapped in plastic and refrigerated. Can also be frozen for up to 3 weeks. Thaw at room temperature or in the refrigerator.

Basic Meringue

Before starting, please review the information under "Beating Egg Whites" on page 11.

MAKES 12 MERINGUES

TIME: 20 MINUTES

LEVEL: MODERATE

3 egg whites, at room temperature
¼ teaspoon salt
1 teaspoon vanilla extract
½ teaspoon cream of tartar
½ cup sugar mix (¼ cup superfine and ¼ cup confectioners')

1. Preheat the oven to 300°F and line a 12 x 15-inch baking sheet with parchment. Using an electric mixer or hand whisk, beat the egg whites, salt and vanilla in a large bowl until foamy. Add the cream of tartar and beat until soft peaks form.
2. Slowly add about half the sugar and beat to stiff peaks. Add the remaining sugar all at once and beat (on low speed if using a mixer) for 3 seconds.
3. Using a large pastry bag fitted with a ½-inch plain tube, pipe the meringue onto a baking sheet 1 inch apart.
4. Bake for 20 minutes. Turn off the heat, open the oven door and let the meringues cool for 30 minutes. Cool completely on a wire rack before storing.

MAKE AHEAD: Stored in an airtight container at room temperature, baked meringues will keep for several weeks.

Basic Puff Pastry

Puff pastry in Italian is mille foglie *or "thousand leaves." The flakiest of all the doughs, puff pastry contains more butter than flour, and when cooked becomes, in fact, thousands (well, maybe not exactly thousands) of layers, each puffed up with air. Patience is the most important ingredient when attempting to make this rather difficult dough. The dough must rest and chill between "turns" and, if the butter softens too much, it must also be returned to the refrigerator until the butter firms. A few hints:*

  Make sure to lift the dough constantly while rolling so it doesn't stick to the work surface.

MAKES APPROXIMATELY 2 POUNDS OF DOUGH

TIME: 7 HOURS

LEVEL: ADVANCED

- Lightly dust the work surface and never place the dough on top of a mound of flour; too much flour will lead to tough dough.
- If butter shows through at any time during turning, lightly cover with flour.
- Each time you "turn" or roll the dough, approach it from a different angle.
- When rolling, start the rolling pin in the middle and work your way firmly to the ends.

2 cups cake flour
1 teaspoon salt
½ cup ice water
2 tablespoons vegetable oil
1 cup unsalted butter, frozen

1. Place 1¾ cups flour, salt, water and oil in a food processor and pulse until a ball has formed. Add a few drops more of water if necessary to form the ball. Form into a 3-inch square, wrap in plastic and refrigerate for 20 minutes.
2. Place the remaining ¼ cup flour in the food processor. Cut the butter into thin slices and drop onto the flour. Pulse until the mixture looks like coarse cornmeal crumbs. Remove, form into a 4-inch square, wrap in plastic and refrigerate.
3. Remove the 3-inch square from the refrigerator, place on a lightly floured work surface and roll into a 10 x 12-inch rectangle. Brush off excess flour. Remove the butter square from the refrigerator, unwrap it and place it on half the rectangle. Fold the other half over, press the edges to seal and roll into an 8 x 15-inch rectangle. Lift and turn the dough occasionally to be sure it's not sticking. Dust the surface with more flour if necessary. Square the corners, stretching the dough with your hands when necessary. Fold the rectangle in thirds, like a business letter. This completes the first turn.
4. Roll the dough into an 8 x 15-inch rectangle and again, fold into thirds. Dust lightly with flour if the dough begins to stick. This completes the second turn. Wrap in plastic and refrigerate for 45 minutes to chill the butter.
5. Remove from the refrigerator and repeat Step 4 twice more. Remember to dust lightly with flour if the dough sticks. Wrap again in plastic and refrigerate for 45 minutes or overnight.

6. Give the dough two final turns. After the sixth and final turn, wrap in plastic and refrigerate for at least 1 hour before using.

MAKE AHEAD: Wrapped in plastic, the dough will keep for 3 days in the refrigerator and up to 2 months frozen. Thaw the dough in the refrigerator before using.

Equivalent Measures and Substitutions

BUTTER
1 pound butter = 2 cups
4 sticks butter = 1 pound
1 stick butter = ½ cup

CREAM
1 cup heavy cream (35–40% butterfat) = 2 cups whipped cream

EGGS
1 US Grade A large egg = 2 ounces or 3 tablespoons
1 large egg yolk = 1 tablespoon
1 large egg white = 2 tablespoons
2 large eggs = ½ cup
2 large eggs = 3 medium eggs
4–5 large eggs = 1 cup

FLOUR
1 pound all-purpose flour = 4 cups
1 pound cake flour or pastry flour = 4½ cups plus 3 tablespoons

DRIED FRUITS
8 ounces dried apricots = 2 cups, packed
1 pound seedless raisins = 3½ cups

FRESH FRUITS
1 large lemon = 2–3 tablespoons juice and 2–3 teaspoons grated zest
1 large orange = 6–8 tablespoons juice and 2–3 tablespoons grated zest
1 pint fresh berries = 2 cups

GELATIN

1 envelope unflavored gelatin = 2¼ teaspoons

NUTS

1 pound whole almonds, shelled = 3½ cups
1 pound walnuts, shelled = 4 cups
1 pound fresh chestnuts, peeled = 4 cups
1 pound dried chestnuts, peeled = 2 cups
1 pound whole hazelnuts, shelled = 3½ cups
1 cup shelled whole hazelnuts = 5 ounces

SUGAR

1 pound granulated sugar = 2¼ cups
1 pound brown sugar = 2¼ cups
1 pound confectioners' sugar = 4–4¼ cups unsifted
1 cup granulated sugar = ⅞ cup honey and decrease recipe liquid by
3 tablespoons
1 cup brown sugar = 1 cup granulated plus 2 tablespoons molasses

CHAPTER TWO

Biscotti, Cookies and Cialde

Coddled from Cradle to Grave

On paper, Tuscan society nestles safely in the bosom of the capitalist world, with a free market economy (give or take a few state monopolies and government subsidies), and a general atmosphere of creative enterprise and individual initiative. And yet anyone peeking in from the outside would never define individual initiative as the precept governing peoples' lives here. Because Tuscany is, for all intents and purposes, a welfare state where everyone is used to being taken care of from cradle to grave: both in terms of legislative policy and—more important—in action and expectation.

Tuscans believe they have an innate right to be coddled from the time they're born until well beyond the moment of death. Their country is like the ultimate Mother, always there, always giving, never playing favorites. But although the government has always been a complicit partner in this mental construct, it is now peddling hard and fast to step back from paying the ever-grander bills such a system entails. "Our people must learn to manage their own lives," says Romano Prodi, the current Prime Minister, who has wagered his career on streamlining the nation's economy in accordance with the demands of the newly created European Economic Union (EEC).

While Prodi has succeeded admirably in slashing the mind-boggling number of Italy's social welfare programs, he has—as far as I can see—not made the tiniest dent in people's attitudes regarding what their "mother" owes them. If anything, his promulgations have merely heightened the genetic tendency of Tuscans to do everything necessary—employing gestures, schemes or interpersonal interaction—to make themselves look even more than ever in need of a mother's care. I say "genetic tendency" because Tuscans have, since time immemorial, played on peoples' sympathies, whether for economic advantage or special treatment or simply to gain attention. It is simply part of who they are.

Let's take my grandmother as an example. She is 93 and in perfect health. But the only people who know she's in perfect health are members of my immediate family, who sometimes catch her off guard. When no one is watching (or when she thinks no one is watching), Nonna Angelina sings, reads and walks normally. But as soon as someone comes to visit, her back bows in a pitiful arch and she begins limping, crying that God has even taken away her eyesight. *"Eh noi poveri vecchi,"* she says with that practiced Tuscan whine, *"che ci stiamo a fare al mondo?"* ("Poor oldsters that we have become, why are we even still alive?")

It always works, the visitor hastening to spread the word that poor Angelina is so sick and so alone. Nobody visits her, nobody cares, even her family is too busy to spend more than a few minutes. How tragic!

Tuscans have a saying: *"Se un piangi, un puppi"* ("If you do not whine, you will not eat"). Few proverbs better define that certain look, posture, hand gesture, tone of voice, choice of words that make Tuscans interactions the dramatic spectacle that they are. Suffice to say that, when in Tuscany, the proper answer to the question "how are you?" is not "fine," regardless of how you're feeling. The only people who might answer "fine" are foreigners, who obviously have no idea how to play the game.

The proper answer is, at best, *"così, così."* ("So, so.") If you really want to pass as an insider, you'll learn to slump your shoulders, shake your head and, in the most pathetic of voices, utter a long drawn-out "ehiiii" (pronounced "eiiiiii"), raised inflection on the end of the syllable. What you're essentially saying is "don't even ask me," which works beautifully, given that most of the time, there is nothing to talk about since there's no actual problem.

Umberto Bossi, the leader of the Lega Party, Italy's Separatist movement, cites just this behavior in his case for splitting the country into three sections: Padania, the northern, most wealthy part of Italy; Etruria, consisting of Tuscany, Umbria, Marche and the northern part of Lazio; and the South, for which he hasn't even bothered to come up with a name. "The North is like a locomotive," he is fond of saying. "With our drive and motivation, we have always pulled the rest of the country along. But people who wait to be taken care of are too heavy to pull and now there's too many of them. It is time to divide the train and let each section find its own locomotive."

Tuscans have been the most vociferous in their demonization of Bossi. "Tourists from all over the world flock to Tuscany and then, if there's time left over, maybe journey north. Without us, your locomotive will most certainly be pulling a lighter load—a load consisting of nothing but air."

I have journeyed to Lucca for the weekly produce market. My routine always begins however, with a pre-shopping foray to the beautiful *pasticcerìa* Di Simo, which serves the very best *caffè macchiato* in the entire province. Today my regular table is occupied by an elegantly mustachioed man in his fifties who is obviously waiting for someone since he spends most of his time craning his neck to look out the floor-to-ceiling windows. I am hoping he will leave soon or at the very least, notice from my disapproving stare that he is sitting where he does not belong.

But it is not to be. He signals the waiter for a large pot of tea and resumes his watchful wait. Ah, here he comes. Another example of old world elegance, this one with a fashionable olive green checked blazer, a paisley ascot and a brown suede fedora. The two exchange greetings, hugs, pats on the back, pecks on both cheeks. They settle themselves over small doily-covered plates of pastries, the one man dusting his with additional powdered sugar.

I cannot help but hear their conversation, sitting as close as I am. Is it about art? Film? The new facade on San Lorenzo Church? *Niente.*

"You know Gianpiero, this business with the *accompagnamento* is really getting out of hand. My mother has had it all her life, but now that she is living with me, the government revoked her voucher." (*Accompagnamento* is a government subsidy paid to sick people to move in with their relatives instead of crowding public nursing homes.)

"That's impossible. Once approved, you're entitled to have it for the rest of your life."

"I know, I know. But my mother already receives two stipends: one for being an invalid, the other because she has diabetes. Moreover, she also gets my father's pension, so the government obviously decided she was already getting too much."

"With three stipends though, she should be comfortable enough to not be worried, no?"

"My mother is not the problem. The problem is *ours* since my wife has so much more to do, what with an extra mouth to feed and an extra bedroom to clean. We had used the money to hire a maid but now I don't know."

"How much was the *accompagnamento*?"

"About $700 a month. A lot of money to suddenly have taken away."

I would like to say that I'm amazed at the conversation between these two obviously well-to-do men. But I am not. The fact is, the Italian government supports just about everybody. Those whose wages are below a certain minimum are eligible for a *sussidio*, which brings them up to snuff. If a family has more than six children and the father is the sole wage earner, they receive *assegni familiari* (supplementary stipends) whether or not they need it. People over 55 with cancer or heart trouble are declared 100 percent invalids and receive stipends that cover rent, food and life's other necessities. If that same person lives with relatives, they get an *accompagnamento*. Prescriptions are covered by the *mutua*, public transportation by another type of mutua, and walk-in health care is free for all. What better way to convince a populace that illness pays?

The two men finally vacate my table, and I stretch out in the richly cushioned window seat, spreading my paper across the white marble table. The lead article describes the new *riccometro* (literally translated: rich meter) which the government has just devised to determine people's income so that, supposedly, they can adjust the amount of entitlement.

That's it. I've had enough talk about stipends and pensions. Time to go out into the brilliant sunshine and bask in the glory of this stupendous walled town. I plop my sunglasses atop my nose and stroll blithely down the Fillungo toward my favorite vegetable vendor, Alberto the porcini mushroom man.

"*Ciao* Alberto, *che mi dai oggi?*" ("What do you have for me today?")

"*Ehiiii,*" he says. "*Che ti do.* What could I possibly have with this dry weather? The forest floor cannot yield magic you know." Alberto is your quintessential complainer. But there's also a certain charm about his acknowledgment of complaining as a national sport.

We are interrupted suddenly by the screams of a woman who has just purchased the paper from the adjacent stall. "*Che vergogna!*" she howls upon reading the headline. ("What shame!") Her wrath is directed toward the headline feature about Francesco DeLorenzo, Italy's Public Health Minister who was jailed in 1994 for negligence in failing to test a large batch of imported blood.

The blood, which turned out to be severely tainted, caused more than twenty cases of AIDS. After a long trial, during which government lawyers depicted DeLorenzo as a selfless, dedicated public servant who had simply made a mistake ("and for this, he is to spend the next ten years in prison?"), he was sent to jail. But ninety days later, he was freed on grounds that being in jail had caused such severe depression as to render him in danger of taking his own life.

"And now they've awarded him a pension!" the woman is screaming. "What's next? A pension for Craxi?" (the former president who was indicted for embezzlement and fled to Tunisia with millions of taxpayer dollars).

"*Dai* Ombretta," says Alberto, egging the woman on. ("Give it to them.")

Ombretta does, in fact, "give it to them"—every market day. Her outrages over the day's events are as much a part of the market routine as the vendors and their stalls.

"I should pay her," Alberto says. "Her rantings attract far more customers than I could ever dream of luring with my simple mushrooms." Actually, he says, the person who should *really* pay Ombretta is Riccardo over there, with the prepared food stand. "And maybe he does," Alberto ventures.

"What do you mean?"

"Look at the time," Alberto says. "It's almost noon, yes? And women have to zoom home to prepare lunch for their husbands. But they cannot hold themselves back from viewing the spectacle in its entirety—in fact, they sometimes hover around the *piazza* waiting for Ombretta to arrive, taking bets on which of the day's stories are going to spark her uncontrollable fury. They talk, they watch, they listen, they join in. And before long, it's too late even to make a fresh plate of pasta. So they buy everything from Riccardo—roasted vegetables, lasagna with béchamel, roast pork, *farro* and ricotta tarts. I'd guess that Ombretta has just about doubled Riccardo's sales."

This is why I live in Tuscany. Not the beauty, not the sunshine, not the food, not even the nearness of my family—although all are certainly potent factors. It's the amusement provided by a society of perpetual children.

I'm reminded of the earthquake in Umbria a few months ago, of the Pope's rush to comfort the people of Perugia and Assisi, where homes and churches had been devastated by the series of quakes. Next thing you know, network news anchors were interviewing homeowners in Marche, an adjacent region that had also been pretty hard hit.

"I can't believe the Pope would go to Umbria and not come here to

Marche," they complained on national television. "Are we not just as worthy of his presence? True the Umbrians have St. Francis, but the Pope has obviously forgotten how the people of Marche long ago fought many battles on behalf of papal sovereignty. A fine way to thank us."

On my way home, I stop in Viareggio to buy some focaccia. As always, I check the parking meter situation, which has seen more flux in the last year than has Pavarotti's weight. For a long time, as long as I can remember in fact, Viareggio had no parking meters anywhere. You simply parked your car wherever you wanted for however long you wanted. Note that when I say "wherever you wanted," I mean exactly that. People would nose their cars into minute spaces and leave their backsides sticking out into the street. In some cases, they would even pull up onto the sidewalk.

Illegal parking practices were somewhat curtailed when the city assigned traffic controllers a few years ago to "bring order to the city's vehicular thoroughfares," which, of course, meant handing out tickets. At the time, I was both pleased and pained. Yes, I wanted to be able to drive from one end of town to the other without having to spend time inching past cars parked in the middle of the street. But on the other hand, I rather liked the childlike qualities implicit in that act of simply pulling over and getting out. There was a basic trust that everything would be okay, that nothing bad could possibly happen ever.

Anyway, the Mayor then decided Viareggio needed money to pay for new tree plantings and installed a host of parking meters throughout the city. But either he had acted like an enraged parent who threatens action without ever following through, or the contractor installed the meter casings and somehow neglected to include the innards because the parking meters were, for a long time, not in service. Last fall, with the expense of Carnival right around the corner, the mayor decided to activate the meters and, true to prediction, almost everyone got tickets.

But then, City Hall became routinely flooded with furious drivers refusing to pay the fines. And so within a week, the meters were restored to nonfunctionality. Lately, however (Carnival time again draws near), there has been talk of trying once more. All this to say, you can never be too sure when parking in Viareggio these days.

But despite my best attempts at monitoring the situation, I, in fact, have a little pink slip on my windshield when I return. "Parked in a no-parking zone," it says apparently referring to the front of my car which sits squarely in a driveway, albeit a nonfunctioning one. Immediately, I search for the police officer who wrote the offensive little summons and crawl toward him with the most penitent of expressions.

"I'm sorry," I tell him. "I know I should not have parked there, but I started to feel sick and had to stop for a pastry. Believe me, I could not have searched any further—I literally thought I was going to faint."

"You stopped because you were hungry?" he asks with great seriousness.

"No," I moan, "I have diabetes." Which is not true, but what other excuse could I offer?

"Oh," he says, suddenly embarrassed. "I'm terribly sorry." And next thing you know, he rips up the ticket and walks me back to my car, telling me how his sister has diabetes and what a serious disease it is and how I should be more careful with my regimen.

And so there you have it. Come to the party and get your slice of cake. But, as our Prime Minister keeps telling us, "The party is over."

How many times have I heard those words from my mother. "That's it Sandra," she would say when, as a teenager, I'd come home much later than agreed. "The party's over." How many times my piano teacher uttered those same words when I failed to put in enough practice hours. The same words, yet again, when my dressmaker has, periodically, to "stretch" my jackets and skirts. Each time, the threat of retribution, of having the Good Mother turn sour.

And yet, I am here to tell you, the party is always just beginning. Mothers never stop being mothers, especially in Tuscany.

⸻ ⸻ ⸻ ⸻

Biscotti, Cookies and Cialde

While Americans have come to know biscotti as those hard, crescent biscuits perfect for dipping in hot chocolate (or, Tuscan-style, in wine), the Italians use the word as a generic term to mean all cookies. The actual meaning of biscotti is "cooked twice" (just as *biscottare* means "the method used when a cake or a particular type of cookies need to be baked a second time"). As such, it is a perfect name for the aforementioned crescent biscuits which, in fact, are cooked twice—once before slicing and once afterwards. Looked at in this light, the only cookies truly worthy of the name biscotti are the ones known to Americans by that very moniker and not cookies at large. So why do the Italians persist with this misnomer? *Chi lo sa!*

Cialde are wafers made with a type of *pizzelle* iron heated over the stovetop or, traditionally, over an open hearth. Generally, they are rolled into cylinders when still hot and wrapped around whipped cream or ricotta—Tuscany's version of Sicilian cannoli minus the frying.

While cookies are generally considered somewhat easier than many other categories of baking, they do require attention to a few details:

- Always grease baking sheets with unsalted butter or a cooking spray. Parchment sheets and reusable nonstick liners can also be used but, in my experience, cookies baked on grease spread more and are thinner than those baked on liners, which tend to limit the flow of the batter.
- Place the cookies on cold baking sheets.
- Fill the entire sheet with cookies; partially filled sheets tend to draw and concentrate heat to the cookies and may result in burning;
- Place the sheets at least two inches from the wall of the oven; when baking more than one sheet at a time, space them equally apart from each other.
- Since oven heat circulates unevenly (if you bake two sheets on separate racks, notice that the bottoms of the cookies on the lower rack and the tops of the cookies on the upper rack bake the quickest), rotate the pans once during baking.
- Although baking times are given for all cookie recipes in this chapter, differences in ingredients, equipment, oven performance, weather and altitude can cause variations in the amount of time actually required. New bakers should keep a close watch on cookies as they bake—30 seconds can sometimes make the difference between perfectly baked cookies and burnt ones. Color and smell are the surest signs of doneness—baked cookies are lightly colored and their aroma is distinctly noticeable.
- When cookies are fully baked, remove them from the baking sheet immediately, or they will continue to cook. The exception to this rule is very delicate cookies such as ladyfingers, which should be cooled for a few seconds on the baking sheet before they're removed.

- Cool cookies on a rack; make sure they are not overlapping.
- Do not place a second batch of cookies on the baking sheet until it has cooled. Brush off leftover crumbs before reusing the sheet.
- Do not store cookies until they are completely cooled, or they will become soggy.

Biscotti, Cookies and Cialde

Cantucci di prato
Crisp Almond Biscuits

Ladyfingers

Biscotti al cocco
Coconut Drops

Biscotti al burro e màndorla all'arancia
Orange-Scented-Butter-and-Almond Cookies

Lingue di gatto
Cat's Tongues

Biscottini al miele e fichi secchi
Honeyed-Fig Cookies

Cialde di montecatini
Meringue-Filled Wafers

Fiorentini
Chocolate-Coated Dried Fruit and Nut Cookies

Ossi di morto
Dead Man's Bones

Nozze
Lemon and Anise Seed Wafers

Biscottini ai pinoli
Pine Nut Crescents

Buchi con fichi
Fig-and-Pine-Nut Cookies

Ravioli dolci
Fruit-Filled Ravioli

Dolcetti di cioccolata e nocciole
Chocolate-Hazelnut Cookies

Cantucci di prato
Crisp Almond Biscuits

These wonderful cantucci are served throughout Tuscany with glasses of Vin Santo, a sherry-like dessert wine. Much softer than the imported versions available in specialty food stores, the cookies are very easy to make and keep for up to 2 months when sealed in an airtight container.

MAKES APPROXIMATELY 24 BISCOTTI

TIME: ABOUT 1½ HOURS

LEVEL: MODERATE

3 cups bread flour, sifted
2 cups sugar
⅓ teaspoon salt
1 teaspoon baking powder
3 eggs, at room temperature
½ teaspoon grated lemon zest
½ teaspoon grated orange zest
½ teaspoon vanilla extract
¾ cup roughly chopped toasted unpeeled almonds
½ cup whole, toasted, unpeeled almonds
Unsalted butter or cooking spray, for greasing

1. Sift together the flour, sugar, salt and baking powder.
2. Using an electric mixer or a hand whisk, beat the eggs, lemon zest, orange zest and vanilla in a large bowl until smooth and creamy.
3. Gradually stir the dry mixture into the eggs. Add the chopped and whole almonds and mix until a soft dough has formed. If the dough seems overly dense, add an extra beaten egg. Wrap the dough with plastic and refrigerate for 30 minutes.
4. Preheat the oven to 400°F and grease a 12 x 15-inch baking sheet.
5. With floured hands, divide the dough in half and shape each portion into a 3 x 12-inch log. Place the logs about 4 inches apart on the baking sheet. Pat each log to smooth the surface.
6. Bake until the loaves are golden, about 10 minutes. Turn carefully with a spatula and bake 10 minutes longer.
7. Remove from the oven, transfer the logs to a cooling rack and cool for 10 minutes. Lower the oven temperature to 325°F.

8. Place the logs on a cutting board and slice each loaf diagonally into ½-inch-thick slices. Return the slices, cut side up, to the baking sheet and bake for 10 minutes, turning each cookie after 5 minutes. When done, the cookies will be golden brown on both sides. Cool on a rack.

MAKE AHEAD: The prepared dough can be wrapped in plastic and refrigerated for 1 day or frozen for up to 3 weeks. Thaw in the refrigerator before using.

Savoiardi
Ladyfingers

MAKES
APPROXIMATELY
25
LADYFINGERS

TIME: 1 HOUR

LEVEL:
ADVANCED

Delicate and refined as their name implies, ladyfingers are generally served throughout Tuscany in the later afternoon with tea. They are also frequently used to line molds for tiramisù or other custards. Their lightness requires working the ingredients quickly; once air is beaten into the eggs, it is a race to get the cookies blended, piped and baked before the mixture starts to deflate. Have a 14-inch pastry bag fitted with a plain, ½-inch nozzle, the bowls on the counter and the confectioners' sugar at hand. Ready, set, avanti!

Unsalted butter or cooking spray, for greasing
2½ cups cake flour
2½ cups potato flour
8 eggs, separated, at room temperature
2 cups sugar
½ teaspoon vanilla extract
¼ teaspoon salt
½ teaspoon cream of tartar
4 tablespoons sugar blended with 2 tablespoons confectioners' sugar,
   for dusting

1. Preheat the oven to 375°F and lightly grease 12 x 15-inch baking sheets. Sift together the flour and potato flour.
2. Using an electric mixer or hand whisk, beat the egg yolks, the sugar and vanilla in a large bowl until smooth, creamy, pale and tripled in volume, about 5 minutes with a mixer (15 minutes by hand). Add the flour mixture and continue to beat until well blended. The consistency will be very thick and stiff.

3. Using an electric mixer or hand whisk, beat the whites and the salt in a large bowl until foamy. Add the cream of tartar and beat until stiff peaks form.

4. Using an electric mixer (set on low) or a spatula, gently fold half the whites into the yolk mixture until just barely blended. Then fold in the remaining whites.

5. Pour the mixture into a 14-inch pastry bag fitted with a plain ½-inch nozzle. Working quickly, pipe 4-inch shapes onto the prepared baking sheets (or dribble the mixture from a spoon). Dust each ladyfinger with the blended sugars.

6. Bake until dry and pale golden, about 20 minutes. Remove from oven, cool for 2 minutes on the pan. Transfer gently to a cooling rack.

MAKE AHEAD: Ladyfingers can be made up to 2 weeks in advance and stored in airtight containers. They can also be frozen for 3 weeks. Thaw in refrigerator and briefly crisp in 350°F oven before serving.

Biscotti al cocco
Coconut Drops

MAKES
APPROXIMATELY
25 COOKIES

TIME: 1 HOUR

LEVEL: EASY

The recipe for these easy-to-make cookies comes from Davide Monferatti of Torre del Lago's famous pasticcerìa *Da Davide. "Anyone can make them—I guarantee success," he said with absolute assurance.*

Unsalted butter or cooking spray, for greasing
5 egg whites, at room temperature
¼ teaspoon salt
½ teaspoon cream of tartar
2 cups cake flour, sifted
1½ cups unsweetened shredded coconut
4 cups confectioners' sugar

1. Grease a 12 x 15-inch baking sheet and preheat the oven to 375°F. Using an electric mixer or a hand whisk, beat the egg whites and the salt in a large bowl until foamy. Add the cream of tartar and beat until stiff peaks form.

2. Mix the flour, coconut flakes and sugar in a large bowl. Gently fold the eggs into the dry ingredients until just blended.

3. Spoon the mixture into a pastry bag fitted with a ribbon tip. Pipe the cookies in S shapes onto the prepared sheet.
4. Bake until lightly golden, about 12 minutes. Cool on a rack.

Biscotti al burro e màndorla all'arancia
Orange-Scented-Butter-and-Almond Cookies

MAKES
APPROXIMATELY
15 COOKIES

TIME: 2 HOURS

LEVEL:
MODERATE

My friend Domenica, who lives in Massa Carrara, used to make these cookies in early autumn, when the almonds ripened on the trees. She gave them as gifts, packed in gold paper boxes tied with red ribbons. "Eat them when the winds begin to blow," she would say and all of us did—with steaming pots of hot tea. Last year, her sister gave me the recipe and, when last I saw Domenica, she complained that it was no longer a secret, that I had gone about spreading it to the four winds. I guess she's right, but I firmly believe a good recipe should be shared widely and as soon as possible. "Chi dorme, non piglia pesci!" ("He who sleeps does not catch the fish!")

½ cup unsalted butter, at room temperature
½ cup sugar
2 egg yolks, at room temperature
½ cup ground toasted almonds
1 teaspoon orange extract
½ teaspoon grated orange zest
1 cup cake flour
½ teaspoon salt
Unsalted butter, for greasing

1. Using an electric mixer or wooden spoon, cream the butter and sugar in a large bowl. Add the egg yolks, almonds, orange extract and orange zest and beat until well blended.
2. Sift together the flour and salt. Stir into the butter mixture and beat until a smooth, soft dough has formed. Wrap in plastic and refrigerate for 1 hour.
3. Preheat the oven to 350°F and grease a 12 x 15-inch baking sheet. Transfer the dough to a lightly floured work surface and, using a floured rolling pin, roll to ½-inch thickness.

4. Using a round cookie cutter approximately 2 inches in diameter, cut the dough into individual rounds and place 1 inch apart on the prepared sheet.
5. Bake until lightly golden around the edges, about 10 minutes. Cool on wire racks.

VARIATION: Lemon extract and lemon zest can be substituted for orange extract and orange zest.

MAKE AHEAD: The dough can be prepared the day before, then wrapped in plastic and refrigerated. The completed cookies can be stored in airtight containers for up to 2 weeks.

Lingue di gatto
Cats' Tongues

These long crisp wafers are thin as cats' tongues (hence, their names) and pair very well with ice creams and fruit salads. Make sure to remove them from the baking sheet as soon as they're cooked or they'll crisp up and stick.

MAKES APPROXIMATELY 30 CATS' TONGUES

TIME: 1 HOUR

LEVEL: MODERATE

Unsalted butter or cooking spray, for greasing
4 tablespoons unsalted butter, at room temperature
½ cup confectioners' sugar
1 teaspoon grated orange zest
½ teaspoon almond extract
½ cup cake flour, sifted
½ teaspoon salt
2 egg whites, at room temperature
¼ teaspoon cream of tartar

1. Preheat the oven to 375°F. Grease and flour two 12 x 15-inch baking sheets.
2. Using a wooden spoon or an electric mixer, cream the butter and the sugar in a large bowl. Add the orange zest and almond extract.
3. Add the flour and half the salt and stir until the batter is smooth and blended.
4. Using an electric mixer or hand whisk, beat the egg whites and the remaining ¼ teaspoon salt in a large bowl until foamy. Add the cream of

tartar and beat until stiff peaks form. Gently fold the whites into the butter mixture.

5. Transfer the batter to a 10-inch pastry bag fitted with a round tip, ¼-inch opening.

6. Pipe the batter into 3-inch-long, pencil-thin strips placed about 2 inches apart (they will spread).

7. Bake until the cookies are golden on the sides and pale in the center, about 7 minutes. Immediately and gently transfer to cooling racks.

Biscottini al miele e fichi secchi
Honeyed-Fig Cookies

MAKES
APPROXIMATELY
24 COOKIES

TIME:
1½ HOURS

LEVEL:
MODERATE

Honey is revered throughout Tuscany as one of nature's most perfect foods. Produce markets inevitably have at least one table featuring chestnut, acacia, thyme, sage, and thousand-flowers honeys. This traditional recipe uses acacia, a mild honey variety. Try experimenting with various flavors—each creates a different cookie experience.

Unsalted butter, for greasing
Flour, for dusting
¼ cup unsalted butter, at room temperature
¼ cup acacia or other mild-flavored honey
2½ cups bread flour
1 egg, at room temperature
½ teaspoon salt
3 tablespoons warm milk
1½ teaspoons baking powder
8 dried figs, stemmed and diced
1 egg yolk, at room temperature, lightly beaten with a tablespoon of milk
Confectioners' sugar, for dusting

1. Preheat the oven to 375°F. Grease and flour a 12 x 15-inch baking sheet.

2. Cream the butter and the honey in a large bowl until smooth. Add the flour, egg, salt, milk, baking powder and figs, and beat until the dough is soft and well blended.

3. Transfer the dough to a lightly floured work surface. Using a rolling

pin, roll the dough out to ½ inch thick. Cut the dough into 1½-inch-long diamonds, place on the baking sheet 1 inch apart, and brush the tops with the beaten egg yolk.

4. Bake until golden, about 20 minutes. Remove from oven and cool on a wire rack. When cooled, dust with confectioners' sugar.

VARIATIONS: Any type of dried fruit—apricots, cherries, dates—can be used in place of figs.

MAKE AHEAD: These cookies will keep for up to 2 weeks when stored in an airtight container.

Cialde di montecatini
Meringue-Filled Wafers

Cialde are paper-thin disks of sweet pastry impressed with ornamental designs. They are made with special wafer irons called testi, *which consist of two iron disks engraved on the inside with the negative of a family's particular crest. The two disks are hinged together and long handles extend from each one for holding over the burners of a stove or the flames of a hearth. During the Renaissance, the irons were embellished with allegorical motifs and often bore, at the center of the disk (marking the occasion for which they were designed) the coat of arms of two families united by matrimony.*

Pizzelle irons can be substituted for testi *and can be purchased in stores selling specialty bakeware.*

MAKES APPROXIMATELY 15 WAFERS

TIME: 1½ HOURS

LEVEL: MODERATE

THE WAFERS

3 egg yolks, at room temperature
4 tablespoons sugar
6 tablespoons unsalted butter, at room temperature
2 cups cake flour mixed with ½ teaspoon baking powder
3–5 tablespoons milk
Cooking spray

THE FILLING

½ cup ground toasted almonds
½ cup sugar

½ teaspoon orange extract
1 egg white, at room temperature
Pinch cream of tartar
Whipped cream or ice cream, optional

1. To make the wafers, using an electric mixer or a hand whisk, beat the egg yolks, the sugar and butter in a large bowl until fluffy, pale and smooth, about 5 minutes with the mixer (15 minutes by hand). Add one-third of the flour and continue beating until completely incorporated. Beat in 3 tablespoons milk and half the remaining flour. When the mixture is well blended, add the remaining flour and continue to beat until the batter is the consistency of melted ice cream. If too dense, add 1 to 2 tablespoons of the remaining milk. Set aside for 30 minutes.

2. Spray the two halves of the *testi* or *pizelle* iron with cooking spray and heat until a drop of water sizzles when sprinkled on one of the surfaces.

3. Working in batches, spoon 2 or 3 tablespoons onto one side of the iron, cover with the other side and cook over low to low-medium heat, turning the iron from side to side until there is no steam coming out, 4 to 5 minutes. Transfer the wafers to a heated platter and cover with a cloth to keep warm. Continue until all the mixture has been used.

4. To make the filling, when all the wafers have been made, blend together the almonds, sugar and orange extract in a large bowl. Beat the egg white and the cream of tartar in a large bowl until stiff peaks form. Gently fold into the almond mixture.

5. Spread 1 tablespoon of the almond-egg white mixture across the surface of one wafer and cover with another. Return the stuffed wafer to the iron, press very gently to close and cook on both sides over medium heat until lightly golden, about 1 minute per side. Serve immediately.

VARIATIONS: The wafers can be served without the almond filling. Roll them around ice cream or whipped cream and sprinkle the tops with fresh berries.

MAKE AHEAD: The batter can be prepared up to 1 day in advance and stored, refrigerated, in a sealed container.

Fiorentini
Chocolate-Coated Dried Fruit and Nut Cookies

These cookies originated in Florence (hence, the name fiorentini) *and trying to get the recipe after I'd tasted them in a bake shop one day was like asking the baker to reveal her most cherished secret. How did I succeed? I finally pretended to be the niece of a famous pastry chef from Florence. Thank God, she will never find out about this book! At least, I hope not.*

MAKES
APPROXIMATELY
20 *FIORENTINI*

TIME: 1 HOUR

LEVEL:
MODERATE

Flour, for dusting
½ cup unsalted butter, at room temperature
½ cup sugar
¼ cup cake flour
¼ cup chopped dried apricots
2 tablespoons golden raisins
1 tablespoon chopped candied orange
1 tablespoon grated lemon zest
10 dried cherries, chopped
1 tablespoon toasted almond slivers
1 tablespoon heavy cream
½ pound bittersweet chocolate

1. Preheat the oven to 375°F. Line a 12 x 15-inch baking sheet with waxed paper and dust with flour.
2. Using an electric mixer or a wooden spoon, cream the butter and the sugar until fluffy and smooth. Sift in the flour, add all the fruits, the almonds and the cream and mix until well blended.
3. Drop the mixture by the tablespoonfuls onto the surface, spacing the cookies 2 inches apart. Dip a spatula into iced water and slightly flatten each cookie.
4. Bake until set, about 10 minutes. Remove from the oven and transfer to a cooling rack.
5. Warm the chocolate in a double boiler until melted. Using a pastry brush, spread the chocolate on one side of each cookie. When the chocolate is almost hardened, use the prongs of a fork to make a wavy pattern on the surface.

VARIATIONS: Dried cranberries can be substituted for the cherries. In place of the flour, try substituting ¼ cup ground almonds.

MAKE AHEAD: The cookie mixture can be prepared up to 1 day in advance and stored, refrigerated, in a sealed container.

Ossi di morto
Dead Man's Bones

MAKES
APPROXIMATELY
20 COOKIES

TIME: 1 HOUR

LEVEL: EASY

This recipe takes its morbid name from the alabaster color and crisp texture of the cookies—duro come un osso (hard as bones). Originally, they were made only on October 31st, All Soul's Day, but now they can be found year round in local bakeries throughout Tuscany.

Unsalted butter, for greasing
Flour, for dusting
1 cup cake flour
1½ cups sugar
2 tablespoons confectioners' sugar
4 egg whites, beaten into stiff peaks
½ cup ground hazelnuts
1 cup ground almonds
½ teaspoon vanilla extract
½ teaspoon grated lemon zest
Butter, for greasing
Flour, for dusting

1. Preheat the oven to 325°F and grease and lightly flour a 12 x 15-inch baking sheet.
2. Sift the flour, the sugar and confectioners' sugar into a large bowl. Fold in the egg whites.
3. Add the ground nuts, vanilla extract and lemon zest and gently stir until a dough has formed. Shape the dough into a circle and cut into ⅜-inch-thick slices.
4. Arrange the cookies approximately 1 inch apart on the sheet.
5. Bake until lightly golden, about 25 minutes. Remove from oven and cool on a wire rack.

MAKE AHEAD: Stored in an airtight container, these cookies will keep for up to 3 weeks.

Nozze
Lemon and Anise Seed Wafers

Every year in mid-June, Calcinaia, in the province of Pisa has a Nozze Sagra—*a country fair devoted to these lemon and anise seed wafers, named* nozze, *which means "weddings." No one really remembers whether they were originally served at weddings or whether the name refers to the perfect marriage between lemon and anise seed that gives this dessert its extraordinary flavor. As with the* Cialde di montecatini *(Meringue-Filled Wafers), recipe on page 59, these wafers require the use of a* pizzelle *iron. The finished wafer must also be rolled around a thin cylinder—cannoli forms are perfect although any cylinder roughly two inches in diameter will do.*

MAKES
APPROXIMATELY
30 WAFERS

TIME: 3 HOURS

LEVEL:
MODERATE

9 eggs plus 1 egg yolk, at room temperature
½ cup sugar
½ cup *rosolio* (rose liqueur)
2 tablespoons anise seeds, soaked in ½ cup extra-virgin olive oil for 3 hours
½ cup cake flour, sifted
2 cups fresh sheep's milk or other ricotta
4 tablespoons confectioners' sugar

1. Using an electric mixer or a whisk, beat the eggs and the sugar in a large bowl until smooth, pale and fluffy, about 5 minutes with a mixer (15 minutes by hand). Add the *rosolio* and the anise seeds with the oil and blend until a smooth batter has formed.

2. Stir in the flour, cover with a cloth and let sit for at least 2 hours. Stir once in a while to prevent a crust from forming.

3. Place the *pizzelle* iron over low-medium heat until a drop of water drizzled on one of the surfaces sizzles. Pour a spoonful of batter into the center of *pizzelle* iron and press closed. Place the iron over the burner and cook for 3 minutes; turn and cook for 2 minutes on the other side. Remove the waffle from the iron and immediately roll it around a cannoli form (or a thin, straight sided glass or bottle) until cooled, less than 1 minute. Place on a dish and set aside. Repeat until all the batter has been used.

4. Using an electric mixer or hand whisk, beat the ricotta and the confec-

tioners' sugar until smooth, about 1 to 2 minutes with the mixer (5 minutes by hand). Fill the waffle rolls with the ricotta mixture and serve.

VARIATION: Whipped cream can be substituted for the ricotta.

MAKE AHEAD: The batter can be prepared the day before and stored, refrigerated, in a sealed container.

Biscottini ai pinoli
Pine Nut Crescents

MAKES
APPROXIMATELY
40 COOKIES

TIME: 1 HOUR

LEVEL:
MODERATE

Five of seven times that these cookies are presented, someone is bound to dredge up the rivalry that has existed for centuries between the Sienese and the Pisani over who was the first to come up with the recipe. This particular version is made throughout the province of Pisa, but the Sienese apparently claim that the Pisani simply copied their famous Ricciarelli di Siena (Christmas Almond Cookies), recipe on page 257, and changed the recipe title dastardly to disguise the deed. The judgments and accusations continue to this day: "I Senesi hanno sei nasi" ("The Sienese have six noses [for lying]"), maintains an old Pisan proverb. To which the Sienese righteously reply: "Il Pisanti rubano il sale e puoi te lo vendano" ("The Pisani steal your salt and then sell it back to you").

Unsalted butter, for greasing
Flour, for dusting
6 eggs, at room temperature
2 cups sugar
½ teaspoon vanilla extract
½ cup ground pine nuts
1 teaspoon grated lemon zest
½ cup unsalted butter, at room temperature
5 tablespoons warm milk
6 tablespoons rum
1½ cups bread flour
1 tablespoon baking powder
5 tablespoons whole pine nuts
Confectioners' sugar, for dusting

1. Preheat the oven to 350°F. Grease and flour a 12 x 15-inch baking sheet.

2. Using an electric mixer or a hand whisk, beat the eggs, sugar and vanilla in a large bowl until a smooth, pale and fluffy, 3 to 4 minutes with the mixer (about 10 minutes by hand). Stir in the ground pine nuts and lemon zest.

3. Beat in the butter, milk and rum until a smooth batter has formed.

4. Sift the flour and baking powder into the mixture and stir to blend.

5. Transfer the dough to a pastry bag fitted with a plain tip and pipe the mixture onto the prepared baking sheet in 2-inch crescents. Press the whole pine nuts lightly into the surface.

6. Bake until lightly golden, about 20 minutes. Remove from the oven and cool on a rack.

VARIATIONS: Cognac or brandy can be substituted for the rum.

MAKE AHEAD: Stored in an airtight container, these cookies keep for up to 2 weeks.

Buchi con fichi
Fig-and-Pine-Nut Cookies

When summer comes to Tuscany, figs are almost everywhere and it is hard to find an appetizer menu not featuring the ubiquitous fichi con prosciutto *(figs and prosciutto). But figs are also used in a great many desserts, especially at the end of summer when they are at their sweetest. There are fig custards, fig pastries, fig preserves and fig tarts. The following cookies are yet another wonderful example of the perfection of figs —in any form!*

MAKES 6 LARGE
COOKIES

TIME: 1 HOUR

LEVEL:
MODERATE

2 recipes Basic *Pasta Frolla* (see page 34)
½ cup fig preserves
1 teaspoon roughly chopped pine nuts
1 teaspoon finely diced candied lemon peel
Confectioners' sugar
3 tablespoons lightly toasted, finely ground hazelnuts

1. Preheat the oven to 350°F. Line two 12 x 15-inch baking sheets with parchment paper.

2. Remove the two disks of *pasta frolla* from the refrigerator and place on

a lightly floured work surface. Using a floured rolling pin, roll each disk into an 8 x 12-inch rectangle, ⅓ inch thick.

3. Using a 4-inch round cookie cutter, cut 12 circles of *pasta frolla.*
4. Using a 1½-inch-round cookie cutter, cut out the center of 6 circles, forming dough rings and cookie holes.*
5. Place the fig preserves, pine nuts and lemon peel in a saucepan and cook over low heat for 5 minutes, stirring constantly until the preserves have melted. Cool to room temperature.
6. Place a tablespoon of the preserve mixture on each whole circle of *pasta frolla,* spreading it to within ½ inch of the edge. Brush the edges lightly with water. Gently top with the *pasta frolla* rings and lightly press the edges to seal. Using a spatula, transfer the cookies to the prepared baking sheet.
7. Bake until lightly golden, about 20 minutes. Cool on wire racks.
8. Cut pieces of waxed paper the same size as the holes in the cookies and cover the preserves. Dust the cookies with sugar and the ground hazelnuts. Remove the waxed paper and serve with ripe figs cut in half.

* The cookie holes make delicious cookies in their own right. Bake on a separate baking sheet until golden brown, about 10 minutes. Cool on a wire rack and dust with confectioners' sugar.

VARIATIONS: Any type of preserves can be used in place of the figs. Try raspberry or apricot.

Ravioli dolci
Fruit-Filled Ravioli

MAKES
APPROXIMATELY
40 RAVIOLI

TIME: 2 HOURS

LEVEL:
ADVANCED

Ravioli are filled with cheese, meat, fish, vegetables, even other grains. But fruit? Yes, fruit. In this case, fresh peach compote. Unlike their savory counterparts, dessert ravioli are made with sweet dough created from a mixture of flour, sugar and marsala.

2 cups cake flour
½ cup unsalted butter, at room temperature
4 tablespoons sugar
3 eggs, at room temperature
3 tablespoons marsala or sherry

½ teaspoon salt
Pinch of ground ginger
Pinch of ground nutmeg
2 pounds peaches, peeled and finely diced
2 cups vegetable oil, for frying
Confectioners' sugar, for dusting

1. Place the flour, butter, 1½ tablespoons sugar, eggs, marsala, salt, ginger and nutmeg in the bowl of a food processor and pulse until a ball of dough forms on the blades. Transfer to a lightly floured work surface and briefly knead into a smooth, soft dough. Put in a bowl, cover with a towel and let rest for 15 minutes.

2. Meanwhile, place the peaches in a large, heavy-gauge saucepan, stir in the remaining 2½ tablespoons sugar, and cook over low heat until reduced to a thick purée, about 30 minutes.

3. Cut the dough into three pieces. Pass one piece at a time through every setting on a pasta machine, wide to narrow, until it emerges from the next-to-last setting.* Allow to dry for 15 minutes on a lightly floured work surface. Continue until all three pieces have been prepared.

4. Spoon ½-teaspoon portions of the peach purée in a straight line along the bottom half of the dough rectangles, about 1¼ inches from the edge and 1 inch apart. Fold the top over the bottom and press down between each mound to seal the dough well.

5. Using a jagged-edged cutting wheel, a 2-inch-diameter ravioli cutter, or a 2-inch-square ravioli cutter, cut the dough into ravioli and trim off excess dough. Transfer the ravioli to a surface dusted lightly with flour.

6. Heat vegetable oil to 375° F. Add ravioli, no more than 5 or 6 at a time, and fry until golden on both sides, turning once. Drain on paper towels, then dust with sugar. Serve hot or cold.

* If you don't have a pasta machine, roll the dough with a rolling pin until it reaches the thickness of 3 sheets of paper (approximately ⅛ inch).

VARIATIONS: Apples, pears, apricots and nectarines can be used in place of peaches. Preserves can also be used in place of fresh fruit.

MAKE AHEAD: The dough can be made the day before, wrapped tightly in plastic and stored in the refrigerator until needed. Return to room temperature before rolling. It can also be frozen for up to three weeks. Thaw in the refrigerator.

Dolcetti di cioccolata e nocciole
Chocolate-Hazelnut Cookies

MAKES
APPROXIMATELY
36 COOKIES

TIME:
1¼ HOURS PLUS
OVERNIGHT
REFRIGERATION

LEVEL:
MODERATE

These extraordinary cookies are an adaptation of a recipe from my grand-mother, Angelina. I have substituted butter for lard in the dough and choco-late for cocoa powder—in other words, I have taken a recipe from her poverty days and gentrified it!

THE CHOCOLATE DOUGH

1 cup bread flour
⅛ teaspoon baking powder
⅛ teaspoon salt
4 ounces finely grated dark chocolate
½ cup sugar
1 teaspoon vanilla extract
1 egg yolk, at room temperature
1 cup blanched hazelnuts
1 egg white, lightly beaten, at room temperature
½ cup unsalted butter, cut into ⅛-inch-thick slices

THE BUTTER DOUGH

1 cup bread flour
⅛ teaspoon baking powder
⅛ teaspoon salt
¼ cup sugar
1 teaspoon vanilla extract
1 egg yolk, at room temperature
1 egg white, lightly beaten, at room temperature
½ cup unsalted butter, cut into ⅛-inch-thick slices
Unsalted butter, for greasing

1. To make the chocolate dough, sift flour and baking powder into a large bowl. Add salt, grated chocolate, sugar, vanilla and egg yolk. Using a pastry blender, cut in the butter until a ball has formed. Transfer to a lightly floured work surface and knead briefly into a smooth dough. Knead in the hazelnuts. Shape dough into a 9-inch square, ½ inch thick and brush with the beaten egg white. Set aside.

2. To prepare the butter dough, sift the flour and baking powder into a large bowl. Add the salt, sugar, vanilla and egg yolk. Using a pastry blender, cut in the butter until a ball has formed. Transfer to a lightly floured surface and knead briefly into a smooth dough. Shape into a 9-inch square, ½ inch thick. Place on top of the chocolate dough square and roll the two into a cylinder. Wrap in plastic and chill overnight in the refrigerator.

3. Preheat oven to 325°F and grease a 12 x 15-inch baking sheet. Slice dough cylinder into ¼-inch-thick slices with a sharp knife. Transfer to prepared sheet, placing cookies 1 inch apart.

4. Bake until golden, 14 to 18 minutes. Cool on a wire rack.

MAKE AHEAD: The dough can be made up to 2 days in advance and kept refrigerated until ready to use.

CHAPTER THREE

Single-Portion Desserts

Art Is Art Is Art

When Michelangelo was asked how he created the David, he simply answered, "I just carved away everything that was not him." Such clarity of vision was extraordinary even for a block of recorded time considered to be one of the art world's foremost "Golden Ages." To listen to this Renaissance master talk about his artistic process, one would think his creations required no effort greater than just showing up at the studio on a daily basis.

"That's the way art should always be," says Silvano Spini, my friend Cinzia's father. "Art is a spirit that uses the body as a medium for its creation. It should never pause in the brain for even a split second."

Silvano is a highly opinionated man—a man who never lets any piece of information go until he has mulled it over six times, analyzed it through every available prism and then calculated his precise position, which he then never fails to share with you in a manner suggesting he has spoken the quintessential word.

I like Silvano. Nothing I say should create any opinion other than that I really and truly like him. It's just that he is Florentine, which is to say conservative, traditional and rule bound. There is not a rule Silvano has trouble with—quite the opposite. Cinzia, his daughter, teasingly refers to him as "Galateo," the Italian Emily Post.

"*Babbo* (Tuscan for "dad") is like Florence itself," she has always maintained. "The perfect representative of a city whose buildings almost all date back to the 1400s without one precious stone ever having been changed."

Cinzia, Silvano and Lubiana, Cinzia's mother, live in Certaldo Alto, a beautiful medieval village that roosts on top of a lush green hill dominating the Elsa river valley. Located just south of Florence, halfway to Siena, Certaldo is the birthplace of Bocaccio, who wrote his Decameron in an ivy-covered stone monastery that has now been turned into a museum. Everyone who lives in the village feels a certain proprietariness about it, as if they have been entrusted with a historical treasure, which, in fact, they have. They walk through the ancient streets with their noses pointing toward God, their spines as straight as the majestic cypresses that define the borders between one property and another.

I have come to have lunch with the Spinis, after which Cinzia and I are scheduled to drive into Florence for an exhibit of our friend Riccardo's paintings. Today is the last day of his show and Riccardo is supposed to receive the prestigious Lauriana award honoring the extraordinary body of work he has created in the past 12 years. There will be a number of celebrities present as well as press people from all over Europe and two from Japan, where his work is extremely well regarded.

Silvano was not pleased when he heard of our plans.

"Who are these people giving Riccardo an award?" he demanded to know. "Do they know anything at all about art?"

In Silvano's mind, what Riccardo does is not art. "It's a simple exercise in pure self-indulgence," he says. "What else can be said about a collection of childlike canvases, each one so nearly identical to the one before it in shape, size, color and theme as to make the word 'repetitive' seem like a gross understatement?"

Riccardo's life work has been about exploring what he calls "the dark personal psyche hidden behind a wall of modern anonymity." He paints people—both familiar and not (although he never hints at identities)—and then hides them under several coats of dark, lacquered veneer so that only the faintest shadow of the person's visage seeps through. The works are almost always large—huge, actually—and standing in a gallery hung with his canvases, one can't help but be struck by the sheer power of the eerie darkness, by the ghostly presence of people peering out from beneath their imposed curtains, begging to be seen, begging to have their identities restored. One reviewer called the work "a masterful metaphor for life in the modern age."

That's not to say I would ever consider buying one and hanging it in my living room. Which is one of Silvano's foremost determinants for whether or not it is art.

"If it's not pleasing to the eye, then it's not art," he says.

"So if I don't like a particular painting done by Bellini, then that painting is not art?" Cinzia asks as we sit down to lunch.

"You would certainly never say that about Bellini," her father clarifies. Even if you don't like his subjects or his technique, no one would say the man is not an artist."

"Why not?" Cinzia presses. "Suppose I don't like any of Bellini's paintings. Using your measurement stick, I would say what he does is not art. Is that what you're saying?"

Cinzia and her father often go head to head on topics. In most cases, it's simply teasing; sometimes, however, there's a great huffing on the part of one or the other and then Lubiana has to intercede. But we're still a long way from that point here.

"You can't judge art using a framework of personal subjectivity," I say because I long ago learned that, in this house, silence is more objectionable than contrariness. "If everyone did that, what's art and what's not art, or more appropriately what's good and what's not good art would be determined solely by a quick, uneducated glance. You need to know something about what you're seeing."

"Ah!" says Silvano. "Now we're throwing mud into waters already saturated with sludge. Now we bring in the concept of 'education'." He sits back in his chair as Lubiana serves the soup. "It's not enough to look at something and say 'I like it, I don't like it.' We have to study it before we can be permitted an opinion."

Cinzia drizzles oil over her soup and then with perfect poise, turns to glare at her father. "No one is saying you have to complete a course of study on a person's work. But it does help to know what you're looking at—to know something about the artist's intent."

"Why should I extend myself toward the artist," Silvano explodes. "It's the artist's responsibility to extend himself to me!"

"Mangiate," says Lubiana, fearing the argument will overshadow her precious chestnut soup. (Eat).

"Why?" Cinzia asks with supreme calm. She takes a small, dainty spoonful of soup and carefully raises it to her lips. Watching her movements out of the corner of my eye, I can't help but smile. This has always been her debate strategy, through all the years we spent together at university. The other person gets louder, she gets softer. At times when she's used it on me, I have become infuriated.

Likewise Silvano. "Because art is about communication," he screams. "There is no purpose to creating art other than to make a statement. And what good is making a statement if no one can hear it?"

I love eating lunch with this family. It's never restful in the way that mealtimes are supposed to be. Everyone jumps in with heart and soul, regardless of who is present or what their views are.

"So what you're saying is that for the statement to be considered valid, it must be understood and therefore appreciated by the lowest common denominator, meaning everyman," Cinzia is saying between sips of soup. "If not, if there's any mystery about it or obscurity or, heaven forbid, a degree of exploration too personal to be immediately obvious, then the artist is reneging on a social contract."

"Cinzia, you know what your father is saying," Lubiana interjects. "No one questions Riccardo's right to create the art he does. It's just hard to understand why reporters are flocking here from Paris and Bonn to celebrate his work while, at the Palatina, no one even notices the stunning works by Titian hanging in the Sala di Venere."

"What about music," I say to forestall poor Riccardo being pitted against Titian. "What about Stravinsky who often relies on passages totally alien to any sense you have of rhythm or melody." I broach the question to Lubiana, an amateur music historian.

"That's a very good question," she says. "Generally I don't like atonal music, but I like it more when I can see it live. Because then I can watch the musician's process." She turns to her husband. "Remember when we went to that concert in the Boboli Gardens?" she says. "The musicians played a series of completely dissonant pieces. And yet we both loved it." She pauses to watch his reaction. "So maybe Riccardo should invite viewers to watch him create?" she says in an obvious effort to bring the conversation to a close.

It doesn't work. "To watch what? Riccardo slapping black paint on canvas after canvas?" Silvano pushes away his soup in preparation for the grilled lamb that is Lubiana's specialty. "The problem with all of this is that we've forgotten what art is. Art is a visceral pleasure afforded by the eyes and—in the case of music, the ears. Not the brain. Never the brain. Once you have to think about what you're seeing, it's no longer art."

I can almost predict Cinzia's next words. "Cite your source for that definition," she says, employing yet another strategy with which I am all too familiar. "Where does it say that art cannot be something considered?"

"It's common sense," says Silvano, trying to bludgeon his way to truth in lieu of having any real evidence. "Art is a creative process. Once you involve the brain, you have a reasoned response. The two are antithetical."

"I'm not sure you're right, Silvano," I say. "What about great literature? Is that not art? And yet, writers routinely draw outlines and impose artificial structures on their creative beginnings." I strive for compromise, remembering how many times Cinzia has teased me for always attempting to make peace. "Why not just say that there are different kinds of art—some forms are purely beautiful, others are . . . , let's use the word *'affascinante.'"*

The show is quite a success. Thirty-eight of Riccardo's paintings dominate the main hall of the Lanzone Galleria on Via dei Calzaioli. The room swarms with journalists, many standing transfixed before the largest of the canvases, entitled *Perdita Espediente* (Medium Loss). The looks on their faces connotes a blend of reverence and confusion, as if they're not quite sure whether to laugh or cry. Beneath the veneer of gray-brown haze, a woman is running off the canvas towards the audience, her sneakers barely visible under the thickly-applied top coats. To me, she looks somewhat like Princess Diana, although Riccardo says no. He often says no when I pose questions about the identity of this one or that one, but he never says who it actually is.

"I never intend any of my subjects to be one specific person," he says. "I work with themes that are larger than the individual."

The comments made by people in the room are much along the lines of that particular one by Riccardo; the meanings all as hazy as the dark curtains on his canvases, the underlying intent hidden by design. When I talk to someone like Silvano about this type of art ("contemporary," one woman chided a man who had called it "modern"), I become fiercely protective of Riccardo's reputation. Not in terms of guarding his honor, but more defending the validity of creating one's own rules.

But when here in the thick of people dressed all in black posing glamorously on bleached wooden floors and discussing the art in hushed, cerebral tones, I find myself stepping back and marveling at the ridiculousness of it all.

At one point a Japanese journalist draws me into a conversation about the one piece in the show I can honestly say I truly detest. It's a floor-to-ceiling, very thin canvas hung in the entranceway so that you see it as soon as you walk in. The subjects seem to be a group of very young girls whose faces are brutally slashed but glowing with vitality. The veneer is overlaid in blotches, as if thrown onto the canvas and hence their bodies, in violent thrusts. I don't like the colors, I don't like the maniacal mood and most of all, I don't like how I feel when looking at it.

This turns out to be the very thing inspiring such a sense of awe in the journalist. "It makes me feel sick," he says with great glee in his voice. "I have rarely experienced such an emotional outpouring of revulsion."

"But would you have it in your house," I say, invoking Silvano's test.

"Certainly," he says. "If I could afford it, I would love to hang it over my couch. The passion would overwhelm the room."

"I think it's a question of one's personal level of stress," I say to Cinzia when the show is over and we're driving back to her house. It is a new theory I've read about somewhere, and I want to try it out conversationally. "I think I'm more open to obscure art when my life is calm enough to be able to accommodate the stress of not understanding."

"That's a good point," she says. "I'm much more able to extend myself toward obliqueness when I don't have to harness all my energy just to cope with daily life."

"How does that apply to your father?" I ask. "Given this new theory we've just developed, your father's life must obviously be too stressed to be able to appreciate anything other than the familiar."

"No," says Cinzia, pulling into her driveway. "*Babbo* is not even one percent stressed. In his case, he is at the opposite end of the spectrum— so supremely comfortable as to just have become lazy."

"*Allora*," Silvano says as Lubiana puts on a pot of coffee. "How was the show?"

"Wonderful," I say, cautiously.

"The truth now," he says. "Did he sell any of his so-called paintings?"

Cinzia puts her arms around her father's neck. "Actually, *caro*, you're not going to believe this, but there were only two left unsold." She gives him a big kiss on the tip of his nose. "I thought about getting one for your birthday, but then Sandra reminded me it wouldn't fit in the car."

He laughs and kisses her back. Then he turns to me. "Seriously now, Sandra. What did you think? My daughter's a little crazy, but I've always thought of you as a sensible, feet-on-the-ground kind of person. Did you like any of them?"

"To tell you the truth, Silvano, I loved each and every one." I look him square in the eye. He looks back at me. His lips curl upward—the beginning of a smile. "I know you for 22 years," it says. "You can't hide behind Riccardo's dark veneers." I lose it and break into an outright laugh.

"Actually, Silvano, I much prefer Michelangelo."

Single-Portion Desserts (Bocconcini)

The first point of impact whenever I enter a Tuscan *pasticcerìa* comes from the overwhelming abundance of dessert options. There they all sit, in perfect little doily cups, side by side in the display case, looking at me as if to say "which of us are you going to choose?" If my eyes had a voice, the answer would undoubtedly be "one of each." But my well-documented tendency toward gluttony and a bulging waistline hovers in a dark corner of my consciousness, and so I demure and choose instead from the case filled with what we call *bocconcini* (single-portion desserts that are somewhat smaller in size than even a piece of cake or tart).

If all goes well, my conscience is so thoroughly assuaged by this rare example of culinary discipline that I can then convince myself to simply have another. After all, they are so much smaller than an entire slice of chocolate tart and, anyway, what value can we assign to an existence completely devoid of the occasional flight of passion?

Bocconcini include everything from chocolate truffles to custard filled cream puffs to miniature sambuca soufflés to creamy chestnut babas and are much more diminutive than the zabaione cake often described in retrospect by those who have chosen large when they should have stuck with small as *un mattone nello stòmaco* (a brick in the stomach).

Single-Portion Desserts
(Bocconcini)

Diti alla crema
Tuscan Cannolis Filled with Ricotta and Pine Nuts

Gocce di neve
Snow Drops

Bocconcini di marzapane
Marzipan Nibbles

Tartufi di castagne e cioccolata
Chocolate-Chestnut Truffles

Tartufi al cocco e mascarpone
Coconut-Mascarpone Truffles

Frittelle di ricotta alla pietrasantina
Lemon-Ricotta Fritters

Piccoli napoleoni con pere calde al cioccolato
Chocolate Napoleons with Warm Pears

Soufflés con cioccolato aromatizzato all'arancia e praline
Individual Soufflés with Orange-Chocolate Sauce and Hazelnut Pralines

Ricottine al mandarino
Ricotta Molds with Cognac-Soaked Clementines

Mimosine con tartellette di banana
Banana Tarts with Mimosa

Bomboloncini riempiti di crema alla lavanda
Miniature Doughnuts Filled with Lavender Cream

Pirottini al cioccolato con arancia candita e mandorle
Bittersweet Chocolate Cups with Candied Orange and Almonds

Tegoline di pistacchi
Pistacchio Leaves with Pistachio Ice Cream

Castagnole
Honey-Glazed Puffs Served with Candied Chestnuts

Diti alla crema
Tuscan Cannolis Filled with Ricotta and Pine Nuts

When we hear the word cannoli, *we generally think of the Sicilians who made the dessert an international favorite. But in Tuscany,* cannoli *are called* diti *(fingers) or* cannoncini *(small cannons) and are made with puff pastry dough that is baked instead of fried. Like their Sicilian counterparts, Tuscan cannoli are filled with fresh ricotta, which has been sieved twice for extra smoothness. If you are unable to find the* ricotta di pecora *(sheep's milk ricotta) used by Tuscans, at least make sure to buy a truly fresh cow's milk variety. The prepackaged supermarket type will simply not give the same flavor. If possible, mix in a little goat cheese ricotta to give a slightly tarter flavor. Most kitchenware stores sell the cannoli forms needed to make the outer shells.*

MAKES
10 *CANNOLI*

TIME:
1½ HOURS

LEVEL:
ADVANCED

Unsalted butter, for greasing
1 recipe Basic Puff Pastry (see page 37)
1 egg, lightly beaten along with 1 tablespoon water, for wash
½ cup fresh sheep's milk ricotta or cow's milk ricotta mixed with a little
    goat's milk ricotta
½ cup Basic Custard (see page 34)
2 tablespoons coarsely ground pine nuts
1 teaspoon vanilla extract
Cocoa powder, for dusting

1. Lightly butter ten 1-inch-diameter *cannoli* forms, line a 12 x 15-inch baking sheet with parchment paper and preheat the oven to 400°F.
2. Remove the prepared dough from the refrigerator and using a floured rolling pin roll the dough into 3 x 20-inch rectangle, ¼ inch thick. Using a sharp knife and working across the width of the dough, cut out ten 2-inch-wide strips approximately.
3. Roll each strip around a cannoli form, overlap the edges and press to seal.
4. Lightly brush the dough with the beaten egg and place on the prepared baking sheet.
5. Bake until lightly golden, about 15 minutes. Remove from oven and cool on a wire rack. Do not remove the tubes until completely cooled.

6. Meanwhile, prepare the filling. Press the ricotta through a fine sieve into a medium-size bowl. Sieve the ricotta again. Stir in the custard, pine nuts and vanilla and mix until well blended.
7. Pour the custard mixture into a medium-size pastry bag fitted with a plain tip. Gently slide the cannoli shells off the tubes. Pipe the mixture into the shells, dust with cocoa powder and serve.

VARIATIONS: For a fruity filling, substitute ½ cup thick fruit purée (pear, banana, apple) for either the ricotta or the custard.

MAKE AHEAD: The cannoli shells can be made up to 4 weeks in advance, wrapped tightly in plastic and frozen until needed. Thaw in the refrigerator, crisp for 5 minutes in a preheated 400°F oven and cool to room temperature before filling.

Gocce di neve
Snow Drops

MAKES
12 DROPS

TIME: 2 HOURS

LEVEL:
ADVANCED

Since Tuscany is a region kissed by the sun, snow is a very rare event. It is especially rare in Lucca province, where I live, because we border the sea. Nevertheless, in 1985, it snowed, paralyzing the entire region to the point where people could not leave their houses. Granted, there was only an inch or two on Viareggio's streets, but for people used to wearing slippers to run around the corner for fresh bread, the sudden need for boots left them somewhat flummoxed.

This recipe is a tribute to that long ago moment. For weeks afterwards, the windows of local pasticcerie all featured these snowball-like puffs, and they became all the rage, which caused me to wonder whether those who screamed so loud about "the tragedy" may secretly have loved it. I certainly did!

THE DOUGH

Unsalted butter or cooking spray, for greasing
½ cup water
¼ teaspoon salt
½ cup unsalted butter
½ cup cake flour
4 eggs, at room temperature

THE FILLING

½ cup milk
2 tablespoons flour
¼ cup sugar
⅛ teaspoon salt
1 egg yolk, lightly beaten
1 tablespoon Cointreau
1 cup whipped cream
Confectioners' sugar, for dusting

1. Preheat the oven to 375°F. Grease a 12 x 15-inch baking sheet.
2. To make the dough, place the water and salt in a medium-size saucepan and bring to a boil. Whisk in the butter and cook over low heat until melted. Remove from heat.
3. Whisk the flour into the saucepan, pouring in a steady stream until incorporated. Cook the mixture over low heat, stirring constantly until the mixture comes away from the sides of the pot and a smooth ball of dough has formed, about 7 minutes. Remove from heat and cool for 10 minutes.
4. Stir in 3 eggs, one at a time and blend well until a glossy and smooth mixture has formed.
5. Drop the dough onto the baking sheet by the tablespoon, spacing the mounds 3 inches apart. In a small bowl, lightly beat the remaining egg. Brush each mound with beaten egg.
6. Bake for 15 minutes or until golden brown. Remove from oven and cool on a rack.
7. To make the custard, heat the milk in a small saucepan until very hot but not boiling.
8. Mix the sugar, flour and salt together in a medium-size bowl, stir in the hot milk and beat until well blended. Pour back into the pan and continue to stir over low heat until very thick and smooth, 4 to 5 minutes. Add the egg yolks and cook for 5 minutes, stirring constantly.
9. Cool, stirring occasionally and then add the Cointreau.
10. Gently fold the whipped cream into the cooled custard. Slice open the puffs and spoon the mixture into each. Dust with the confectioners' sugar.

VARIATIONS: The puffs can be filled with ice cream, chocolate cream or other types of sweet custards; they can also be served with savory fillings.

MAKE AHEAD: The custard can be prepared the day before and refrigerated in a sealed container.

—————

Bocconcini di marzapane
Marzipan Nibbles

MAKES
APPROXIMATELY
24 NIBBLES

TIME: 1 HOUR

LEVEL:
ADVANCED

"Se metti buono, levi buono," maintains an old Tuscan proverb. ("If you use good ingredients, you will get good results.") In this case, the reference is to making your own marzipan instead of buying already prepared. Marzipan is almond paste combined with egg whites and sugar to make a smooth blend that can be molded. Very easy to prepare, the homemade variety is infinitely fresher and easier to shape than the tubes of paste sold at baker's supply stores. In lieu of a muffin tin, use disposable miniature baking cups.

1 cup almond paste
5 egg whites, at room temperature
2 teaspoons almond extract
2 cups confectioners' sugar
2 tablespoons amaretto liqueur
½ cup apricot or apple preserves
½ teaspoon salt
½ teaspoon cream of tartar
½ cup almond slivers

1. Preheat the oven to 350°F. Grease a miniature muffin tin with capacity for 12 muffins that are 1⅝ inch in diameter and ⅝ inch deep (or use disposable miniature muffin cups).
2. Crumble the almond paste into a bowl, add 1 egg white, the almond extract and sugar. Using an electric mixer or sugared hands, mix until the ingredients form a ball. Knead for a few minutes until smooth and satiny.
3. Place the marzipan in a bowl and stir in the amaretto and preserves until well blended.
4. Using an electric mixer or hand whisk, beat the 4 remaining egg whites and the salt until foamy. Add the cream of tartar and beat until stiff peaks form. Fold the egg whites into the marzipan mixture just until blended.

5. Spoon the mixture into the muffin cups. Top with the almond slivers.
6. Bake until lightly golden, about 15 minutes. Remove the muffins from the tin and transfer to a cooling rack. Repeat with the remaining batter.

MAKE AHEAD: The marzipan can be prepared the day before through Step 2.

Tartufi di castagne e cioccolata
Chocolate-Chestnut Truffles

MAKES
APPROXIMATELY
30 TRUFFLES

TIME: 1 HOUR

LEVEL: EASY

When it comes to trees, Tuscany has more chestnuts than olives, which is why chestnut fruits have always been one of the region's essential sources of food. I still remember stories told by my grandfather, Celso, a partisan, who spent much of the declining years of World War II hiding in the woods of northern Tuscany. His only source of food was what the woods offered—berries, mushrooms and, of course, chestnuts.

These delectable truffles take their creaminess from chestnut purée, which takes the place of butter and cream. Dried chestnuts can be found in specialty and Italian gourmet stores.

1 pound dried chestnuts, soaked for 6 hours, drained and rinsed
2 cups milk
½ teaspoon vanilla extract
5 ounces bittersweet chocolate in chunk form
1 ounce bittersweet chocolate, finely grated
2 tablespoons sugar
2 tablespoons *Vin Santo* or Cointreau

1. Place the chestnuts and milk in a medium-size saucepan, and cook for 30 minutes over very low heat, stirring occasionally. Don't worry if the milk looks curdled.
2. Stir in the vanilla, add the chocolate chunk and cook until melted.
3. Purée the mixture in a food processor until smooth and creamy. Add the sugar and *Vin Santo* and process for 1 minute. Transfer the mixture to a bowl, cover and refrigerate until firm, about 5 hours.
4. Place the grated chocolate in a medium-size bowl. To form the truffles, pinch off a walnut-size piece of chocolate-chestnut dough and roll into a ball using the palms of your hands. Roll in the grated chocolate until

completely coated and place on a serving platter. Repeat until all the truffle mixture has been used. Sprinkle any remaining grated chocolate on top and serve.

MAKE AHEAD: The truffles can be made up to 1 week in advance and refrigerated in a sealed container. They can also be frozen for up to 3 weeks.

Tartufi al cocco e mascarpone
Coconut-Mascarpone Truffles

MAKES
APPROXIMATELY
30 TRUFFLES

TIME: 1 HOUR

LEVEL: EASY

"Truffles are the diamonds of the kitchen," wrote Anthelme Brillat Savarin, the famous French gourmet and politician, in his 1825 Physiologie du Gout. *I firmly agree with him, especially when I look at the price. Those truffles are, of course, the pungent tubers that attach themselves to the roots of certain trees. In the glittering, no-holds-barred 80s, they were suddenly propelled from relative obscurity in the larders of field-workers to $2000 per pound essentials as restaurateurs began using them on everything from fried eggs to creamy risottos. Their popularity was so all encompassing that this dessert version was created. The original dessert truffles were simply made with mascarpone and rolled in chocolate. How far we have come since those days of innocence!*

Although very similar in preparation to the chestnut-chocolate truffles on the previous page, these coconut and mascarpone nibbles have a completely different, albeit equally delicious, flavor. Their richness comes from a blend of mascarpone, which is a triple-cream cheese native to northern Italy, and sheep's milk ricotta. Coffee, chocolate, coconut, ground nuts and amaretto impart a rich, complex flavor.

1 pound mascarpone cheese or cream cheese
½ cup fresh sheep's milk ricotta or other fresh ricotta
½ cup confectioners' sugar
3 cups coconut flakes
½ pound unsweetened chocolate, grated
1 teaspoon finely ground coffee
½ cup ground toasted hazelnuts or almonds
6 tablespoons amaretto or rum
5 tablespoons cocoa powder

1. Place the mascarpone and ricotta in a large bowl and add the confectioners' sugar, stirring until the mixture is creamy and fluffy.
2. Gradually stir in the 2 cups of coconut flakes, the grated chocolate, ground coffee and ground hazelnuts. Pour in the amaretto and mix until all ingredients are well blended.
3. Place the remaining 1 cup coconut flakes in a small bowl. Pinch off a walnut-size piece of truffle mixture and roll into a ball in the palms of your hands. Roll the ball in the coconut flakes until completely coated. Place on a serving platter. Repeat until the truffle mixture has been used up. Dust the finished truffles with the cocoa powder.
4. Transfer each truffle to individual petit four cups and refrigerate for at least 2 hours before serving.

MAKE AHEAD: The truffles can be made up to 1 week in advance and refrigerated in a sealed container. They can also be frozen for up to 3 weeks.

Frittelle di ricotta alla pietrasantina
Lemon-Ricotta Fritters

Pietrasanta is a small town near the coastal resort of Viareggio. Its name means "holy stone" and the stone in question is marble, pure white Tuscan marble. In olden days, when marble workers climbed up to the quarries in the morning, they carried enough food to last the entire day—no lunch-time siestas for these quarry denizens. Naturally, the foods they carried had to be nutritious enough to propel them through the rigors of the job; they also had to withstand the lack of refrigeration. These ricotta fritters fared well in both categories. They also had the advantage of being easy to eat and—since Tuscans are probably the world's most unforgiving gourmets—of being absolutely delicious.

MAKES APPROXIMATELY 30 FRITTERS

TIME: 1¾ HOURS

LEVEL: EASY

1 whole egg plus 1 egg yolk, at room temperature
¼ cup sugar
1 tablespoon freshly grated lemon zest
1 tablespoon milk
½ teaspoon vanilla extract
1 tablespoon cake flour, sifted

1½ cups fresh sheep's milk ricotta or other fresh ricotta
Vegetable oil, for frying
Confectioners' sugar, for dusting

1. In a medium-size bowl beat the eggs, egg yolk and sugar until fluffy and smooth. Stir in the grated lemon zest, milk, vanilla, and flour, and mix to blend all ingredients.
2. Press the ricotta through a fine sieve directly into the egg mixture and stir until creamy. Cover the bowl and refrigerate for 1 hour.
3. Heat 1 inch oil in a large non-stick skillet over high heat until a bread cube immersed in the center sizzles around the edges.
4. Drop the chilled ricotta mixture by the tablespoonful into the hot oil. Fry until golden brown on all sides, turning once. Drain on paper towels, dust with the confectioners' sugar and serve.

VARIATIONS: Two tablespoons cognac or brandy can be added in Step 1.

Piccoli napoleoni con pere calde al cioccolato
Chocolate Napoleons with Warm Pears

MAKES
4 NAPOLEONS

TIME:
40 MINUTES

LEVEL: EASY

Napoleon was a great general, no doubt, but he is remembered as much for his diminutive height as for his military strategy. That is why I have always been confused by the elegant dessert named in his honor—a rather tall assemblage of puff pastry and cream. To me, this shorter version is more to the point. Caramelized pears replace the puff pastry and the filling is a mixture of unsweetened chocolate and basic custard.

2 ounces unsweetened chocolate
1 cup Basic Custard (see page 34)
⅓ teaspoon vanilla extract
1 teaspoon orange extract
4 tablespoons unsalted butter
4 medium pears, peeled, cored and thinly sliced, lengthwise
1 cup raspberries or other berries

1. Melt the chocolate in a double boiler over simmering water. Transfer to a large bowl, add the custard, vanilla and orange extract and stir until smooth and glossy.
2. Melt the butter in a large skillet over low heat. Working in batches, add the fresh pears in one layer and cook until golden on both sides. Transfer the pears to a heated plate and cover to maintain the heat.
3. Place two pear slices on each of four plates and top with chocolate custard. Repeat the layering: two slices of pears topped with custard. End with a layer of pear slices. Scatter the berries over each Napoleon and serve immediately.

VARIATIONS: One tablespoon of a liqueur such as cognac, brandy and rum can be added along with the custard in Step 1.

Soufflés con cioccolato aromatizzato all'arancia e praline
Individual Soufflés with Orange-Chocolate Sauce and Hazelnut Pralines

Soufflés are always thought of as a French invention; and yet, they were another of those marvelous culinary innovations (along with the fork) brought to France by Catherine de Medici when she married Henry II and became the mother of those three obstreperous French kings.

These are rather grand soufflés, but well worth the time and effort. The combination of flavors—chocolate, orange, and sugar-coated hazelnuts—is an extraordinary finish to the no-holds-barred meal you will undoubtedly prepare as a prelude.

MAKES
3 SOUFFLÉS

TIME: 1 HOUR

LEVEL: EASY

THE HAZELNUT PRALINE

Cooking spray, for greasing
¾ cup sugar
½ cup water
5 ounces hazelnuts, toasted and husked

Unsalted butter, for greasing
Confectioners' sugar, for dusting
1 cup milk
½ cup sugar
1 teaspoon vanilla extract
2 tablespoons sambuca or other anise-flavored liqueur
5 tablespoons unsalted butter, at room temperature
3 tablespoons cake flour, sifted
2 tablespoons cornstarch
½ teaspoon grated lemon zest
4 egg yolks, at room temperature
8 egg whites, at room temperature
¼ teaspoon salt
1 teaspoon cream of tartar
Confectioners' sugar, for dusting

THE ORANGE-CHOCOLATE SAUCE

10 ounces bittersweet or semisweet chocolate, grated
1 cup heavy cream
4 tablespoons corn syrup
½ teaspoon vanilla extract
1 teaspoon orange extract
1 teaspoon Cointreau

1. To make the hazelnut pralines, lightly grease a baking sheet.
2. In a medium-size saucepan, mix the sugar and water and bring to a boil over very low heat, stirring frequently until the syrup turns amber, about 8 minutes.
3. Pour in the hazelnuts and stir until well coated, about 1 minute.
4. Gently pour the hot mixture onto the prepared baking sheet. Cool until the praline has hardened, about 10 minutes.
5. Transfer to a plastic bag and crush by rolling with a rolling pin.
6. To make the soufflés, preheat the oven to 350°F. Grease eight 6-ounce soufflé molds and dust with confectioners' sugar, shaking off the excess.
7. Place the milk and sugar in a small saucepan and heat through but do not boil. Stir in the vanilla and sambuca.

8. Melt the butter in a double boiler. Sift in the flour and cornstarch and whisk until smooth.

9. Add the warm milk to the butter mixture, pouring in a steady stream and whisking until the mixture is creamy and well blended. Cook over low heat until thickened, 5 to 7 minutes.

10. Remove from heat. Stir in the lemon zest and egg yolks (one at a time) and blend until smooth.

11. Using an electric mixer or hand whisk, beat the egg whites and the salt in a large bowl until foamy. Add the cream of tartar and beat until stiff peaks form.

12. Using an electric mixer (on low) or spatula, gently fold the whites into the egg mixture until just blended. Divide the mixture among the 8 prepared soufflé molds. Place the molds on a baking sheet.

13. Bake until puffed and golden, about 25 minutes.

14. To make the orange-chocolate sauce, while the soufflés are baking, place the chocolate in a medium, heavy stainless steel bowl.

15. Place the heavy cream in a saucepan and slowly bring to a gentle boil over very low heat.

16. Gently stir the hot cream into the chocolate. Add the corn syrup, vanilla, orange extract and Cointreau, and stir until smooth and glossy, about 5 minutes. Cool to room temperature, stirring occasionally to maintain liquidity.

17. Using an electric mixer, whip the mixture until thickened and well blended, about 8 minutes.

18. Gently scrap a butter knife around the outside edges of the soufflés to pry them loose. Transfer to individual serving plates, drizzle with the Orange-Chocolate Sauce, surround with the Hazelnut Pralines and serve immediately.

VARIATIONS: Almond, pecan or macadamia nuts can be substituted.

MAKE AHEAD: The praline can be made up to 1 month in advance and stored in an airtight container.

Ricottine al mandarino
Ricotta Molds with Cognac-Soaked Clementines

MAKES
EIGHT 6-INCH
DESSERTS

TIME:
1½ HOURS

LEVEL:
MODERATE

In Tuscany, ricotta is used in everything from soups to sauces to ravioli fillings to cakes to mousses to this wonderful recipe for small soufflé-like molds filled with a light chocolaty ricotta cream. I first encountered this dessert at I Due Cippi in Saturnia. Fortunately, the owner, Michele Aniello, is my friend and was too embarrassed to do what Tuscan chefs normally do when asked for recipes: refuse! But then again, I had eaten three portions: mine, my partner's and a smaller third helping delivered by Michele's wife when she noticed my enthusiasm. "Tu non sei una donna, sei uno struzzo!" Michele teased me. ("You are not a woman; you're an ostrich!")

6 clementines, skinned, peeled and pith removed
1 cup cognac
Unsalted butter, for greasing
Confectioners' sugar, for dusting
5 egg yolks, at room temperature
½ cup sugar
1½ cups fresh sheep's milk ricotta or other fresh ricotta
5 ounces unsweetened chocolate, grated
1 teaspoon grated orange zest
1 teaspoon vanilla extract
5 egg whites, at room temperature
¼ teaspoon salt
½ teaspoon cream of tartar

1. Divide the clementines into individual segments and marinate in the cognac for at least 1 hour, turning occasionally.
2. Preheat the oven to 350°F. Grease eight 6-ounce ramekins and dust with confectioner's sugar, shaking out the excess.
3. Using an electric mixer or a hand whisk, beat the yolks and the sugar in a large bowl until fluffy, pale and smooth, about 5 minutes with the mixer (15 minutes by hand).
4. Press the ricotta through a fine sieve and stir into the egg mixture. Stir in the grated chocolate, orange zest and vanilla extract.
5. Using an electric mixer or a hand whisk, beat the egg whites and the

salt in a large bowl until foamy. Add the cream of tartar and beat until stiff peaks form. Gently fold the egg whites into the ricotta mixture.

6. Spoon the mixture into the prepared ramekins. Line a large baking pan with a kitchen towel and top with the ramekins. Pour enough boiling water into the pan to reach halfway up the sides of the ramekins.

7. Bake the molds until puffed and golden, about 20 minutes. Remove from the oven and place on individual dessert plates surrounded by marinated clementines. Serve immediately.

VARIATIONS: Oranges can be substituted for the clementines.

MAKE AHEAD: The clementines can be prepared earlier in the day and left in the cognac until needed

---

Mimosine con tartellette di banana
Banana Tartlets with Mimosa

Mimosa trees herald the imminent arrival of spring. Covered in bright yellow flowers weeks before the roses have even thought about blooming, mimosas are to Tuscany what daffodils are to the Dutch. In Viareggio, before the pre-Lenten Carnival, women carried bunches of mimosa to wave at the passing floats, themselves decorated bountifully with sprigs. Mimosa is also the symbol of the Italian woman and, in fact, on March 8, Woman's Day, Italian women crowd the nation's piazzas holding sprigs of mimosa to celebrate their freedom and emancipation.

The following poem was written by Franca Costa, a contemporary Italian poet and the same woman who gave me the recipe for these wonderful tarts associated with National Woman's Day.

MAKES
FOUR 4-INCH
TARTS

TIME:
1½ HOURS

LEVEL:
MODERATE

La Mimosa
Nel piccolo sentiero lungo il fiume
fra mille sterpi, rovi e pratoline
s'innalza su nel cielo come un lume
una pianta robusta e maestosa
e' la bellissima e splendida mimosa
Il suo profumo inebria tutta l'aria

e ubriaca le farfalle e le zanzare
che fra i rametti iniziano a danzare.
Lieta e' la danza fra le gialle corolle
morbide e leggere come bolle
E le fanciulle ne tagliano un rametto
come un gioiello, per adornarsi il petto.
O nobil fiore, simbolo dell'Eva
tu hai il colore del sole e dall'avena
e tu biondeggi nel terso dell'aurora
nell'alba a illuminar la sera.

In the narrow path along the river
Among thousands of thorns, brambles and early spring daisies
A robust and majestic tree
Rises up toward the sky like a light
The beautiful and splendid Mimosa
Its scent inebriates the air
And butterflies and mosquitoes dance among its boughs
As if they were drunk, skipping among the yellow flowers
Soft and light as bubbles.
Girls cut a little sprig and use it like a jewel to adorn their chests
Oh, noble flower, Eve's symbol
Colored like oatmeal, like the sun itself,
You shine in the clear aurora from dawn to sunset.

THE TART SHELLS

1 cup cake flour
½ teaspoon salt
½ cup cold unsalted butter, cut into ⅛-inch slices
3 tablespoons ice water

THE FILLING

2 ripe bananas
½ cup ground hazelnuts
1 teaspoon vanilla extract
¼ cup sugar
⅓ cup apricot preserves
Mimosa sprigs or mint, for garnish

1. To make the shells, sift the flour and the salt. Cut in the butter until the mixture resembles coarse crumbs.

2. Add the water, one tablespoon at a time, turning the dough with a fork just enough to dampen it. Gather into a ball, adding another tablespoon or two of water, if necessary, for the dough to hold together. Wrap in plastic and refrigerate for 30 minutes.

3. Preheat the oven to 350°F. On a lightly floured surface, roll out the dough to ⅛-inch thickness. Cut out four 6-inch rounds. Transfer each to a 4-inch-diameter tart pan with removable bottom and press the dough against the sides. Roll the rolling pin over the top of the pans to level the edges. Line the tarts with waxed paper and weight with raw rice, dried beans or commercial pie weights.

4. Bake for 6 minutes. Remove the waxed paper and weights, and prick each tart bottom with the tines of a fork. Return to the oven and bake until crisp and lightly browned, about 8 minutes. Remove from the oven and cool completely.

5. Meanwhile to make the filling, cut one of the bananas into ¼-inch segments. Purée the remaining 1 banana, the hazelnuts, vanilla and sugar.

6. Fill each shell with 1 or 2 tablespoons of banana pureé. Arrange the banana slices on top. Heat the apricot preserves in a saucepan over low heat until dissolved, 2 to 3 minutes and baste the surface of the tarts with the syrup. Remove the sides of each tart pan. Place the tarts on individual dessert plates and garnish with the mimosa sprigs.

MAKE AHEAD: The dough can be prepared the day before, wrapped in plastic and refrigerated, or it can be frozen for up to 3 weeks. Thaw in the refrigerator before using. The tart shells can be baked early in the day and filled when needed.

Bomboloncini riempiti di crema alla lavanda

Miniature Doughnuts Filled with Lavender Cream

**MAKES
APPROXIMATELY
50 SMALL
DOUGHNUTS**

**TIME: 4 HOURS
INCLUDING
RISING TIME**

**LEVEL:
ADVANCED**

It is hard to think of anyone eating a doughnut without breaking into a smile. Just the mental image of a small child raising to her lips this wonderful round creation makes me happy. I'm even happier, of course, when the person eating the doughnut is me. Fact is, doughnuts are one of my many weak points when it comes to culinary discipline. Even with a clothespin clamped to my nose, I cannot stop fantasizing about their crisp fragrance and heavenly flavors. This recipe is one of my favorite varieties.

THE DOUGHNUTS

1 tablespoon fresh yeast
½ cup warm water
2 cups bread flour
2 eggs, at room temperature
4 tablespoons sugar
1 tablespoon grated lemon zest
2 tablespoons unsalted butter, at room temperature
¼ teaspoon salt
Vegetable oil, for frying

THE FILLING

3 cups heavy cream
½ cup milk
¼ cup sugar
¼ tablespoon vanilla extract
2 egg yolks
4 fresh lavender sprigs or 1½ tablespoons dried lavender
10 fresh lavender sprigs, for garnish

1. To make the doughnuts, dissolve the yeast in the warm water.
2. Heap the flour onto a flat working surface, make a well in the center and add the eggs along with the sugar, lemon zest, butter and salt. Using a fork, beat the ingredients until well blended.
3. Add the water-yeast mixture and continue to beat, incorporating in-

creasing amounts of flour from the edges of the well. When a soft dough has formed, begin kneading with floured hands. Knead until the dough is smooth and elastic, about 5 minutes. Transfer to a large bowl, cover with a cloth and let rise in a warm place until doubled in volume, about 1½ hours.

4. To make the filling, place 1 cup of the cream, the milk, sugar and vanilla in a saucepan and bring to a simmer.

5. In a large bowl, whisk the egg yolks until smooth and pale, 7 to 10 minutes. Slowly whisk in the cream mixture, a little at a time until smooth and thick, about 10 minutes. Remove from heat. Tie the lavender in a square of cheesecloth and add it to the custard. Set aside until cool.

6. Knead the dough for another 5 minutes. Return to the bowl, cover and let rise a second time for 1 hour.

7. Transfer the risen dough to a floured working surface and using a floured rolling pin, roll the dough out into ⅓-inch thickness. Using a floured circular 1½-inch-diameter pastry cutter, cut the dough to form little doughnut rounds. Arrange them on a lightly floured board and cover with a cloth. Recycle the remaining dough by kneading, rolling and cutting again.

8. Pour the oil to a depth of 3 inches into a large, heavy gauge skillet and heat to 375°F. Fry the doughnuts, a few at a time until all sides are golden and well-puffed, about 2 minutes. Remove with a slotted spoon and drain on paper towels. Repeat until all the doughnuts have been fried.

9. Using an electric mixer or hand whisk, beat the remaining 2 cups cream. Remove the lavender from the custard and fold in the whipped cream. Gently pour the cream into a large pastry bag fitted with a round tip. Make a small slit in each doughnut and fill with the lavender cream.

10. Arrange the filled doughnuts on a serving platter and garnish with lavender sprigs. Serve immediately.

MAKE AHEAD: The lavender cream can be made up to 1 day in advance through Step 5. Remove the lavender, then store in a sealed container in the refrigerator.

Pirottini al cioccolato con arancia candita e mandorle
Bittersweet Chocolate Cups with Candied Orange and Almonds

MAKES
10 PETIT FOURS

TIME: 1 HOUR

LEVEL:
MODERATE

A good Tuscan host always offers her guests coffee or tea—sometimes wine or liqueurs, depending on the time of day—accompanied by something to quell the stomach. Having on hand little sweets such as the following allows you to save face if someone drops in unexpectedly. Otherwise, you will have made a brutta figura (a bad showing) and not even all the water in the Arno River can wash away your shame. These chocolate cups are generally served, in the late afternoon or early evening, with a glass of chilled sparkling wine.

2 pounds bittersweet chocolate
½ cup heavy cream
1 tablespoon finely diced candied orange peel
2 tablespoons Cointreau
1 tablespoon almonds, lightly toasted and thinly sliced

1. Place the chocolate in the top of a double boiler and melt over gently simmering water, stirring occasionally.
2. Using a pastry brush, brush ten 2-inch-diameter petit four paper cups with the melted chocolate and cool to room temperature. Repeat the routine three more times, each time brushing with another layer of chocolate and cooling. When the cups have a thick, hardened coating, chill for 20 minutes. Reserve the remaining chocolate.
3. Place the heavy cream along with orange zest in a small heavy-gauge pot and slowly bring to a boil over very low heat, stirring constantly.
4. Mix in the remaining chocolate, stirring constantly until creamy and smooth.
5. Stir in the candied orange peel and Cointreau, and continue to stir until the mixture starts boiling. Remove from heat and cool to room temperature, stirring occasionally.
6. Peel the paper cup from the chocolate shells and arrange them on a serving platter.
7. Spoon the cooled orange mixture into the chocolate shells, decorate with sliced almonds and chill for 30 minutes before serving.

MAKE AHEAD: The chocolate shells can be prepared up to 2 days in advance and stored, refrigerated, in a sealed container.

❧ ❧ ❧ ❧

Tegoline di pistacchi
Pistacchio Leaves with Pistachio Ice Cream

In Tuscany, pistachios are usually added to cured meats such as mortadella or blended into stuffing mixtures for turkey and chicken. As a dessert ingredient, their use is limited to two recipes: one for pistachio ice cream, the other for the unusual pistachio leaves generally served alongside the ice cream.

MAKES
APPROXIMATELY
20 LEAVES

TIME: 1 HOUR

LEVEL:
MODERATE

½ cup unsalted butter, at room temperature
5 tablespoons confectioners' sugar, sifted
4 tablespoons cake flour, sifted
3 tablespoons ground pistachios
2 egg whites, at room temperature
¼ teaspoon salt
¼ teaspoon cream of tartar
1 pint pistachio ice cream
2 tablespoons roughly chopped pistachios, for garnish

1. Preheat the oven to 300°F. Line a 12 x 15-inch baking sheet with parchment.
2. Cream the butter and the sugar in a large bowl. Sift in the flour and ground pistachios and mix until well blended.
3. Using an electric mixer or hand whisk, beat the egg whites with the salt until foamy. Add the cream of tartar and beat until stiff peaks form. Fold the egg whites into the pistachio mixture until just blended.
4. Drop the mixture by teaspoonfuls onto the baking sheet approximately 2 inches apart and flatten with a wet spatula.
5. Bake for 10 minutes. Remove the leaves from the oven, transfer immediately to a flat work surface and gently flatten each leaf with a rolling pin. Cool on a wire rack. Serve four leaves per person with a small bowl of pistachio ice cream. Scatter the chopped pistachio over the leaves.

MAKE AHEAD: The leaves can be made 6 hours in advance.

Castagnole
Honey-Glazed Puffs Served with Candied Chestnuts

MAKES
24 TO 30 PUFFS

TIME:
1½ HOURS

LEVEL:
MODERATE

Castagnole *are small balls of fried dough poached in acacia honey and often served during pre-Lenten Carnival. The name means "little chestnuts" and refers to the fact that mountain people used to pair this simple, humble dessert with boiled chestnuts. In updating that tradition, I have paired the finished* castagnole *with* marron glacés *(candied chestnuts), which can be found in specialty stores.*

1 cup cake flour
1 tablespoon sugar
1 tablespoon unsalted butter, at room temperature
2 eggs, at room temperature
1 tablespoon dry white wine
Vegetable oil, for frying
⅓ cup chestnut or acacia honey
½ cup sugar
marron glacés (available at specialty food shops)

1. Heap the flour onto a flat work surface and make a well in the center. Place the sugar, butter, eggs and wine in the well and stir the ingredients with a fork, incorporating increasing amounts of the flour wall until a smooth dough has formed.

2. Knead for 1 minute and then divide the dough into 24 to 30 walnut-sized balls.

3. Pour the oil to 1½ inches deep into a frying pan and heat to 375°F. Fry the dough balls a few at a time until golden. Remove with a slotted spoon, drain on paper towels and transfer to a large plate.

4. Place the honey and sugar in a saucepan and simmer over very low heat, stirring until the sugar is completely dissolved and the liquid has turned amber, about 6 minutes.

5. Slowly pour the honey mixture over the fried dough and turn the puffs with a spoon until each is completely coated.

6. Place 3 or 4 on individual serving plates and garnish with *marron glacés*.

MAKE AHEAD: The dough can be prepared up to 2 days in advance, wrapped in plastic and refrigerated until needed.

CHAPTER FOUR

Rustic Cakes and Vegetable Tarts

Right, Wrong and That Troublesome Shade of Gray

Guardati dal Toscan o Rosso. (Beware the Red Tuscan.) The slogan is an old one dating back to the days when Tuscany (along with its neighbor Emilia-Romagna) was Italy's revolutionary hotbed—the national center for communist and socialist fervor. The Italian communist movement was born here, and it flourished here after World War II, when workers abandoned family farms for the promises of the Industrial Revolution.

But in the past few years, party loyalty has been dealt a severe blow by the ongoing government investigations into political corruption *(tangentopoli)*. Suddenly, no one is sure any longer which party is right and which one wrong—that is, when anyone can tell which party is which.

Italian politics has always been made up of a dozen or so competing parties, which means that for anyone to gain a plurality and, hence, rule, it has to form coalitions with competing ideologies. A hard enough reality when ideologies were clearly defined. But nowadays parties are constantly metamorphosing to attract the greatest number of disciples. From one day to the next, a party will go from one point of view to its complete opposite, changing in the process its name, logos and colors to the point where no one is sure whether they're voting for the extreme right or the extreme left.

Currently, the country is governed by a shaky coalition of socialists, democrats, and communists who call themselves The Olive Tree Party. The fascist party is now "Allies for Democracy" with a new platform designed to demonstrate relevance and rationality. The PDS (which means Democratic Party of The Left) is a group of so-called new communists who have broken historical ties with established communism and espouse corporate tax exemptions along with worker's rights. Old-style communists have taken shelter in the *Partito di Rifondazione Comunista*, which embraces such nostalgic philosophies as the distribution of wealth and the power of the common person. The old reliable hammer and sickle is now a fresh, green olive sprig.

"Era meglio senza le maschere," says Mariano Michetti. ("Things were better before everyone started hiding behind masks.")

Mariano is the caretaker at Camporomano, the hilltop wine and olive oil estate that houses our cooking school, Toscana Saporita. A 72-year-old lifelong communist, Mariano spent the war years hiding out in the hills above Lucca, enduring everything from physical torture to daily starvation in his fight against the fascists. From 1938–1945, he fought as a partisan, as part of that ragtag alliance of communists and socialists whose cunning and perseverance cleared the way for the triumphant arrival of the Allied Forces.

As much as he hated the fascists, however, Mariano respected the purity of their ideological beliefs. "You knew what they stood for," he says with a certain amount of pride. "The divisions between us were clear and recognizable. When you made a choice to go one way or the other, there was no doubt which side was which."

He remembers the ultimatums—the days when the fascists would sweep into town and demand that everyone declare allegiance to a certain person or cause. "There was no confusion over who was who because the fascists always wore black shirts and we wore brown," he explains. "So there was never even the need to ask 'what side are you on?' They would come right up to us and say 'you must do this,' or 'you must support him.' And we, of course, would refuse, which always meant the same thing—a brutal beating." He laughs at the memory as if it were a pleasant thing. "Afterwards, your entire body would ache, but you felt so incredibly proud that you had stood up and declared yourself."

The problem today, he says, is that no one is willing to do that. "It almost seems as if people are afraid to disagree. My daughter always tells me not to talk about politics when she has company. Why? I ask her. 'Because not everyone feels the same way you do,' she says. Well, doesn't that make politics the perfect choice of topic then? If everyone feels the same way, there's nothing to talk about."

It's hard to explain things like this to someone like Mariano. How to make him understand that the world is no longer divided into clearly defined categories labeled right and wrong, good and bad, passion and cowardice. How to make him see that there's enough confrontation in the world, that people seek peace and tranquillity in their social interactions.

His daughter has certainly done her share of trying. "Papa is constantly giving his opinion," she says in a way that immediately lets you know she's not pleased. "If he's out working in the garden with Marco and Mirella (his grandchildren), he harangues them into planting what he wants, how he wants. There is no room for another opinion." She rolls her eyes and starts to laugh.

"Once Mirella came rushing back into the house, crying and screaming that she just couldn't take it anymore. That Papa was pulling out each of her onion bulbs because the rows were not absolutely straight. 'The book says to stagger them,' she wailed. 'And anyway, what *difference* does it make—are onions going to realize they're not in a straight row and refuse to grow?' *Poverina*, she was absolutely distraught.

"But did that make a dent in Papa's thinking? Absolutely not. Later, when he came in for coffee, he began lecturing me about how thick-headed Mirella was. 'Not like Marco,' he said, siding for that moment with my son. 'Marco listens. You tell him the right way to do things and he does them without wasting time trying out methods that we all know are not going to work.'"

According to his daughter, Mariano is the last of a breed. "Born shortly after Mussolini took charge of a completely impoverished nation in 1922, Papa comes from a generation with virtually no options. You ate, went to work, took care of your family and went to bed. On Sundays you went to church and for entertainment you played cards at the local coffee bar. The only decision you ever had to make was whether you were a fascist, a socialist or a communist. That's why politics have always been so important to people here—because it was the only arena in which they might differ one from the other."

Talk to Mariano about this aspect of his personality—his obstinacy—and he merely shrugs. "What should I do, watch the people I love make mistakes and say nothing? If you ask me, there's far too much saying nothing in the world today. Just look at the situation with Fidel."

Mariano's position regarding his beloved Fidel Castro is that America is engaged in a personal vendetta. "Everybody knows Fidel is the last of the world's great leaders. Even if you disagree with his politics, you have to appreciate the man's integrity—the fact that he has stuck to his beliefs no matter what." Sadness replaces his enthusiasm. "When I saw him in that blue suit he put on to greet Mitterand, I almost cried."

The blue suit incident transpired when Fidel—"pushed to the wall by those American imperialists"—decided to meet with France's Francois Mitterand to discuss economic partnership. The result was Law 77, which allowed foreign businesses to locate in Cuba. Within weeks, Italian firms such as San Pellegrino, Benetton and Fiat had established a Cuban presence.

"I was not happy to see Fidel do it," Mariano says of that law. "In fact, we took up a collection and sent him a check for over $3000 (Mariano is the chapter head of his communist party caucus). But everyone has to bend sometime—that's what we used to say during the war: 'Sometimes it is better to bend and let the tanks roll over you than to stand up straight and be mowed down.'" He thinks about it again. "Only sometimes though. And it has to be on behalf of a greater principle."

This week, our cooking school is playing host to six teenage miscreants enrolled in one of Tuscany's youth rehabilitation programs. The idea is to expose social offenders to as many educational influences as possible, both to show that someone cares and to stimulate crucial interaction with community institutions. Contrary to American theories of youthful offenders as the by-products of socioeconomic inequity or the lack of educational opportunities, Tuscans place the blame on inadequate family and community support. The solution, as they see it, lies in creating a complex web of interpersonal connections that ensnares the young people in a net of social place.

This particular group of six has already worked behind the scenes at the local movie house, assisted neighborhood bar owners in serving coffee and pastries, catalogued books at the church library and gone along on ambulance missions with volunteers of Massarosa's *misericordia* (local social service agency). The goal is not job training but interaction. If the young people know and are known by people in their communities, the theory goes, they will be watched and guided like all the rest of Massarosa's teenagers. The part of the program I find most interesting is the "home invitation" aspect. Three times a week for nine months, each teenager is scheduled to spend time with various families in the town. They are either invited to their homes for dinner, taken out to the movies or simply asked to come over to watch television—in other words, all the things that make up life in a small Tuscan village.

Apparently, the system works. More than 68 percent of youthful offenders who have been through this nine-month program never again appear on police rolls. "They become too entrenched in the life of the town," says Paolo Sfuzzi, one of the program's creators. "Suddenly, they have dozens of parents and grandparents and cousins and friends and it becomes just too hard to let all those people down."

When the teenagers arrive, we are all on the main law to greet them—Elena, the owner of the estate; her father Baron Gianfranco; Pasquina and Dorinda the maids; Anerino, the groundskeeper. Mariano is not there, although I can swear I see him at one point peeking out the door to the olive press room.

He was not pleased to know they were coming. "What these kids need is a good kick in the pants, not an expensive program that disturbs everybody in town." He points his index finger at my shoulder. "My brother was like that when he was young—always in trouble. But he straightened out very quickly when my father started taking him to work. Before that he had too much time. That's what needs to be done with these kids. Make them clean the streets from morning till night. The problem will be solved in a lot less time than nine months."

I have decided to start the week by teaching them basic knife skills. The onions and carrots have just about been divided when Mariano comes rushing into the room with a box of latex gloves. "Give everyone a pair and make sure you use them yourself," he whispers in my ear. "You never know. And one more thing. Make sure you lock up everything and never ever give them the keys. They'll rob you blind."

That evening, I take Mariano to the optician because he needs new glasses. Normally, the Baron would drive him, but he had to go to Florence this afternoon, and his daughter, Elena, is meeting with the plumbers about a long-standing problem with the water pipes in the school's kitchen.

"Those kids could have done anything they wanted," Mariano says predictably as soon as I start up the motor. "But they chose the easy way out, and now they blame the state because they have no future. They should have lived through the war; then they'd know what it means to have problems." He buckles his seat belt reluctantly—I have long made it clear that we go nowhere unless he is buckled in. "You didn't leave them with the keys, did you?" he says struggling under the chest restraint. "That kind of kid, they'll go right into town and make copies, and then we'll have an infinite string of petty thefts."

I turn on the radio in a way that, I hope, will not make it seem as though I'm trying to shut him up. Which is precisely what I'm trying to do. The lead story is on the Pope's trip to Cuba.

"Will the Pope change Fidel's mind?" the announcer is asking.

"Change Fidel's mind?" screams Mariano. "If anyone should have their mind changed, it should be the Pope. I can't believe that people treat this as a mission of mercy. As the Lion of the Church going to help out the poor pussycat who is lost in a dark forest and needs guidance finding his way."

Mariano is one of those combination Catholic and communists, whom people outside Italy have trouble understanding. They think one precludes the other and, in terms of absolute doctrine, they do. But Italians have managed to refashion the communist doctrine of atheism into one that is simply anti-religion. Believing in God is fine; the problem is the Church.

I drop Mariano off at the front door of the optician's office and tell him I'll be back in a half hour. I have to go to the *polleria* to buy six chickens; tomorrow I am teaching the teenagers how to debone them.

Unfortunately for me, the person ahead of me in line is Ugo, Mariano's best friend and his second in command at the communist caucus. And even more unfortunate, Ugo and the butcher are already thick into a conversation about, what else, the Pope and Fidel.

"Did you see he signed more than 50 entry visas for new priests?" Ugo says shrilly.

"I know, but what choice did he have? As compromises go, that was not a bad one," the butcher responds.

"Agostino, what kind of communist are you? Letting priests come into Cuba is the beginning of the end."

"Ugo, you don't know what you're talking about. Listen to me. Fidel is no longer the *Atheist Lider Maximo*. It is a fantasy, a myth to continue to think of him as that romantic revolutionary head of a functioning Marxist state." He breaks off a piece of string to tie up a veal roast. "I went to Cuba 50 years ago," he says, now including me in the conversation. "It was beautiful. My son went last year and said everything is falling apart. The people apparently are desperate. Yes, they still love Fidel, but they have to eat and Fidel knows that. He won't let them down."

"I'll come back," I say, realizing there's no way I'm going to get my chickens and be back to get Mariano in time.

"How many do you want?" Agostino says, turning businesslike.

"Six."

"I'll get them right now." He pushes the veal roast to the side and lays a large piece of waxed paper on the counter. "What do *you* think of the Pope's trip?" he says, lifting the chickens out of the bin.

I'm not sure whether to say "great," which would signify anti-Castroism and lead to a spate of evangelizing on their part, or "can't believe it," which would politically pull me to their bosoms. Either way, I'd have to spend at least five minutes in discussion.

"Amazing," I say as congenially as possible. It works. They are completely puzzled and decide to wait until I leave to resume their conversation.

When I finally get back to the optician, Mariano is holding a press conference in the outer office. "Eighty dollars," he is complaining. "Eighty dollars for these glasses, can you believe? The lenses come from Germany, that's why. We should have settled things in Germany when we had the chance. Now look at the situation. Everyone in Europe has to bow to the German marc. Not right."

"Oh Sandra," he says when we get outside. "I thought you'd gotten lost. I was waiting and waiting."

"How are the glasses?" I ask to forestall any further whining. "Are you going to be able to work tomorrow?"

"Of course I can work. Even if I can't see very well because of the drops the doctor gave me."

In case you hadn't already figured it out, Mariano is the type of man who loves to complain. But he would never think of saying, "I can't come to work today." His way of handling the situation is to start a job and then, when it becomes clear he's not capable of doing it, have to be taken home. No favor requested. Honor preserved.

As soon as we approach the top of the hill, I can see something is wrong. All the lights are on in the kitchen, and the front door is wide open.

"What's going on?" Mariano says, leaning forward in the front seat. "I bet it's those teenagers. Who was watching them while we were in Viareggio?"

I park the car and run as fast as I can. When I get to the front door, I see water streaming out onto the grass. The pipes! After four months of threatening to burst, they have finally had enough.

"Sandra! Sandra! The teenagers race towards me, all in a panic, all talking at once. "We were upstairs, looking through some of those cookbooks you lent us, when we heard a huge clanging noise. We came racing down to the kitchen and saw the water pouring through the floor." They point to a hole in the terra-cotta where the problem apparently originated. "A few of us went to get somebody, but Pasquina, the maid, said everyone had gone home and the Baron's daughter was in town."

"Osvaldo said he had learned something about plumbing from his father," says Ernesto. He points to Osvaldo, who is mopping up the far side of the room. "He figured out how to turn off the water and then we all started mopping. There was about a foot of water on the floor when we first got here."

I rush into the pantry, to see if anything was ruined. "Don't worry," says Lucia, the youngest of the three girls. "Marzia and I put all the pots and pans on the higher shelves so they wouldn't get rusty."

Mariano appears at the door. "What's going on here?" he yells in what can only be described as an accusatory voice.

"The pipes burst while we were gone and no one was here," I tell him. The kids have been mopping for hours."

He looks as though he has not heard me. Clearly this is not what he was expecting.

"How did the hole get in the floor?" It is his one last hope in terms of blame.

"Osvaldo pulled up the tiles, hoping to be able to fix it," Ernesto tells him. "But it's beyond repair; the plumbers are going to have to put in a new joint," he says with the distinct air of one man talking to another.

They all stop what they're doing to see what Mariano will say.

I am speechless. Until this moment, I had not understood how well they'd read the situation—how clearly they'd picked up his resentment, his lack of trust, his aversion to having anything to do with them. But of course, they had spotted who he was. Most of the people who populate their lives are exactly like that. The Marianos of the world are familiar figures, instantly recognizable. It's the rest of us they have to learn to read.

"You did a great job," I tell them, hoping Mariano will echo my praise.

He does not. But he picks up one of the extra mops and begins cleaning up the area by the sink. "The calcium in the water is going to streak the floors if we don't get it all off," he says brusquely.

He points to Osvaldo. "Go to my storeroom and get the thinner."

And then he stuffs his hand into his jacket. "Here are the keys," he says without looking up.

Rustic Cakes and Vegetable Tarts (Dolci Rustici)

Although Tuscany is one of Italy's largest regions, especially when compared with Molise, Liguria or Umbria, it is very small when one thinks of it in terms of individual provinces, in terms of its ten separate areas, each with its own traditions and cuisine. Call it rivalry, call it arrogance, the differences among Tuscany's ten provinces have always been, and continue to be, significant enough to qualify each as a distinctly unique geographic entity. Most of the differences, especially with respect to food, have to do with landscape, with the physical determinants that, for example, make Lucchese cuisine so dependent on fish as opposed to Florentine fare, which leans far more heavily on meat. But much is due to tradition.

Northern Tuscany is much more rugged and mountainous than any other area. As you drive through the countryside, you forget almost completely about art and architecture and nobility and the Renaissance. What you get instead are winding narrow roads, dense chestnut forests, magnificent national parks and gorgeous, snow-capped peaks stretching toward clear blue skies. The villages that dot this region are exquisitely tiny and it is clear after spending even a small amount of time in any one that its occupants are living life the same way they have for centuries, give or take a cellular phone or two. It's not so much about money or modern comforts (both in adequate supply), but rather about attitude, specifically with respect to tradition.

More so than any other area in Tuscany, the mountainous north is where one goes to see the last remaining vestiges of village life. Where people depend on each other by virtue of their isolation. Where outsider influence is minimal. Where things are done locally and without a high degree of technical sophistication. Where the only refuge, apart from church, is the kitchen for women and the marble quarry for men. Where food depends on what is grown and gathered. Where recipes are kept secret and passed from mother to daughter.

The mountain villages of northern Tuscany are structured tightly around the generosity of the land, whether for food or employment. Obviously this has created a cuisine unlike any other Tuscan province, unlike Siena with its rolling hillside farms and Livorno with its fleet of commercial fishermen. But more so than what the land actually provides is the lack of outside influence that might otherwise cause an evolution in the use of certain ingredients. Women in mountain villages cook exactly what their grandmothers cooked, using exactly the same ingredients and in exactly the same way. *Nuova cucina* has no sway here.

When I traveled north and south, east and west collecting these extraordinary recipes I stopped one day in a beautiful mountain village called Isola Santa. Perched on the edge of a cold, emerald green lake, Isola Santa (Holy Island) resembles every fairy kingdom ever envisioned by the masters of children's fantasies

I stayed with my friend, Ida, who owns the local *locanda* (inn), and when I awoke the following morning, she presented me with an old wooden tray that was lined with a white, hand-embroidered cloth topped with *ogni ben di Dio* (every grace from God). There was a huge porcelain plate bearing three types of vegetable cakes: carrot, pumpkin and zucchini. There was also a full pot of hot espresso, a decanter filled with creamy fresh milk (she owns two hefty cows) and a cup of hot chocolate with whipped cream. A few sprigs of lavender tied with a red grosgrain ribbon garnished this exquisite assemblage.

When I finally made my way downstairs, she asked what I'd thought of the cakes and I, obviously, glowed. But then I made the mistake of saying I'd previouly tasted a similar version of the carrot cake. *"Come e possibile?"* she said, springing out of her chair. *"E dove?"* ("How is it possible? And where?")

"In Careggine," I answered. "I stopped there on the way here for a cup of coffee."

"Where?" she continued with drill-like precision.

"I think the name of the bar was...Da Ernesto."

"Ah," she said, relaxing back into her chair. "Ernesto is my son."

Rustic Cakes and Vegetable Tarts
(Dolci Rustici)

Sbrisolona
Almond and Hazelnut Crumble Cake

Torta di carote
Tuscan Carrot Cake

Scarpaccia di zucchine
Zucchini Blossom Focaccia

Ciambella di mais e ricotta
Corn Flour and Ricotta Wedding-Ring Cake

Torta di patate
Potato and Almond Tart

Budino di zucca
Butternut Squash Pudding

Crostata di zucca
Butternut Squash Tart

Pan perduto
Tuscan Bread Pudding

Dolce di stracchino e pere
Farmer's Cheese Cake with Pears and Hazelnut Crumb Topping

Torta del Vescovo
Bishop's Cake

Torta coi becchi di riso e spinaci
Spinach and Rice Cake

Crostata alle arance amare
Blood Orange Tart

Crostata ai frutti di bosco
Wild Berry Tart

Torta di semolino
Baked Semolina Tart

Sbrisolona
Almond and Hazelnut Crumble Cake

Sbrisolona *comes from the verb* sbriciolare *("to crumble"). To call someone a* sbriciolona *is to say they are a mess maker—whether because they are covered in crumbs or because their life is in complete disarray. The appropriateness of the term as applied to this cake is obvious the moment you try to cut it. The recipe comes from Ida Perini who lives in Piazza al Serchio.*

MAKES
ONE 9-INCH
CAKE (8 SLICES)

TIME: 1 HOUR

LEVEL:
MODERATE

Unsalted butter, for greasing
4 large egg yolks, plus 1 large egg, at room temperature
1 cup sugar
1½ cups cake flour, sifted
½ cup unsalted butter, melted
1 teaspoon grated lemon zest
½ teaspoon salt
¼ cup thinly-sliced toasted almonds
¼ cup toasted pine nuts
24 orange segments, peeled, pith removed and marinated overnight in
    Cointreau, for garnish

1. Preheat the oven to 350°F. Grease a 9-inch-diameter springform baking pan.
2. Using an electric mixer or a hand whisk, beat the eggs and the sugar in a large bowl until fluffy, pale and smooth, about 5 minutes with the mixer (15 minutes by hand).
3. Gradually sift in the flour and beat until completely blended.
4. Melt the butter in a saucepan and stir into the flour mixture. Add the grated lemon zest, salt, 2 tablespoons almonds and 2 tablespoons pine nuts and mix until all ingredients are well-blended.
5. Pour the mixture into the prepared pan, sprinkle with the remaining 2 tablespoons almonds and 2 tablespoons pine nuts.
6. Bake until lightly golden, about 25 minutes. Remove the sides of the pan and let the cake cool to room temperature. Serve with the orange segments.

VARIATIONS: Two tablespoons grappa or cognac can be added in Step 4.

MAKE AHEAD: The cake will stay fresh for up to 1 week if wrapped in foil or kept in a glass-domed cake plate.

Torta di carote
Tuscan Carrot Cake

MAKES
ONE 8-INCH
CAKE (8 SLICES)

TIME: 1 HOUR

LEVEL:
MODERATE

In the mountains, carrots are like parsley: everywhere at once. This simply delicious recipe comes from my friend Lorenza's grandmother, who advocated its consumption as a cure for just about anything that could possibly ail you, including standard eye problems. "Mangia la torta di carote, vedrai che poi ti togli gli occhiali" ("Eat carrot cake and you'll throw away your eyeglasses"). As in almost everything else, Lorenza followed her grandmother's advice—but she still wears glasses!

Unsalted butter, for greasing
3 eggs, separated, at room temperature
¾ cup sugar
½ cup grated raw carrots
¾ cup ground almonds
1 teaspoon grated lemon zest
½ cup potato starch
½ tablespoon baking powder
¼ teaspoon salt
½ teaspoon cream of tartar
1 tablespoon whole toasted almonds, for decoration
Confectioners' sugar, for dusting
Lemon peel curls, for garnish

1. Preheat the oven to 375°F. Grease an 8-inch-diameter springform pan.
2. Using an electric mixer or a hand whisk, beat the egg yolks and the sugar in a large bowl until smooth and fluffy, about 5 minutes with the mixer (15 minutes by hand).
3. Stir in the grated carrots, ground almonds and lemon zest and mix until creamy and light orange.
4. Sift in the potato starch and baking powder, and stir until well blended.
5. Using an electric mixer or a hand whisk, beat the egg whites and the salt in a large bowl until foamy. Add the cream of tartar and beat until stiff peaks form. Gently fold the egg whites into the cake batter.
6. Pour the mixture into the prepared pan, and decorate with whole almonds.

7. Bake until a tester inserted in the center of the cake comes out clean, about 35 minutes. Remove the sides of the pan and cool completely. Dust with confectioners' sugar and garnish with the lemon peel.

VARIATIONS: One-quarter cup grated butternut or acorn squash can be substituted for half the carrots.

Scarpaccia di zucchine
Zucchini Blossom Focaccia

Scarpaccia means "bad shoe," and since this cake is almost as flat as a worn shoe sole, it is a perfect descriptor. This delectable recipe from San Pellegrino also has a savory counterpart using thin slices of onion, thyme and fresh basil.

MAKES
ONE 12-INCH
TART
(10 SLICES)

TIME:
1½ HOURS

LEVEL:
MODERATE

Unsalted butter, for greasing
Flour, for dusting
2 eggs, at room temperature
¾ cup sugar
½ teaspoon vanilla extract
½ teaspoon salt
1 tablespoon unsalted butter, at room temperature
3–4 tablespoons milk
3 teaspoons grated lemon zest
1 cup bread flour
½ tablespoon baking powder
7 medium zucchini, scraped and cut into thin rounds
7 zucchini blossoms, stems removed, washed, drained and cut into strips
2 tablespoons extra-virgin olive oil
6 zucchini blossoms, for garnish

1. Preheat the oven to 350°F. Grease and dust with flour a 12-inch-diameter tart pan with removable bottom.
2. Using an electric mixer or hand whisk, beat the eggs and sugar in a large bowl until the sugar is dissolved, about 2 minutes with the mixer (5 minutes by hand). Add the vanilla, salt, butter, 3 tablespoons of the milk and 1 teaspoon of the lemon zest and mix until creamy and smooth.

3. Sift the flour and baking powder over the mixture and continue to beat until the batter is well blended. The batter should have the consistency of a thick syrup; if too dense, add the remaining 1 tablespoon milk.
4. Add the sliced zucchini and zucchini blossoms, drizzle with olive oil and mix by hand until well blended.
5. Pour the mixture into the prepared pan.
6. Bake for 40 minutes. Remove the sides of the pan and cool to room temperature. Dust with the remaining 2 teaspoons lemon zest and garnish with zucchini blossoms.

MAKE AHEAD: This cake is almost better if made the day before.

⊰•—⊱

Ciambella di mais e ricotta
Corn Flour and Ricotta Wedding-Ring Cake

MAKES
ONE 8-INCH
CAKE (8 SLICES)

TIME: 1 HOUR

LEVEL:
MODERATE

Rings, rings, rings! In mountain culture, they mean only one thing: trouble! When you give a ring of any kind, you are promising nonplatonic love and there is only one direction after making such a pronouncement. A silver or white gold ring is used for engagements and the simple golden band known as fede *(faith) or* vera *(true) is exchanged at the actual wedding Mass.*

This delicious ring cake is generally used to celebrate engagements; the woman getting engaged gives the party (which can include hundreds of people) and makes the dessert. "Too much work," says my friend, Cinzia. "Better to stay single."

Unsalted butter, for greasing
2 tablespoons cocoa powder, for dusting
4 eggs, at room temperature
½ cup sugar
1 teaspoon grated orange zest
½ teaspoon vanilla extract
½ cup fresh sheep's milk ricotta or other fresh ricotta
1 cup corn flour, sifted
½ tablespoon baking powder
1 recipe Basic Custard (see page 34), optional

1. Preheat the oven to 350°F. Grease and dust with cocoa powder an 8-inch tube pan

2. Using an electric mixer or a hand whisk, beat the eggs and the sugar in a large bowl until smooth, fluffy, and pale, about 5 minutes with the mixer (15 minutes by hand).

3 Stir in the orange zest, vanilla and ricotta and mix until blended. Sift in the corn flour and baking powder, stirring constantly, until thoroughly incorporated, about 5 minutes.

4. Pour the mixture into the prepared pan.

5. Bake until a tester inserted in the center comes out clean, about 30 minutes. Remove from oven, cool for five minutes and then invert onto a cooling rack. Serve plain or with lemon custard.

VARIATIONS: One-quarter cup golden raisins soaked for 20 minutes in ½ cup rum and then drained can be added in Step 3 before the addition of the corn flour.

Torta di patate
Potato and Almond Tart

The best potatoes in Tuscany come from the Garfagnana—more precisely, from San Romano, the same place that grows the best farro (a barley-like grain used for soups, stews and desserts). Garfagnine potatoes are a large white variety with a medium starch content that makes them a perfect binding agent. Obviously, this town has as many recipes for potatoes as Naples does for pizza, but the following is my favorite of all.

MAKES
ONE 9-INCH
TART (8 SLICES)

TIME: 2 HOURS

LEVEL:
MODERATE

Unsalted butter, for greasing
1 cup sugar
¼ cup ground toasted almonds
½ teaspoon salt
2 tablespoons rum
2 tablespoons warm milk
2½ cups medium starch (boiling) potatoes, boiled, peeled and passed
    through a ricer or food mill
1 teaspoon grated lemon zest
5 eggs, at room temperature
3 tablespoons unsalted butter, melted

1. Preheat the oven to 350°F. Grease a 9-inch-diameter springform baking pan.
2. In a large bowl, beat the sugar with the ground almonds, salt, rum and milk until smooth.
3. Add the mashed potatoes and blend well.
4. Add the lemon zest and eggs (one at a time) and continue stirring until a soft dough has formed.
5. Pour in the melted butter and mix for another 5 minutes. Let the mixture sit for 10 minutes.
6. Transfer the mixture to the prepared baking pan.
7. Bake until golden, about 40 minutes. Remove the sides of the pan and cool on a rack.

MAKE AHEAD: The potatoes can be boiled 1 day in advance, mashed, and stored, refrigerated, in a sealed container.

Budino di zucca
Butternut Squash Pudding

MAKES
1 PUDDING
(8 SERVINGS)

TIME: 2 HOURS

LEVEL:
MODERATE

Italians refer to butternut squash simply as zucca (squash). A beautiful and delicious winter squash, zucca is used throughout Tuscany as the main ingredient in soups, risotto and sauces. Its sweetness pairs well with both savory dishes and desserts. Pre-Renaissance artists routinely anthropomorphized zucca, substituting it for human heads in paintings satirizing the vanities of the aristocracy. Dante often lashed out at patrons, calling them zucca vuota (empty-headed squashes).

1½ cups sugar
3 tablespoons water
10 ounces butternut squash, peeled, seeded and cut into small chunks
1 tablespoon confectioners' sugar
4 eggs plus 1 egg yolk, at room temperature
½ teaspoon vanilla extract
2 cups milk
2 tablespoons heavy cream
1 tablespoon rum
16 thin slices butternut squash, caramelized in butter, for garnish*

1. Preheat the oven to 350°F.

2. Place ½ cup sugar and 2 tablespoons water in a small saucepan and cook over very low heat, stirring constantly until the sugar turns amber. Immediately remove from heat and transfer to an 8-inch-diameter (2-quart) soufflé dish, swirling to coat the sides.

3. Place the squash and the remaining 1 tablespoon water in a medium-size saucepan, cover and cook over low heat until soft, about 20 minutes.

4. Transfer the cooked squash to the bowl of a food processor add the confectioners' sugar; pulse until puréed. Pour into a large bowl and set aside.

5. Using an electric mixer or hand whisk, beat the eggs, the remaining 1 cup sugar, the vanilla, milk, cream and rum in a large bowl until smooth. Add to the squash and stir until blended.

6. Strain the mixture through a sieve to smooth the texture, then pour into the caramel coated soufflé dish.

7. Place the dish in a large baking pan filled with enough water to come halfway up the sides of the dish.

8. Bake until a tester inserted in the center comes out clean, about 1 hour. Remove from heat, let cool and refrigerate for 2 hours.

9. Using a thin metal spatula, loosen the sides of the pudding and invert it onto a serving platter. Garnish with the caramelized squash and serve.

* To caramelize the squash slices, melt 3 tablespoons butter in a large skillet, add as many pieces of squash as will fit in one layer and cook over low heat until very lightly browned on both sides.

MAKE AHEAD: The butternut squash can be cooked up to 2 days in advance and stored, refrigerated, in a sealed container.

Crostata di zucca
Butternut Squash Tart

MAKES
ONE 8-INCH
TART (8 SLICES)

TIME: 2 HOURS

LEVEL:
MODERATE

"Maggio va e poi ritorna," is an old Garfaganino saying. ("May departs but always returns.") But in the meantime, winter in the Tuscan mountains meant there were no peaches or cherries or sometimes even apples or pears if they had all already been eaten. What to substitute to make a perfect winter dessert tart? Why, butternut squash of course. I have substituted pasta frolla for the lard-based dough traditional to this dessert. I have also added crumbled amaretti, almonds and walnuts, which I think give the tart a wonderful added complexity.

Unsalted butter, for greasing
1 recipe Basic *Pasta Frolla* (see page 34)
2 pounds butternut squash, peeled, seeded and cut into small chunks
3 eggs, at room temperature
½ cup amaretti, crumbled
1 teaspoon grated lemon zest
1 teaspoon lemon juice
2 tablespoons roughly chopped candied orange peel
1 teaspoon vanilla extract
2 tablespoons golden raisins, soaked in ½ cup rum for 20 minutes and
    drained
3 tablespoons semolina
4 tablespoons sugar
3 tablespoons cake flour
½ teaspoon salt
½ teaspoon ground nutmeg
½ cup coarsely chopped toasted almonds
½ cup coarsely chopped shelled walnuts
½ cup apricot preserve

1. Preheat the oven to 400°F. Very lightly grease an 8-inch-diameter tart pan with removable bottom.
2. Remove the *pasta frolla* from the refrigerator, unwrap and roll into a 9 inch circle on a lightly floured work surface. Arrange the circle in the bottom of the prepared pan, piercing it with a fork and pressing the ex-

cess against the sides. Roll a rolling pin over the top of the tart pan to level the sides.

3. Press a sheet of aluminum foil into the pan, top with raw rice, dried beans or commercial pie weights and bake for 5 minutes. Remove the weights and foil and bake until the crust is pale golden, about 7 minutes.

4. Place the butternut squash in the bowl of a food processor and purée. Transfer the purée to a large bowl, stir in the eggs, crumbled amaretti, zest, lemon juice, candied orange peel, vanilla and drained golden raisins. Stir for 5 minutes to blend all the ingredients.

5. Sift together the semolina, sugar, flour, salt and nutmeg. Stir the dry ingredients into the squash mixture, a little at a time until a well blended batter has formed.

6. Fill the tart pan with the batter. Mix the almonds and walnuts, and top the batter with the mixture.

7. Bake for 40 minutes. Remove the sides of the pan.

8. While the tart is baking, melt the apricot preserves in a saucepan over low heat. Brush the melted preserve over the surface of the tart while still hot. Serve lukewarm.

VARIATIONS: Acorn or another winter squash can be used in place of the butternut.

Pan perduto
Tuscan Bread Pudding

Tuscany's mountain people are reputed to be extremely thrifty. Some would say cheap. But when it comes to food preparation, this tendency to use everything results in some wonderful creations, among them, this clever version of bread pudding. Bread pudding it is, but bread pudding of a dramatically different sort by virtue of the quality of bread and ingredients such as raisins soaked in Vin Santo.

SERVES 6

TIME: 2 HOURS

LEVEL: MODERATE

Unsalted butter, for greasing
8 slices rustic-style bread, preferably stale
4 cups warm milk

2 eggs, at room temperature

¾ cup sugar

½ cup unsalted butter, at room temperature

¼ teaspoon ground cinnamon

1 teaspoon grated lemon zest

1 tablespoon golden raisins, soaked in ½ cup *Vin Santo* for 20 minutes
    and then drained

2 tablespoons pine nuts

1 tablespoon almond slivers

1 cup lightly whipped cream, for garnish

1. Preheat the oven to 350°F. Grease a 2-quart soufflé dish.
2. Place the bread in a large shallow pan in one layer, pour in the milk and soak for 20 minutes, turning the bread once or twice.
3. Squeeze the bread slightly (it should still be quite soggy and dissolved into clumps) and discard the milk.
4. Using an electric mixer or a hand whisk, beat the eggs and the sugar in a large bowl until smooth, fluffy and pale, about 5 minutes with the mixer (15 minutes by hand). Add the butter, cinnamon and lemon zest and continue to beat until all ingredients are well blended.
5. Add the bread, raisins, pine nuts and almonds and mix well. Pour the mixture into the prepared soufflé dish.
6. Bake for 1 hour. Serve warm, topped with the whipped cream.

MAKE AHEAD: The pudding can be made up to 2 days in advance and reheated in an oven when needed. Leftover pudding can also be reheated in a double boiler over simmering water.

Dolce di stracchino e pere
Farmer's Cheese Cake with Pears and Hazelnut Crumb Topping

During winters, when mountain children asked for cake, and mothers could not go to the market because it was too far to walk in the snow, this wonderful cheese and pear confection perfectly filled the void. Stracchino (a type of soft, creamy farmer's cheese) was always on hand as were eggs and some type of fruit. I have added the hazelnut-crumb topping purely because I believe that too much of a good thing is simply a starting point.

MAKES
ONE 9-INCH
CAKE (8 SLICES)

TIME:
1½ HOURS

LEVEL:
MODERATE

Unsalted butter, for greasing
Dry bread crumbs, for dusting
2 eggs plus two egg yolks, at room temperature
3½ tablespoons sugar
½ teaspoon vanilla extract
8 ounces *stracchino* or other soft farmer's cheese
2 medium pears, peeled, cored and finely diced
2 egg whites, at room temperature
¼ teaspoon salt
¼ teaspoon cream of tartar
4 tablespoons unsalted butter
½ cup ground hazelnuts
Clusters of grapes misted slightly with water and dipped in sugar,
    for garnish

1. Preheat the oven to 350°F. Grease and dust with bread crumbs a 9-inch-diameter springform pan.
2. Using an electric mixer or hand whisk, beat the eggs, egg yolks and sugar in a large bowl until smooth, creamy and pale, about 5 minutes with the mixer (15 minutes by hand).
3. Stir in the vanilla, cheese and pears, and mix until well blended.
4. Using an electric mixer or hand whisk, beat the egg whites and the salt in a large bowl until foamy. Add the cream of tartar and beat until stiff peaks form. Gently fold the whites into the cheese mixture until just blended.
5. Pour the mixture into the prepared pan and tap against a countertop to level the surface.

6. Melt the butter in a skillet and add the ground hazelnuts, toasting over low heat and stirring constantly for 5 minutes.

7. Spread the toasted hazelnut crumbs evenly over the surface of the cake.

8. Place the cake pan in a larger one filled with enough water to come halfway up the sides of the cake.

9. Bake for 35 minutes. Remove from oven, let cool and then refrigerate for 2 hours.

10. To serve, release the spring, cut the cake into wedges, gently remove each slice and arrange on individual plates garnished with a cluster of sugared grapes.

VARIATIONS: Apples can be used instead of pears.

Torta del Vescovo
Bishop's Cake

MAKES 1 CAKE
(8 SLICES)

TIME:
1½ HOURS

LEVEL:
MODERATE

The sixteenth century Bishop of Lucca used to spend his weekends at Casone di Profecchia, a picturesque inn located in the Garfagnana Mountains. It is said that he always arrived with a woman, but nobody will swear to it. What people do swear to is how much he used to eat. His favorite proverb was: "Prayers are the food of the soul and the bigger the prayer the richer the soul." This delicious nut and chocolate cake was apparently his favorite.

5 egg yolks, lightly beaten with 2 tablespoons milk and 1 tablespoon sugar
1½ cups unsalted butter, softened, at room temperature
1 cup sugar
6 tablespoons ground almonds
6 tablespoons ground walnuts
6 tablespoons grated unsweetened chocolate
20 ladyfingers
8 tablespoons rum
8 tablespoons cherry liqueur
5 tablespoons brandy
1 cup finely ground hazelnuts
Fresh mint, for garnish

1. Place the egg mixture in the top of a double boiler and cook over simmering water (the water should not touch the bottom of the egg pan), stirring constantly until the temperature reaches 160°F. Transfer to a bowl and let cool to room temperature.
2. In a large bowl, cream the butter and the sugar until smooth.
3. Add the egg mixture, a little at a time, stirring constantly until creamy.
4. Stir in ground almonds, walnuts and chocolate and mix until well blended.
5. In a small bowl, mix together the rum, cherry liqueur and brandy.
6. Briefly dip the ladyfingers into the blended liqueurs, turning them to moisten both sides. Drain them on a plate. Place a layer of soaked ladyfingers in a deep round serving bowl, spread the egg and chocolate mixture over them and level with a spatula. Continue to layer until all ingredients have been used.
7. Dust the top layer with ground hazelnuts, cover with foil and chill for two hours. Garnish with the fresh mint.

MAKE AHEAD: The custard mixture can be made through Step 4 up to 1 day in advance and stored in a sealed container in the refrigerator.

Torta coi becchi di riso e spinaci
Spinach and Rice Cake

Since chocolate was once so prohibitively expensive, Tuscany's shrewd mountain dwellers invented this thriftier version of the traditional torta coi becchi *which includes a large amount of unsweetened chocolate blocks. The recipe uses all the ingredients native to the area: the freshest eggs from their backyard hen house, soft wheat flour ground fresh in their kitchens, and tender spinach picked minutes earlier from their kitchen garden.*

MAKES
ONE 8-INCH
CAKE (8 SLICES)

TIME: 2 HOURS

LEVEL:
ADVANCED

THE DOUGH

2 cups bread flour, sifted
½ teaspoon salt
1 teaspoon baking powder
½ cup unsalted butter, at room temperature
⅓ cup sugar
1 tablespoon confectioners' sugar

2 eggs plus 1 yolk, at room temperature
1 teaspoon grated lemon zest
1 tablespoon warm milk
1 tablespoon extra-virgin olive oil
1 teaspoon vanilla extract
Unsalted butter, for greasing

THE FILLING

1 cup arborio rice
1 quart milk
1½ teaspoons salt
2 teaspoons grated lemon zest
1 cup sugar
1 teaspoon vanilla extract
3 eggs plus 1 egg yolk, at room temperature
3 tablespoons warm milk
½ cup pine nuts
½ cup diced candied fruit
½ cup golden raisins, soaked in 1 cup of rum for 2 hours and then
    drained
1 cup boiled and coarsely chopped spinach
6 tablespoons amaretto

1. To make the dough, sift together the flour, salt and baking powder.
2. In a large bowl, cream the butter, sugar and confectioners' sugar until smooth and fluffy. Beat in the eggs, one at a time; beat in the egg
   yolks, lemon zest, milk, oil, and vanilla.
3. Sift the flour mixture into the creamed butter a little at a time and stir
   until blended into a smooth, soft dough.
4. Shape the dough into a ball, wrap in plastic and refrigerate for 1 hour.
5. Preheat the oven to 350°F. Grease a 9- inch-diameter springform pan.
6. To make the filling, cook the rice, milk, 1 teaspoon salt, and 1 teaspoon lemon zest in a saucepan over medium heat until tender,
   about 18 minutes.
7. Drain the rice and place it in a large bowl along with the sugar, the
   remaining ½ teaspoon salt, the vanilla, the remaining 1 teaspoon
   grated lemon zest, eggs, egg yolk, milk, pine nuts, candied fruit,
   golden raisins, spinach and amaretto and gently stir until all the ingredients are thoroughly blended.

8. Pinch off a 2-inch-diameter piece of dough and set aside. On a lightly floured surface and using a rolling pin, roll the remaining dough into a 10-inch-diameter circle, ⅛ inch thick. Arrange in the prepared pan, patting the excess against the sides.

9. Work the side crust so that the top edge is even all around. Pour the filling into the pan, tapping it against a counter to level the surface. Using a knife, cut the crust into a pattern resembling a series of small towers. Add the excess dough to the reserved dough and roll into a rectangle approximately 9 x 4 inches. Cut into ½-inch-wide strips. Arrange on top of the cake in a lattice pattern.

10. Bake until the center is set, about 50 minutes. Remove the sides of the pan and serve at room temperature.

MAKE AHEAD: The dough can be prepared in advance, wrapped in plastic and refrigerated for 2 days or frozen for up to 3 weeks. Thaw in refrigerator before using.

Crostata alle arance amare
Blood Orange Tart

When I was a young girl, tradition dictated that every household plant an orange tree in the front garden so that in the spring the blossoms would scent the air with their tantalizing perfume. The orange trees planted in those days were a particular type of bitter orange that is, nowadays, hard to find. I have substituted blood oranges in this recipe, for both their brilliant color and slightly tart flavor.

MAKES
ONE 9-INCH
TART (8 SLICES)

TIME: 2 HOURS

LEVEL:
MODERATE

Unsalted butter, for greasing
1 recipe *Pasta Frolla* (see page 34)
4 blood oranges, peeled, seeded, pith removed and thinly sliced
2 lemons, peeled, seeded, pith removed and thinly sliced
2 tablespoons confectioners' sugar
6 tablespoons Cointreau
1 recipe *Pasta Genovese,* or Basic Sponge Cake (see page 36)
⅓ cup apricot preserves

1. Preheat the oven to 400°F. Grease an 8-inch-diameter springform pan.

2. Remove the chilled *pasta frolla* from the refrigerator, unwrap and roll it into a 9-inch-diameter circle on a lightly floured surface. Arrange the circle in the bottom of the prepared pan, pierce with a fork in a few places and press the excess against the sides.

3. Cover the *pasta frolla* with aluminum foil and top with raw rice, dried beans or commercial pie weights. Bake for 10 minutes, remove the weights and aluminum foil and continue to cook for another 5 minutes. Remove from oven and let cool to room temperature.

4. Place the sliced oranges in a nonreactive (enamel, nonstick or stainless steel) saucepan along with the lemons, sugar and 2 tablespoons of the Cointreau. Cook over very low heat for 10 minutes, stirring constantly. Remove from heat and using a slotted spoon transfer the cooked fruit to a small bowl. Reserve the cooking liquid.

5. Cut the sponge cake to fit the pastry shell and place in the pan over the baked crust. Brush the remaining 4 tablespoons Cointreau over the surface of the sponge cake along with 3 tablespoons of the fruit cooking-liquid.

6. Arrange the lemon and orange slices on the sponge cake.

7. Melt the preserves in a saucepan over low heat. Using a pastry brush, paint the fruit with the melted preserves.

VARIATIONS: Any type of orange or mandarin can be substituted for the blood oranges.

<hr>

Crostata ai frutti di bosco
Wild Berry Tart

MAKES
ONE 10-INCH
TART (8 SLICES)

TIME:
45 MINUTES

LEVEL: EASY

The fragrant flavor of wild berries is unforgettable. Come August, they scent the mountain air and draw thousands of foragers into the dark forest underbrush, each hoping to leave with a basket full of berries to make tarts. This particular tart recipe comes from Mariella Mertosi, who lives in Castiglione, an eleventh century town with magnificently preserved walls.

Unsalted butter, for greasing
1 recipe Basic *Pasta Frolla* (see page 34)
1 cup Basic Custard (see page 34)
2 cups blackberries or raspberries, stemmed and washed

⅓ cup fig preserves
Fresh mint leaves, for decoration

1. Preheat the oven to 375°F. Grease a 10-inch-diameter tart pan with removable bottom.
2. Remove the *pasta frolla* from the refrigerator, unwrap and roll into a 12-inch-diameter circle on a lightly floured work surface. Arrange the circle of *pasta frolla* in the bottom of the prepared pan, pressing the excess against the sides. Line the pastry shell with foil and add raw rice, dried beans or commercial pie weights.
3. Bake for 10 minutes, remove the foil and the weights and bake until lightly golden, about 5 minutes. Cool slightly.
4. Spread the custard over the pastry, leveling the surface with a spatula.
5. Arrange the berries in 1 layer on top of the custard. Cover with foil.
6. Bake for 10 minutes. Remove the foil and bake for 5 more minutes.
7. Melt the preserves in a saucepan over low heat. Using a pastry brush, paint the surface of the tart. Remove the sides of the pan, let cool to room temperature and decorate with the fresh mint.

VARIATIONS: Other seasonal fruit can be substituted for the berries.

Torta di semolino
Baked Semolina Tart

Semolina is cream of wheat. There is always a great deal of confusion regarding this product since Tuscans also use semolina flour in making pasta and refer to it with the same name. Mountain cooks make frequent use of semolina (cream of wheat) for soups or a particular type of baked gnocchi. In this unusual and totally delectable recipe, the semolina is simply mixed with butter, milk, eggs and a little seasoning and baked into a tart. Paired with fresh fruit or drizzled with a fruit purée, it serves as the perfect finale to a rustic dinner of, perhaps, pasta with chickpeas and a mixed greens salad.

MAKES
ONE 8-INCH
TART (8 SLICES)

TIME: 1 HOUR

LEVEL: EASY

Unsalted butter, for greasing
1 cup toasted almonds
1½ cups sugar
4 cups milk
6 tablespoons unsalted butter, at room temperature

1 cup cream of wheat
½ teaspoon salt
4 eggs, lightly beaten, at room temperature
2 teaspoons grated lemon zest
½ cup ground almonds
½ cup raspberry purée

1. Preheat the oven to 350°F and grease a 9-inch-diameter springform pan.
2. Place the almonds and 1 cup sugar in a food processor and pulse until the mixture is completely granular. Set aside
3. Place the milk in a medium-size saucepan and bring to a gentle boil over very low heat. Add 3 tablespoons of the butter, and when melted, whisk in the cream of wheat and the salt, pouring in a steady stream and stirring constantly until thickened, about 3 minutes. Let cool to room temperature.
4. Cream the remaining 3 tablespoons butter with the ground almonds and the remaining ½ cup sugar until a thick paste has been created.
5. Add the eggs to the semolina a little at a time, stirring constantly until well blended. Stir in the lemon zest. Pour the mixture into the prepared pan. Dot with the almond-sugar mixture.
6. Bake for 30 minutes. Let cool to room temperature and remove the pan sides. Slice the tart and center each slice on a bed of fruit purée.

MAKE AHEAD: The cake can be assembled up to 1 day in advance, wrapped and stored, refrigerated, until ready to bake.

CHAPTER FIVE

Spoon Desserts

What Price Paradise

L'Incanto Circeo

Tra I due porti, tra l'uno e l'altro faro
Bonaccia senza vele e senza nubi
Dolce venata come le tue tempie
Assai lungi di lá dell'Argentaro
Assai lungi le rupi e le paludi
Di Circe, dell'iddia delle molte erbe
E ci incantó con una stilla d'erbe
Tutto il Tirreno, come un suo lebete!

Between the two ports, between the two lighthouses
Calm winds with no sails or clouds
Sweetly veined as the temples of your face
Far enough beyond the Argentaro
Far beyond Circe's cliffs and moors
The goddess of the earth
Enchants with sprig of herb
The whole of the Tyrhennian, making it one of her many vials!

by Gabriele D'Annunzio

Very few people who come to Tuscany ever venture beyond the mainland to the spectacular archipelago of islands located just off its southern coast. There are seven large isles—Gorgona, Capraia, Pianosa, Montecristo, Giglio, Giannutri and Elba—and a smattering of smaller ones appropriately called *formiche* (ants). The entire assemblage floats on the warm, blue-green waters of the Tyrrhenian and each belongs to either Livorno or Grosseto, two provinces that make up the heart of what was once the land of the Etruscans.

Judging for myself, I would say that the five accessible islands (Gorgona and Pianosa are off limits) are all equally extraordinary, but then it has always been difficult for me to parse the finer points of paradise. And yet, guidebooks routinely engage in just that kind of comparative analysis, elevating Giglio above Giannutri (or the other way around) on the basis of things such as services, accommodations, roads, or length of available beach front. But guidebooks can't even approach the criticisms and nit-picking of the parent regions themselves when it comes to the relative charm of one island over another. The Livornesi, of course, claim there is no island anywhere in the world more perfect than Elba, which lies within its regional boundaries. "Even Napoleon thought so," they say, begging the point just slightly. It is true that Napoleon chose Elba over a list of other Mediterranean outposts presented for his consideration upon being exiled after the 1814 Treaty of Fountainbleau (ergo the Napoleonic palindrome: able was I ere I saw Elba). His stated reason was "the gentleness of both climate and inhabitants." I suspect it also had to do with the fact that, on clear days, he could look across to his beloved Corsica.

Located slightly farther south than Elba, Giglio is the second largest island in the Tuscan archipelago. To the Grossetani however, there is nothing second rate about their Tyrrhenian jewel. Giglio means "lily," which is the island's symbol and the most popular flower in its many public gardens. With red and green lighthouses to welcome the ferries and pink and beige villas straggling up the hills, Giglio is a colorful and welcoming place. In recent years, it has acquired a strict environmental consciousness; signs are posted everywhere stating its aversion to camping, noise, riding over the wildflowers, uprooting plants, picking flowers, even collecting rocks.

There is a fierce rivalry between Livorno and Grosseto over their respective island holdings. For starters, you can only reach Giglio, Montecristo and Giannutri (which lie within Grosseto's administrative boundaries) from Grosseto—from ferries docked at Porto Santo Stefano. Elba and Capraia (part of Livorno), on the other hand, can only be reached via ferries leaving Livorno. The arrangement makes some sense, given that each group of islands is technically closest to the specified point of departure. But if you look at a map, you realize that the archipelago is so incredibly compact that it would make much more sense for both ferry terminals to service all five of the islands. Especially in vew of the fact that, in summer, ferries must be booked a month in advance and turn away half as many customers as they actually carry.

One of the most serious confrontations between the two regions has nothing to do with the islands per se but is such a wonderful story that I feel compelled to include it here. At the center of the incident is Amedeo Modigliani, the great nineteenth century sculptor, who was born in Livorno and revered by the Livornesi in a manner befitting a deity. Well, in 1984, a group of artists from Grosseto sculpted two giant heads in the Modigliani style and threw them into the water off Porto Mediceo. As they later stated, "We just wanted to tweak the Livornesi for always holding their alleged cultural supremacy under our noses."

After a few months had gone by, newspapers printed an amazing story that had been leaked to them from "anonymous" sources: Before moving to Paris, the young Modigliani had created two heads from local stone but, disappointed in the results, had flung them off the end of a pier.

The port was dredged and the heads retrieved under the reverant stare of the international media. "No doubt, we are witnessing the return to our bosom of authentic Modigliani sculptures" said the eminent art critic, Maria Durbe. Many agreed with her, although there was doubt on the part of Federico Zeri and Carlo Argan, famous Florentine art historians. Their questions led to months of examination and testing and finally, the story once again made the front page; this time revealing the scandalous fake as well as the unmasking of the Grossetani artists, who were all students at the nation's foremost art college, the Accademia di Belle Arti. Needless to say, given the Italian aversion to incarcerating anyone short of violent criminals (and even then...) the artists were never brought up on charges; in fact, they enjoyed a brief but intense period of national adulation over both their artistic talents and the unbridled gaul they had demonstrated in spoofing the Livornesi.

I am treating myself to a three-day holiday at the home of my friend, Lucrezia Palmiri, whose villa is located directly across from one of Elba's most beautiful beaches. "The water is warm and I'm already tanned," she said by way of luring me across the sea. As if I needed luring!

The crossing from Piombino takes an hour—five minutes more than usual because someone changed their mind at the last minute ("I forgot to turn off my computer!" she screamed just before running off the boat). It is a beautiful day and I sit on the main bridge, watching the flock of seagulls chasing our wake in hopes of fish. In the distance, I can see Gorgona, a lush green island on its way to being converted into a national park after serving for centuries as a penal colony. The closest of all the islands to Stiava, where I live, Gorgona has more myths spun about it than the island of Atlantis.

Lucrezia is waiting for me at the outer gates, having calculated almost to the minute how long it would take to drive from the ferry.

"Guess who arrived last night?" she says with equal does of enthusiasm and regret.

That can only mean one thing. "Caterina?"

"She came straight from Milan where she just finished the Versace show. I was already in bed when the caretaker came running in, saying a visitor had just pulled into the garage."

"I thought you were also scheduled to show for Versace," I say. Lucrezia and Caterina are both models and often they work the same shows. The two are good friends but sometimes you'd never know it from the way they compete against each other to be the star of the show.

"I was, but then I got this haircut and dye job when I did the Prada show," she points to an adorable cap of brilliant red hair, "and the Versace people didn't want to use wigs." She lowers her voice, even though we're about 100 yards from the beach where Caterina has stretched out her lithe feline body. "I'm not really thrilled about her being here. But what could I do? She showed up at my door."

I'm not thrilled about Caterina being there either, not because I don't like her—it's impossible not to like Caterina with her sarcastic wit and relentless optimism. But the two of them together make me tired. If Lucrezia orders a certain entrée, Caterina says she wouldn't think of eating the food in that particular restaurant. If Caterina swims out to the jetty, Lucrezia says she's tired and why don't we just head back to the house. Besides being models and always having to be the center of attention, the two of them also exhibit an inescapable tendency toward regional rivalry: Caterina is from Grosseto and pitted against Lucrezia from Livorno, so the battle becomes an epic struggle for supremacy in everything from which region has the greater number of Titians to which one makes the best fish soup.

"It will be great to see her," I say hesitantly. "When's the last time we all got together—maybe for Fabiola's wedding?"

"There was a marriage made in hell," says Lucrezia signaling for the gardener to take my bags. "Fabiola waited all through his involvement with that other woman and when they finally got together, she realized he was just like every other Grossetano—a great big jerk."

"Don't start," I say, throwing myself on the divan just outside the front door. I kick off my shoes, my brain swirling with visions of a long bountiful lunch beginning with a chilled glass of wine, which I'm hoping someone will bring me in the next twenty seconds. But Lucrezia grabs my hands and pulls me back to my feet.

"We're going fishing," she announces. "Armando and Delfo (her brothers) are joining us and we're all going out for lobsters."

She picks up a huge basket filled with covered bowls of food (and three bottles of nicely chilled wine) and yells to Caterina. "Come on Miss Bathing Beauty, the guys are waiting!"

We board a small motorboat belonging to Lucrezia's parents and head out to the open waters. The Tuscan archipelago is a haven for lobsters and shrimp and all kinds of crustaceans and tonight, according to Armando, we're going to have a lobster feast guaranteed to swear us off lobster for the next twenty years. On the deck are four *nassa* (cages) and the announced plan is this: We three women will lie on the boat and sun ourselves while the men dive for dinner.

"How very 90s," says Caterina, slathering sunscreen on her legs. "All that trying to be equal was much too tiring anyway."

"As if you ever exerted any effort," Armando teases her.

The boat is fast and extremely quiet as it slices its way through the placid waters of the lower Tyrrhenian. We dock on the west side of Elba, and the two men immediately put on their goggles. "We're getting out of here as fast as we can," says Armando, heaving himself backwards off the stern. "Come on, Delfo," he calls from the waters. "You're preventing these women from being able to talk about us."

"Don't flatter yourselves," Caterina yells. She picks up the cages and begins heaving them into the water, one by one. "Don't come back unless these are full!"

Lucrezia throws herself into the nearest chaise. "*Dio mio,* what a month of work it has been," she says wearily. "I'm going to just lie on this deck for the rest of the afternoon and read my book."

"Actually, I think I'll swim a few miles," says Caterina predictably. "The water is soooo warm."

"You're crazy," Lucrezia tells her. "I wouldn't put my toe in there until August."

"Of course you wouldn't. You're one of those thin-skinned Livornesi."

"Meaning what—that the Grossetani are tough? We saw how tough you were four years ago after the shark attack. It took two years before anyone from Grosseto ventured back to Elba—and that included the people who owned houses here. For us, of course, it was wonderful."

I'd forgotten about this incident, about the three tourists who were killed by a white shark just off the beach at Marina di Campo, on the southern end of Elba. "Thanks," I tell Lucrezia. "I was just planning on going in for a swim."

"It's fine," says Caterina. "Don't listen to her."

I can tell from Lucrezia's face that she's about to bring up something else. Only God knows the specifics of what it will be, but I feel comfortable wagering on it having something to do with confrontation.

"*Basta!*" I tell them. ("Enough!") "When are you two going to stop competing? If it's not 'look at me, look at me,' it's 'my mother's better,' 'no, mine is.' I don't know how I ever made it through all those years we went to school together."

"Now who's trying to grab the highest ground?" laughs Caterina as she dives into the water.

"You know, you're right," says Lucrezia, adjusting her sunglasses. "Caterina and I always seem to be competing." A frown crosses her face. "Mainly it's because of the way we were raised—the way all Tuscans are raised. All you ever hear is 'we're better than them,' them meaning anyone not from our immediate area. Even those in our immediate area who exhibit the tiniest bit of difference are judged not quite as good." She shakes her head. "It's terrible!"

Much as I'd like to say "Oh Lucrezia, you're always exaggerating" (which in most cases is true), this time, she is, unfortunately, right on target. The fact of the matter is that Tuscans have never moved beyond the mindset of feudal duchies warring with each other over titles and land. In modern times, the warring focuses on safer things, like recipes and cultural holdings, but the spirit remains the same.

"What to do?" I throw up my hands. "I guess we're just doomed!"

The rest of the afternoon goes by too quickly and soon the sun becomes a fire ball plunging into the sea. We make our way back to Rio Marina, where Lucrezia lives, and unpack the lobsters, whose red and black claws are poking nervously through the metal sides of the cages. I feel a little sorry for them and wonder about the glee with which we all greeted their capture.

We eat on the wide granite terrace behind the villa, the scent of summer roses enveloping us as we dig into a profusion of bright red claws. "Hmmmm," says Caterina, taking what will most likely be her first and last bite, given her neurotic attention to calories. "These are so incredibly delicious."

"Eat more," urges Lucrezia's brother Armando. "You can't get these in Grosseto."

"We can so, " says Caterina. "What do you think—there's a vast boundary line laid on the floor of the Mediterranean? That lobsters can only stay on the Livorno side?"

Her snideness surprises Armando, but only for a second. "It's just that Elba is farther out in the water than Giglio and the water is considerably cooler. Lobsters prefer cold water you know."

"What are you talking about?" Caterina is now on her feet. "There's twenty miles between us. How much colder can the water be?"

"It's not only temperature, " adds Lucrezia. "The waters here are clearer too, by virtue of the tidal stream."

I've had it. Twenty years of this has worn me down to the point where I simply can no longer listen to them joust. I love these two women, truly. But enough is enough. "I'm going home," I announce to the table at large. "There must be a late boat to the mainland. If not, maybe I'll swim. Anything is better than dangling in the cross current of your battles."

I fold my napkin over my plate and look around for a response. There is none. Everyone is silent, looking at me as if the culprit resided in *my* words, *my* attitude.

"What battles?" says Caterina. "Lucrezia is my best friend. We *never* fight, never have."

I turn toward Lucrezia. Well? my look says.

"I can't believe you think we fight," she says. "We tease each other. A lot, in fact. But fight? Why would we?"

"Exactly!" I say loudly. "That's what I'm always asking myself—why would you? Why would you try to outdo each other over who has more artwork, more history, more lobsters for God's sake. Professionally, I can even somewhat understand, but over number of beaches? Why?"

Caterina stretches her hands across the table. "Poor Sandretta," she says, wrapping her palms around my wrists. "Tuscan and not Tuscan. I've always told you that American cousin of yours was a bad influence. Here's the proof."

Everyone nods their heads. "You've become too much like Anna," Lucrezia adds. "You know how Anna is always trying to analyze situations?"

"They're joking," Delfo pleads. "It's just for fun. Don't take it wrong."

Suddenly, the problem is me. Everyone is standing around my chair, hugging me, embracing me, patting me on the back as if I were being somehow unreasonable. Petulant. Unable to comprehend the reality of the situation.

Lucrezia whispers over my head to Caterina. "What are we going to do," she says mockingly. "We can't let her swim across to Piombino."

I think it's too late," Caterina whispers back. "She hates us."

Suddenly Armando puts a lobster in front of my face. "We're sorry," he says, pretending to be a ventriloquist. "We've been very very bad." He shakes the lobster and begins to sniffle. "Can you ever find it in your heart to forgive us?"

I turn around to chase them away and see Caterina and Lucrezia standing hip to hip with their arms around each other's shoulders. They're right, I think. I'm wrong and they're right. There have never been any arguments, only the kind of make-believe carping that becomes a habit between lifelong friends—the Italian *argomento* means "discussion" after all.

"So shouldn't you be getting ready?" says Lucrezia, winking at her two brothers. "It's going to be a long swim to Piombino."

"Well, maybe she should swim to Grosseto," suggests Caterina. "After all . . ." she plops herself into my lap and cups my face in her hands, ". . . the water is so much warmer that you probably won't have to worry about being grabbed by a lascivious lobster."

Spoon Desserts

Dolci al cucchiaio (spoon desserts) is what Tuscans call that entire category of custards, sorbets, gelatos, flans, *zabaiones*, mousses, puddings and individual soufflés that are—surprise!—eaten with a spoon. They are among the most elegant of desserts, both because of their rich, creamy texture and their appearance—generally small compact rounds that can be beautifully centered on a plate of fruit purée or garnished with fruit slices or herb sprigs.

Spoon desserts are also easy to make—despite all the negative publicity about curdled custards and fallen soufflés. A few things however, are worth noting:

- Custards separate (curdle) when heated too long or over high temperatures. Depending on the ingredients, the separation of egg proteins and liquids takes place somewhere between 170 degrees Fahrenheit and 190 degrees Fahrenheit. To avoid curdling, warm the milk or cream before mixing with the eggs, sugar and other ingredients. Warming acclimates (or tempers) the eggs and speeds the custard's setting.

- Custard ingredients are best heated in double boilers over hot water until they reach 160 degree Fahrenheit. The heating should be a slow process. If warmed too quickly, the custard will not thicken properly. If heated too long, it will curdle.

- Custards cook in a *bagno maria* (double-boiler) so that they are insulated from the direct heat of the oven. Place the custard cups in a roasting pan filled with enough water to come halfway up their sides. To further insulate the custard from direct heat (in this case, the hot pan bottom), place the cups on a towel laid on the bottom of the roasting pan. The cups should be placed far enough apart so that they don't touch.

- Low-fat and skim milk can be substituted for whole milk in custard recipes; the recipe will work just as well although the consistency will be thinner and less dense. Also, three egg whites can be substituted for two whole eggs without compromising the setting process.

- Soufflés have an undeserved reputation for being hard to make. Nothing could be farther from the truth. Once the egg whites have been beaten (see "Beating Egg Whites" page 11) and mixed with the remaining ingredients, all that remains is for the oven to expand the air trapped in the beaten whites and create that beautiful puffed creation known as the perfect soufflé. Soufflés must be served at once, however, or they will fall. Also, soufflé molds should be buttered and dusted with a layer of sugar before using them.

- To test whether a soufflé is done, open the oven door slightly at the end of the required cooking time and touch the soufflé with your hand. If the soufflé feels firm, it is set. If a tester is inserted, it should come out dry. It is important to be brief when testing; if too much cold air rushes into the oven, the soufflé will fall.

- Mousses require three to five hours of refrigeration before serving in order to gel the ingredients. When ready to serve, unmold them onto a serving plate or eat them with a spoon directly from the molds in which they were made. To unmold a mousse, dip the bottom of the mold into a tub of hot water for two to three seconds and then invert the mold onto a plate.

- When making gelatos, mousses or custards, always cook the eggs in a double boiler over hot water to kill harmful bacteria. Eggs should be combined with a few tablespoons of milk when cooked. The fat in the milk enables the eggs to be cooked to a fairly high temperature, in this case, 160 degrees Fahrenheit, which effectively kills salmonella and other bacteria. An alternate strategy is to buy pasteurized liquid eggs (which come both whole and separated into yolks and whites). Increasingly, pasteurized eggs can found in specialty and gourmet stores.

Spoon Desserts

Timballo di castagne
Chestnut Timbale with Warm Fig Sauce

Sorbetto al limone e salvia
Lemon and Fresh Sage Sorbet

Gelato agli amaretti
Amaretto Gelato

Gelato di pinoli e zucca
Pine-Nut-and-Butternut-Squash Gelato

Tiramisù
Mascarpone Custard

Latte alla portoghese
Espresso Flan

Panna cotta al torrone con salsa al cioccolato
Cream and Nougat Tarts with Orange-Chocolate Sauce

Budini di riso e mandorle
Rice and Almond Pudding

Yogurt di cioccolato al caffè con arancia candita
Chocolate Yogurt with Coffee Liqueur and Candied Orange Peel

Crema al balsamico
Balsamic Vinegar and Vanilla Gelato

Budino al mandarino
Creamy Mandarin Pudding

Ricotta all'caffè
Espresso Ricotta

Timballo di castagne
Chestnut Timbale with Warm Fig Sauce

MAKES
4 TIMBALES

TIME:
2 HOURS PLUS
REFRIGERATION

LEVEL:
MODERATE

I would love to live in the Maremma (the moorlands of southern Tuscany) for two reasons: (1) It has the most beautiful landscapes in all of Tuscany; and (2) my favorite restaurant I Due Cippi is located there in Saturnia and run by Michele and Bianca Aniello, whose motto is "Ci vuole un occhio di riguardo dall'inizio alla fine di ogni pasto" ("One must watch over the food from the first ingredient to the final presentation")! The recipe for this timbale comes from Bianca Aniello and is the living proof of how a simple ingredient like the chestnut can be transformed into a dessert worthy of a king.

1 pound chestnuts
1 teaspoon salt
1 bay leaf
2 cups milk
2 tablespoons grated unsweetened chocolate
2 eggs plus 2 egg yolks, at room temperature
1 cup sugar
2¼ teaspoons (1 envelope) gelatin dissolved in ¼ cup warm water
1 cup fig or apricot preserves

1. Place the chestnuts, salt, bay leaf and enough water to cover by 2 inches in a large pot. Bring to a boil and cook for 40 minutes. Using a slotted spoon remove the chestnuts from water and place in a large bowl to cool. Discard the bay leaf.
2. Peel and skin the cooled chestnuts and place them in a large saucepan with the milk. Cover and cook over low heat until the milk has been completely absorbed, about 20 minutes.
3. Transfer the chestnuts to the bowl of a food processor, add the chocolate and purée.
4. Place the eggs and sugar in the top of a double boiler and cook over simmering water, beating constantly, until the egg mixture reaches 160°F, about 10 minutes. Remove from the heat and let cool to room temperature. Add the puréed chestnut-chocolate mixture and mix until well blended. Stir in the dissolved gelatin.
5. Pour the mixture into four 4-ounce custard cups and refrigerate for 3 hours before serving.

6. Just before serving, place the preserve in a small saucepan and melt over very low heat. Pour 1 tablespoon on each plate, then gently invert the timbales into the center.

MAKE AHEAD: The chestnuts can be cooked up to 3 days in advance, peeled and refrigerated in a sealed container until ready to use.

⚬──⚬──⚬──⚬

Sorbetto al limone e salvia
Lemon and Fresh Sage Sorbet

Sorbets are the ancestors of ice cream. Their common usage can be traced to sixteenth century Florentine architect Bernardo Buontalenti, who invented a new method of refrigeration using water and nitrates to preserve water ices for a few hours.

In Tuscany sorbets are generally served as "mouth cleaners" after a fish course or when segueing from fish to meat. In this case, the choice is generally between mint or citrus fruit sorbets. The following recipe is for traditional lemon sorbet updated by adding finely chopped fresh sage.

MAKES
APPROXIMATELY
1 QUART

TIME:
1 HOUR PLUS
REFRIGERATION

LEVEL: EASY

7 tablespoons sugar
3 cups water
1 teaspoon vanilla extract
Juice and rind of 3 lemons
1 tablespoon very finely chopped fresh sage
3 lemons, halved and hollowed
6 sprigs fresh sage, for garnish

1. Place the sugar, water, vanilla and lemon rind in a medium-size saucepan and cook over low heat for 10 minutes, stirring constantly. Remove from heat and let cool to room temperature.
2. Stir in the lemon juice and sage and let sit for 20 minutes.
3. Using a slotted spoon, remove the lemon rind from the syrup.
4. Transfer the syrup to an ice cream maker and process according to manufacturer's directions.
5. Remove the sorbet from the ice-cream maker and place in a covered metal container. Refrigerate for 1 hour.
6. Serve the sorbet in the hollowed out lemon halves. Garnish with the sage.

MAKE AHEAD: The sorbet can be made up to 1 week in advance and frozen until ready to use. Thaw in the refrigerator for 20 minutes before serving.

Gelato agli amaretti
Amaretto Gelato

MAKES ABOUT
1 QUART

TIME:
1¼ HOURS PLUS
REFRIGERATION

LEVEL: EASY

The young Napoleon Bonaparte had just arrived in Paris when he discovered the already famous Café Procope. Unfortunately, the future emperor was broke, but the tempting view of the jasmine, violet and pistachio scented sorbets proved irresistible. He ordered a double bowl of his favorite flavor and immediately consumed it. When the owner realized that the young man had no money, he became furious, but after a long talk, accepted his hat as payment. Napoleon was not the cafe's only famous client. Moliere, Rousseau, Diderot and Voltaire were habitués and Alfred de Musset used to meet George Sand at this particular locale. Its founder was, nevertheless, a Sicilian gentleman, Procopio de' Coltelli, who opened the first gelateria in Rue des Fossés Saint-Germain. His famous gelatos even reached the table of Louis XIV, the Sun King, who personally received Procopio at Les Tuileries. The art of making gelatos and sorbets is, however, historically Italian. The Emperor Nero was well known for his love of honey and rose sorbets, which he consumed while Rome was burning. And when Caterina de Medici left Florence to marry Henry II in 1533, she brought with her personal cooks and pastry chefs who introduced gelati all'acqua (water ices) to the French.

3 egg yolks, at room temperature
½ cup sugar
1 teaspoon vanilla extract
1 teaspoon grated lemon zest
2 cups milk
½ cup heavy cream
1 cup finely crumbled amaretti
Amaretto liqueur

1. Using an electric mixer or a hand whisk, beat the egg yolks and sugar in a medium-size bowl until creamy, smooth and fluffy, about 5 minutes with the mixer (15 minutes by hand). Place the mixture in a double boiler and cook over simmering water stirring constantly, until

the temperature reaches 160°F, about 10 minutes. Do not let the water touch the bottom of the pan. Remove from heat and let cool to room temperature.

2. Stir in the vanilla and lemon zest. Gradually whisk in the whole milk, heavy cream and the crumbled amaretti. Transfer the mixture to an ice cream maker.

3. Process the mixture according to the manufacturer's directions. Remove from the ice cream maker, place in a sealed container and refrigerate for 2 hours. Serve with amaretto liqueur.

VARIATIONS: Ground almonds or walnuts can be added halfway through the freezing time.

MAKE AHEAD: The gelato can be made up to 1 week in advance and frozen until needed. Thaw in the refrigerator for 20 minutes before serving.

Gelato di pinoli e zucca
Pine-Nut-and-Butternut-Squash Gelato

The province of Pisa is famous in culinary circles for its wealth of recipes involving pine nuts. The reason has to do with the huge pinewood forest that stretches from Viareggio to Livorno. In fact, there's an ancient tongue twister that says "PISA PESA I PINOLI AL PAPA, I PAPA PESA IL PINOLI A PISA" ("Pisa weights pinolis for the Pope, the Pope weights pinolis for Pisa"). This is a wonderful gelato, flavored with pine-nut paste. Unlike the previous recipe, it is made without eggs.

MAKES ABOUT
1 QUART

TIME: 20
MINUTES PLUS
REFRIGERATION

LEVEL: EASY

2 cups pine nuts
6 tablespoons sugar
1 teaspoon vanilla extract
2 cups heavy cream
1 cup milk
2 cups puréed cooked butternut squash
1 teaspoon cinnamon
⅛ teaspoon crushed cloves

1. Place 1½ cups of the pine nuts and the sugar in a food processor and process to a thick paste.

2. Transfer to a large bowl, add the vanilla and cream and stir with a wooden spoon until well blended.

3. Whisk in the milk, then add the squash, cinnamon and cloves, stirring until all ingredients are well blended. Transfer the mixture to an ice cream maker and process according to the manufacturer's directions.

4. A few minutes before the ice cream is ready, add the reserved ½ cup pine nuts. Transfer the ice cream to a metal container and freeze for 2 hours.

MAKE AHEAD: The pine nut paste can be prepared up to 2 days in advance and stored, refrigerated, in a sealed container.

Tiramisù
Mascarpone Custard

SERVES 4

TIME: 45 MINUTES PLUS REFRIGERATION

LEVEL: MODERATE

Although this dessert now seems to be part of just about every Tuscan or even Italian cookbook, I still want you to try mine, which is much creamier and more of a custard than a layered cake. For this recipe, Pavesini biscuits (which can be found in Italian specialty and gourmet food stores) are best since they are sturdier and smaller than ladyfingers, but ladyfingers make a fine substitute.

4 eggs, separated, at room temperature
½ cup sugar
2 tablespoons milk
1 pound mascarpone
⅛ teaspoon salt
½ teaspoon cream of tartar
20 ladyfingers or 40 *Pavesini*
1 cup brewed espresso
3 tablespoons unsweetened cocoa powder

1. In a large bowl, beat the egg yolks and the sugar until smooth and fluffy. Add the milk. Place the mixture in a double boiler and cook over simmering water, stirring constantly with a wooden spoon until the temperature reaches 160°F, about 10 minutes. Transfer to a bowl and cool to room temperature.

2. Add the mascarpone and beat until well blended.

3. Using an electric mixer or hand whisk, beat the egg whites and the salt in a large bowl until foamy. Add the cream of tartar and continue beating until stiff peaks have formed. Gently fold the egg whites into the mascarpone mixture. Set aside.

4. Quickly dip the ladyfingers, one by one, into the brewed coffee, turning once so that both sides are soaked, and place on a plate to drain.

5. Line the sides of four 4-ounce dessert bowls with the ladyfingers. Fill the center with the mascarpone mixture. Dust with cocoa powder and refrigerate for two hours before serving.

VARIATIONS: Fresh sheep's milk ricotta and brewed orzo (chicory coffee substitute) can be used in place of mascarpone and brewed coffee.

Latte alla portoghese
Espresso Flan

Why do recipes have certain names? In the case of this flan, the title translates to "Milk Portugese Style," and the only reason is because the French have a similar version called "Creme Caramel." And since Italy and France are culinary "enemies," this version was simply tagged "Portugese Style." Following is my variation of this classic—flan with espresso.

SERVES 10

TIME:
1½ HOURS PLUS
REFRIGERATION

LEVEL:
MODERATE

7 eggs, at room temperature
¾ cup sugar
1 teaspoon grated lemon zest
½ teaspoon vanilla extract
3½ cups milk
½ cup brewed espresso
1 teaspoon water
Espresso beans, for garnish

1. Using an electric mixer or hand whisk, beat the eggs and ¼ cup sugar until fluffy, smooth and pale, about 5 minutes with the mixer (15 minutes by hand). Add the zest and vanilla.

2. Pour in the milk and the espresso and stir until all ingredients are well blended.

3. Place the remaining ½ cup sugar and 1 teaspoon water in a small heavy saucepan. Place the pan over low heat and cook until the sugar

dissolves into a clear syrup, about 5 minutes. Increase the heat and continue to cook, swirling the pan until the sugar turns amber, 3 to 5 minutes. Quickly pour the caramelized sugar into ten 4-ounce custard cups. Preheat the oven to 375°F.

4. Divide the custard mixture among the 10 cups. Lay a towel in a large baking pan, arrange the custard cups on top and fill the pan with enough boiling water to come halfway up the sides of the cups.

5. Bake until the centers are set, about 40 to 50 minutes.

6. Let cool to room temperature and refrigerate for at least 3 hours. To unmold, dip the bottoms of the cups briefly into hot water and invert onto individual plates. Garnish with coffee beans.

VARIATIONS: Can be made in 1 large dish instead of in individual portions.

MAKE AHEAD: The flans can be made the day before, wrapped loosely with foil and refrigerated until ready to serve.

Panna cotta al torrone con salsa al cioccolato

Cream and Nougat Tarts with Orange-Chocolate Sauce

MAKES 8 TARTS

TIME: 40 MINUTES PLUS REFRIGERATION

LEVEL: EASY

Panna cotta is now as traditionally Tuscan as ribollita, the famous bean and vegetable soup. This version is somewhat different in both flavor and texture because of the addition of crumbled nougat.

THE TARTS

2 envelopes (4½ teaspoons) gelatin
¼ cup cold water
4 cups heavy cream
1 cup sugar
½ teaspoon vanilla extract
8 ounces nougat candy (or Heath Bar Crunch), crumbled

½ pound unsweetened chocolate
5 tablespoons Cointreau

1. To make the tarts, in a small bowl, sprinkle the gelatin over the water to soften.
2. Pour the heavy cream into a large saucepan, stir in the sugar and vanilla and stir until the sugar is dissolved. Add the crumbled nougat. Cook over very low heat, stirring constantly until warm, about 5 minutes.
3. Add the gelatin to the warm mixture and stir until well blended
4. Pour the mixture into eight 2-ounce ramekins and refrigerate for 3 hours.
5. To make the sauce, just before serving, melt the chocolate in a double boiler over hot water. Add the Cointreau and stir until blended.
6. Remove the cream tarts from the refrigerator and bring to room temperature, about 10 minutes. Loosen with a spatula and invert onto individual plates. Drizzle with sauce and serve.

VARIATIONS: Any kind of fruit purée can be used in place of chocolate sauce.

<hr />

Budini di riso e mandorle
Rice and Almond Pudding

Budini are small puddings cooked in custard cups and sold in pastry shops, generally as breakfast items. This particular pudding is one that brings back memories of my childhood, when the owner of the local pasticceria *would walk over with a sliver tray bearing steaming cups of cappuccino and this tiny budino—light and fluffy and just the perfect size for the abstemious eater I used to be.*

Unsalted butter, for greasing
2 tablespoons cocoa powder, for dusting
1 cup arborio rice
4 cups milk
1 teaspoon grated lemon zest
1 teaspoon vanilla extract

MAKES
FOUR 6-OUNCE
PUDDINGS

TIME:
1½ HOURS

LEVEL:
MODERATE

1 teaspoon salt
3 tablespoons sugar
3 eggs, at room temperature
3 tablespoons finely ground toasted almonds
10 amaretti, crumbled
1 teaspoon almond extract
1 teaspoon grated orange zest
3 tablespoons bread flour
1 teaspoon baking powder
Confectioners' sugar, for dusting
Sliced almonds, for garnish

1. Preheat the oven to 370°F. Grease four 4-ounce ramekins and dust with cocoa powder, shaking out the excess.
2. Place the rice in a saucepan with the milk, lemon zest, vanilla and salt and cook over low-medium heat until the rice is tender, about 20 minutes. Remove from heat and drain in a colander.
3. Transfer the cooked rice to a bowl and stir in the sugar, eggs, almonds, crumbled amaretti, almond extract, orange zest, flour and baking powder. Mix until all ingredients are thoroughly blended.
4. Spoon the mixture into the prepared ramekins.
5. Bake until puffy and golden, about 25 minutes. Remove from heat and cool for 15 minutes. Invert onto serving plates, dust with confectioners' sugar and serve, garnished with sliced almonds.

VARIATIONS: Golden raisins, grated chocolate and candied fruit can be added or substituted in Step 3.

MAKE AHEAD: The rice can be cooked 1 day in advance, stored in a sealed container and refrigerated until ready to use.

Yogurt di cioccolato al caffè con arancia candita

Chocolate Yogurt with Coffee Liqueur and Candied Orange Peel

This very easy dessert capitalizes on Tuscany's growing love affair with frozen yogurt. I have paired it with strips of candied oranges, which can be prepared in quantity and stored for up to three months.

SERVES 4

TIME: 30 MINUTES PLUS OVERNIGHT AIR DRYING

LEVEL: EASY

2 cups frozen chocolate yogurt
3 teaspoons coffee liqueur
Peel from 2 medium-size navel oranges
1½ cups sugar
1 cup water

1. Stir the liqueur into the yogurt until blended. Refreeze for 15 minutes before serving.
2. To make the candied peel, cut the peels into ¼-inch-wide strips.
3. Bring 1 cup sugar and 1 cup water to a boil in a large, heavy-gauge saucepan, and add the strips of peel. Reduce heat to low and simmer for 15 minutes. Drain. Arrange on waxed paper and separate with damp toothpicks. Let cool for 10 minutes; toss with the remaining ½ cup sugar until coated. Let air dry overnight.
4. Serve a dollop of yogurt sprinkled with candied peel.

VARIATIONS: The peel can also be left unsugared, frozen, minced and sprinkled over desserts.

MAKE AHEAD: The candied peel can be made up to 3 months in advance and stored in an airtight container in a dry dark place. Since candied peel keeps so long and can also be used in many other dessert recipes, it is a good idea to double or even triple the recipe.

Crema al balsamico
Balsamic Vinegar and Vanilla Gelato

SERVES 4

TIME:
10 MINUTES

LEVEL: EASY

Good balsamic vinegar is sweet and musty-tasting with overtones of wild berries. As such, it is a perfect flavor pairing for vanilla gelato and makes a wonderfully simple dessert when garnished with bunches of champagne grapes. This recipe is adapted from "In Cucina con l'Aceto Balsamico" by Renato Bergonzini, a great friend and Italy's foremost expert on balsamic vinegar.

1 pint vanilla gelato, ice cream or frozen yogurt , slightly softened
2 teaspoons aged (the older, the better) balsamic vinegar
Champagne grapes or other grapes or berries, for garnish

1. Place the gelato in a large bowl. Stir in the vinegar until completely blended. The final consistency should be slightly soupy.
2. Divide among 4 dessert goblets and garnish with the grapes.

VARIATIONS: Balsamic vinegar also pairs well with fruit gelatos and dark chocolate versions.

Budino al mandarino
Creamy Mandarin Pudding

SERVES 6

TIME: 2 HOURS
PLUS TIME FOR
REFRIGERATION

LEVEL:
MODERATE

Tourists have only recently discovered the Garfagnana area of northwest Tuscany, with its breathtaking mountains, picturesque villages and authentic traditions—chief among them, il bar del paese *(the village bar), where men meet to play* briscola *or* scopa *from 8:00 in the evening until 4:00 in the morning and where the prevailing dictum is: "un bicchiere tira l'altro" ("one glass calls for another"). The two most common drinks in mountain bars are* caffè corretto alla grappa, *(coffee "corrected" with grappa) and hot mandarin punch made with mandarin juice and brandy.*

Mandarins are also used in making this wonderful pudding, often served along with the punch, especially around 2:00 in the morning, when the rhythm of the card games heats up and a shot of energy is required to continue.

Unsalted butter, for greasing
Brown sugar, for dusting
½ quart milk
1 teaspoon grated mandarin or tangerine zest
½ stick unsalted butter, at room temperature
¾ cup sugar
¾ cup unbleached all-purpose flour
2 tablespoons mandarin or tangerine juice
5 tablespoons mandarin liqueur or Grand Marnier
4 egg yolks, at room temperature
4 egg whites, at room temperature
¼ teaspoon salt
½ teaspoon cream of tartar
Fresh mandarin segments, for garnish

1. Preheat the oven to 375°F. Grease 6 individual ramekins and dust with brown sugar.
2. Heat the milk in a medium-size saucepan until warm and add the mandarin zest. Let cool at room temperature.
3. Using an electric mixer or a wooden spoon, cream the butter and the sugar in a large bowl until fluffy and pale. Sift in the flour and stir until completely incorporated.
4. Gradually pour in the milk, stirring continuously to prevent lumps. Transfer the mixture to a double boiler and heat over simmering water. Beat in the juice, liqueur and egg yolks (one at a time) until the custard is smooth and creamy.
5. Using an electric mixer or hand whisk, beat the egg whites and the salt in a large bowl until foamy. Add the cream of tartar and beat until stiff peaks form. Gently fold the egg whites into the custard until just blended.
6. Pour the pudding into the prepared ramekins. Place a towel on the bottom of a baking pan. Arrange the ramekins on top and pour in enough hot water to reach halfway up the sides. Bake until the pudding is set, about 35 minutes.
7. Remove from the oven and let cool to room temperature. Refrigerate for two hours before serving. Invert the ramekins onto individual plates and garnish with fresh mandarin segments.

VARIATIONS: Orange or other citrus fruit juice can be substituted for the mandarin juice.

Ricotta all'caffè
Espresso Ricotta

SERVES 6

TIME:
10 MINUTES

LEVEL: EASY

This extremely simple recipe was served often when I was growing up. Sometimes, on special occasions, it would be a kind of predessert served after the cheese course; other times it would be the dessert itself, served in beautiful goblets and accompanied with a biscotti or two. Either way, dessert has never been easier.

1 pound fresh sheep's milk ricotta
2 tablespoons finely-ground espresso
2 tablespoons sugar
Fresh mint sprigs, for garnish

1. Place all the ingredients in a large bowl and beat with an electric mixer until creamy and smooth. Serve in stemware goblets on plates garnished with fresh mint.

VARIATIONS: Various liqueurs such as cognac, framboise or apricot brandy can also be added.

CHAPTER SIX

Sunday Desserts

The Problem with Italian Men

Di mamme ce nè una sola. Everyone has only one mother, and to that I say, thank God. Especially when talking about *Italian* mothers. Now let's understand that I have absolutely nothing against showing love to she who gave you light; it's just that Italians—especially Italian men—turn what should be a substantial sideshow into a grandiloquent, three-ring extravaganza.

Italian men revere their mothers—a statement that, on the surface, sounds quite lovely in a dutiful, altruistic kind of way. It's only when one looks at the underpinnings, at the behavioral manifestations of that statement, that one begins to realize something is seriously wrong.

Witness this: When in physical pain or emotional distress, Italian men call not on God, not on a favored saint, not even on the vast lineup of flamboyant antichrists so perfect for those troubled moments. It's "Mamma!" spoken with that pathetic, drawn-out, whiney moan. "Mamma!"

Or this: Italians have always shown more reverence for the Virgin Mary than they have for either God or Jesus Christ. Entire months, sometimes years, are devoted to her honor. Her many miraculous appearances have been codified and legitimized by the Church purely because of pressure from the Italian electorate. Italian Catholics, in fact, conceded the ultimate unity of Christendom rather than yield to Protestant secessionists not as convinced of Mary's importance.

Or this: Most cultures define the psychological aspect of male puberty as separating from the mother figure in order to move closer to Dad and, hence, develop one's necessary sense of masculinity. But Italian boys manage to grow to manhood without ever quite getting around to the nuts and bolts of splitting. Which is fine, since their fathers never did either. As Italian psychologist Maria Bandini puts it: "Italian males and their mothers travel through life in an emotional tandem that forever binds them one to the other in a relationship based on need. Since Italians have chosen to elevate family above all other social or political units, this mutual dependence serves to avert what would otherwise herald the reality of separateness."

I have been invited to dinner at the home of my friends Rita and Carlo. Actually, the friendship is between me and Rita, Carlo having entered the picture only last year when the two were married in what everyone viewed as "a perfect match." I had a slightly different opinion.

To me, Carlo was, and still is, another of those typical Italian male specimens who will always be tied to his mother's apron strings. Suffice to say that on the day of the wedding, just before Rita was set to walk up the aisle, the entire Church was greeted to the sight of Carlo's mother racing to the altar—where her beloved son was standing with his best man—to wipe a smudge from his face with (I couldn't believe this) a lacy pink handkerchief.

"I'll bet you he has never even bought himself a pair of briefs," I said when Rita told me the relationship was getting serious.

"What Italian man has?" she countered with what I had to admit was bull's-eye accuracy.

As soon as I walk through the front door of their house, I realize there's something wrong. But Carlo is just about to pour the champagne and I somehow sense it's not the time to ask. When he leaves the room to get another bottle, she grabs my arm and pulls me out to the verandah.

"Guess who is joining us for dinner?" she says frantically.

"Don't tell me. Carlo's mother"

She gives me a quizzical look. "Do I seem that despairing that you figured it out right away?"

Actually, she does, in fact, seem that despairing. And I don't blame her. As mothers-in-law go, Giulia is among the worst—never thinking before she opens her mouth.

But sometimes it's better to make a joke rather than fuel the fire. "So," I say lightly, "Which is the glass with the poison?"

"Oh please," she answers. "They have not yet invented a poison that would silence that *boccaccia* (bitch). Do you know what she did last Wednesday?"

She launches into a story about how Giulia canceled their traditional Wednesday night dinner at the last minute, saying she was sick. "I think it was a setup," says Rita, who was later told by a friend that Giulia had been seen having coffee at the local bar.

"Wednesday is when Carlo [a political science professor] teaches in Florence," Rita tells me. "That's why we have always dined at Giulia's. It's a very long trip going back and forth in one day, and he's too exhausted when he comes home to wait for me to get out of work and throw dinner together."

"Well," she says, "of course I had no food in the house and while I was out picking up a few things, he called to see how his mother was doing." Rita narrows her stare and peeks down the hall, checking on Carlo's whereabouts. "You're not going to believe what she said to him. (Not true of Giulia, I'd believe anything.) She said she couldn't believe I'd had to go out to get preparations for dinner; she *always* has something in her refrigerator, she said. Because you never know when someone is going to drop in and a good wife should always be prepared."

"Why did Carlo tell you?" I ask incredulously. Right now, he actually seems more at fault than his mother.

"He wasn't trying to stir me up, if that's what you're thinking."

It is precisely what I'm thinking, and her attempts at shielding him only make me feel even more strongly that I'm right.

"The only reason Carlo mentioned it is because he then went on to muse about how people of the last generation who went through the war never leave their refrigerators empty no matter what." She cups my face in the palms of her hands. "Carlo is not like that," she says tenderly. "His mother, now that's another story. What possible motive could Giulia have had other than to suggest I am a negligent wife?"

Fortunately for the continuity of my friendship with Rita, Carlo returns in just that moment. And in the next moment, the door opens and Giulia waltzes in without so much as ringing the doorbell, elegantly coifed and beaming at her son.

"Look who has joined us," she says grandly when her gaze moves beyond her beloved son. "Sandra, what a long time it has been since we have been together in the same room. Since the wedding, yes?"

"*Buona sera,* Signora Malvasio," I say with an air of resignation.

The first course is served, a delicious antipasto consisting of shrimp and scallops coated with a light batter of bread crumbs, minced garlic and crushed chilies and cooked in white wine. With every morsel I raise to my lips, I am thinking I have never had better.

But Giulia apparently has a different opinion. "Where did you buy this fish?" she asks Rita. "It was delicious but it doesn't seem as tender as it should be."

Visibly embarrassed, Rita says she went to Augusto's along the pier.

"Aha," says Giulia. "That's the problem. Augusto buries his fish in so much ice that it inevitably tastes as if it has been frozen."

Carlo is nodding his head. "I thought you shopped at Arturo's," he says. "That's where my mother goes and I don't think she has ever had a problem."

Can he truly be so stupid, I wonder. It's either that or he's deliberately baiting his wife. At this point, I'm not sure which is worse.

Rita also seems to be angry at him, but she answers calmly that Arturo's is simply too far to travel.

"Too far!" Giulia exclaims. "You cycle farther than that every other day for exercise. And besides, what difference does it make? The important thing is setting the table with the best, is it not? That is how I was taught by my mother, and I have always tried to live up to her example."

I'm trying very hard to say nothing, but suddenly my voice takes on a life of its own. "Yes, but you did not have to go to work, Signora Malvasia."

Giulia jumps up from the table as if she has been stung by a bee. "I had two children and a husband who came home every day for lunch," she says authoritatively. "How *could* I have worked? Even if I had wanted to, my husband would not have approved. And with good reason. Who would have taken care of the home if I had been out from morning till afternoon?" Her decibel level increases. "I know that today people think home is not important. That both men and women should work. But look around you. Everything is suffering because nobody has time for anything."

"But we're no longer living in the fifties," I say because, at this point, there's no turning back. "Life has changed. Why should a woman bother going to university if all she's going to do is stay home and cook?"

"Of all people to be lecturing in favor of change," she hisses. "You, a divorced woman. Did you ever think of your husband all that time when you were claiming to be so suppressed? What about your poor mother? What has your need for freedom done to her? Given how your life has turned out, I should think you'd be too embarrassed to say anything."

Rita comes to stand between me and her mother-in-law. *"La frittata e fatta,"* she says. ("The frittata is cooked.")

What an appropriate choice of words, I think to myself. But it is fine. I am fine, this dinner is fine, and I rise from my chair to help her with the serving.

Giulia, however, is not ready to let the argument go. "What about your son?" she asks, upping the ante. "Just last year, a study came out showing that children are irreparably harmed by divorce. What about his feelings, his needs, his future?" She begins stacking the plates to place them on the breakfront. "Italy should never have passed that divorce law, but if we have to have it, thank God the Pope has now clarified the issue."

I can tell by the look on Carlo's face that he is praying for this discussion to end. But it sounds like Giulia is referring to some recent piece of Vatican dogma and I have to know what it is, if only to fuel my religious cynicism. "What did the Pope do? Something regarding divorce?"

Giulia looks triumphant. "Last week, he issued a dictum stating that divorced people can no longer receive Communion."

"I thought that dictum had been issued ages ago," I tell her.

"It has, but now the Pope has decided to point an even stronger finger at the guilty party."

"Which means he is still pointing a guilty finger at both parties even though one might have done the leaving against the other's wishes?"

"No, no, no. The innocent party is now deemed to be a passive sinner and can receive Communion, but he or she has to go to a different church."

The ridiculousness of this statement causes even Carlo to join the conversation. "Another church? Mamma, what are you talking about?"

"It makes perfect sense," his mother says soothingly. "This way, passive sinners are only partly penalized. They can still receive, but there is no danger that they will serve as bad examples to people who might not know whether or not they were the perpetrating party or the party that was wronged."

I am speechless. What a perfect solution for a society that revolves around the *bella figura* (the need for making a good showing). A person's moral redemption now hinges on the *appearance* of their Christian practice.

An American film, *Oh God,* that I saw about 20 years ago comes to mind. In it, George Burns, playing the Almighty, comments on modern-day ministers who claim to speak on his behalf. "Do you think if I had something I wanted conveyed to my children, I'd choose one of these jokesters as a messenger?"

I am nonetheless as fascinated by these promulgations as I am about those emanating from our government. Neither have any real effect on my life, but after a while, it becomes like a soap opera: every day a different ridiculous plot line. "What if these so-called passive sinners remarry?" I ask her. "Can they still receive if they go to a different church?"

"Oh no. If you get married again, you become an *elected* sinner," says Giulia with great seriousness.

One look in Rita's direction and I can tell she is very close to breaking out in hysterical laughter.

"But," Giulia continues solemnly, "if you have no sex with your husband or wife, then you can both receive Communion in your home church."

This I truly cannot believe. "How is anyone going to know whether or not you're having sex?" I ask with as much propriety as I can muster. "Since the whole purpose of marriage, according to the Church, is to have sex and procreate, wouldn't most people assume that if I got remarried I'm engaging in sex? What if I then walked up to the altar of my local church and received Communion, wouldn't that be an extremely bad example?"

I really want to know the answer, but Rita is now standing next to me, saying we should go get the roast. Much as I truly, and unbelievably, would rather stay and talk to Giulia, I follow her into the kitchen.

"I hope you're done," she says with a hearty laugh. "Next thing you know, Giulia is going to start believing we're really interested in what the Pope has to say about relationships between the sexes."

"You're not?" I tease her. "Why get married then?"

"A good question," she says. "Unfortunately, you only realize the answer after you've gone beyond the point of no return—unless, of course, you're you and opt for a second chance." She scrapes the leftovers into the dog's dish. "Do you think you'll ever remarry?"

"I'm not sure," I answer. "If I do, it will be to an orphan."

The next morning, I awaken early to take my 93-year-old grandmother to Mass. Nonna Angelina never misses Mass unless she is very ill, in which case she listens to Radio Maria, a local station, that broadcasts nonstop masses for those deemed unable to make an actual appearance. When I say "deemed," I mean exactly that. The gravely ill must receive a clerical dispensation or chance becoming—what? A passive sinner? An elected one? A sinner by virtue of illness?

As I exit the Church en route to the local *pasticcerìa* where I wait for Mass to be over, I spot my cousin Amelia coming up the road.

"Are *you* going to Mass?" she asks with great surprise.

"No, I only drop off my grandmother. I wouldn't dare go to Mass, passive sinner that I am."

"Passive sinner? What do you mean?"

"Never mind. Where's Edoardo (her husband)?"

"Where could he be? At his mother's, of course. Last night, she called him at midnight, saying her heart felt weak. You know Edoardo. He went right over and slept there."

"What about your father-in-law? Wasn't he home?"

"Of course, he was home. But every time his mother feels a little flutter, she thinks it's the end and wants her son at her side. For his part, Edoardo would never be able to sleep, knowing his mother might die from one minute to the next. *A questo punto, ci ho fatto il callo.* (At this point, I've become hardened to it.) But the fact is, her heart will probably go on forever and meanwhile, mine feels like it's going to explode."

Hard words but spoken in a lighthearted way. But then again, Amelia is not one to make actual waves.

"Big mistake," she had said when I announced I was getting a divorce. "You'll never find anyone better. Not to say Allesandro was such an exemplar of wedded bliss, but husbands are to be tolerated. Patience is the secret of a good marriage, not expectation."

I finally reach the pastry shop, which is, of course, filled with men (the women are all in church), and settle myself in a corner with a cappuccino, a *brioscia* (brioche), and the newspaper.

The lead article catches my eye: a feature exploring the growth of Buddhism in Tuscany, especially in light of Richard Gere's now frequent journeys to nearby Pomaia, a Buddhist temple where he met last year with the Dalai Lama. Apparently, there has been a 200 percent growth in the number of people now turning to Buddhism's promise of inner peace as a vehicle for solving problems in their own lives.

My cappuccino is just about finished, when a frazzled-looking Amelia pokes her head through the door. "Still here?" she says. "Mass is almost getting out."

"By the time my grandmother makes it down the aisle and out the door, I could have eaten three more *brioscie*," I say. "Where are you off to in such a hurry?"

"To pick up a chicken for my son. He and his wife are coming over for lunch today and I want to give him a good meal. It's clear he doesn't get many at home, what with his wife always on a diet."

"Don't start, Amelia, you'd think your own mother-in-law problems would cause you to be more sympathetic."

"It has nothing to do with sympathy. The facts are the facts. Francesco is getting thinner and thinner. And it's not only a question of food. That woman really has no idea how to take care of him. I can see it when I wash his shirts—tears everywhere."

"What do you mean, when you wash his shirts? Why are *you* still washing his shirts? At the very least, his wife should be doing it."

"At first she did. But then he could no longer deal with the fact that she knew nothing about removing stains. He thought about taking them to the dry cleaner's, but I said, bring them over here. I can do them when I do your father's. It's no extra work."

"But don't you see that you're contributing to the same problem you have with your own mother-in-law? What is Francesco's wife supposed to think when you're doing the shirts she's supposedly not good enough to do? And where was his head in the first place, letting you do them? How can his wife see that as anything other than a betrayal?"

"Believe me, Sandra, that one doesn't care. 'You want to wash his shirts,' she said when she found out. 'Fine. Less work for me.' Next I'll be cleaning her house."

Fortunately, I can see my grandmother out of the corner of my eye. "I have to go, Amelia," I say, hurrying off. "Give my love to Edoardo."

Mass is over and a river of people flows out into the church piazza. I can see my grandmother impatiently tapping her cane on the marble stones while searching for me in the bustling crowd. I leave my pastries and hurry over to grab her arm. We head toward the car, she lecturing me yet again on how terrible it is to know my soul is damned. At home, my mother waits for us along with my brother and sister-in-law. Today, after all, is Mother's Day.

Sunday Desserts

Sundays in Tuscany are dedicated to family and, like all such celebratory occasions, has its associated foods. Chief among these foods are special desserts too complicated to make during the week. Women usually go to mass early, then change into their sober aprons as soon as they get home and start cooking for their sons and daughter-in-laws and grandchildren and cousins. This is our tradition, or, as some people might call it, our condemnation.

According to theory, when sons marry, they are starting a new life different from the one they'd been living at home. False! When Tuscan men marry, they simply take their wives home to their mothers on alternate Sundays and as many other days in between as is feasible. In olden days, the daughter-in-law went to live with the son's parents; today, the new family lives on its own, but since most women work, they go to his family's for dinner one week, hers, the next. Simple, clear, and everyone is happy.

The Sunday cooking marathon begins just after dawn, after every good rooster awakens every good mother and mother-in-law. First, Holy Mass and the blessing of the Lord. Then, the dilemma: What to cook? My Alfredo loves cannelloni but last week I heard him say that his wife made a very good lasagne. Ok, I will make both, so he will see that there's no woman equal to his mother. He also said her mother does a wonderful job with roast pork and stuffed veal cutlets. Then I will make fried rabbit and chicken. No meat courses can compare to mine.

The funniest thing is that mothers and mothers-in-law routinely keep diaries where they record what their children ate last Sunday at the respective parents' house. It is a competition with no less a prize than the heart and soul of the beloved son (daughters maintain close ties as a matter of course; sons, on the other hand, must continuously be wooed). The goal is to see them eat, heartily and in great quantity. If a married son is a little overweight, it means the daughter-in-law is a good wife (although never as good a caretaker as the mother). If on the other hand, six months go by after the wedding and he is still thin (or, God forbid, *thinner*), it means the daughter-in-law cannot cook well, which means the marriage is in trouble. *Povero figlio mio! Io sì che ti trattavo bene!* (My poor son! I'm the only one who treats you the right way!)

Whatever is decided on for the appetizer and entrée, the dessert is where the cook makes her statement. The dessert must be perfect. How perfect? Perfect enough to shine brighter than any confection created by the "other" mother. Of course, sometimes the saints intervene and a miracle happens. For example, the son mentions that his mother-in-law prepared a tiramisù and he had a hard time digesting it. Aha! The course of action is now clearer than ever. She will make the most delicate, airy, lightest cake of her baking career. Perfection has many levels after all.

The desserts in this chapter are ones I make in my house on Sundays. Why these and not others? All I can say is that Sunday desserts are that perfect blending of tradition and novelty—a show of grandeur without visible ostentation—a collection of flavors designed to pair well with long cups of coffee and after-dinner liqueurs. They must be like Sunday itself—peaceful, special and about family.

Sunday Desserts

Torta di mele e crema frangipane
Apple Pie with Frangipane Cream

Colomba Pasquale
Dove-Shaped Easter Sweet Bread

Frittelle di pere
Pear Fritters made with Beer Batter

Zuppa lucchese o dell'Ariosto
Strawberry Custard Cake

Mousse meringata al cioccolato
Chocolate Mousse Meringue

Torta di riso coi becchi
Easter Sunday Rice and Chocolate Cake

Gattò Aretino
Chocolate Roll from Arezzo

Tartellette di cioccolata
Chocolate Hazelnut Tartlets

Torta primaverile
Fresh Lemon Cake for Springtime

Babà di cioccolata alla crema di rum
Chocolate Baba Cake with Rum Cream

Crespelle con fragole
Strawberry Crepes

Torta di mele e noci
Apple Nut Cake

Crostata di pere e lamponi
Bosc Pear and Raspberry Tart

Torta al caffè con salsa di nocciole
Espresso Amaretto Cheesecake with Hazelnut Espresso Sauce

Torta di mele e crema frangipane
Apple Pie with Frangipane Cream

Apple pie, apple pie! Americans are famous for their beloved apple pies. But so are Tuscans, especially on Woman's Day, which always falls on a Sunday. The apple is, after all, Eve's symbol. But basic apple pies are somewhat too simple for Sunday dinners; hence this delicate creation topped with frangipane cream, which is a basic vanilla custard blended with brushed almonds.

MAKES
ONE 9-INCH PIE
(8 SLICES)

TIME:
1½ HOURS

LEVEL:
MODERATE

Unsalted butter, for greasing
½ cup unsalted butter, at room temperature
½ cup sugar
2 eggs
½ cup ground almonds
1 teaspoon vanilla extract
2 tablespoons amaretto liqueur
4 tablespoons unbleached all-purpose flour
1 recipe Basic *Pasta Frolla* (see page 34)
4 medium red apples, peeled, cored and thinly sliced
2 cups raspberries

1. Preheat the oven to 375°F. Grease a 9-inch-diameter tart pan with removable bottom.
2. Using an electric mixer or a wooden spoon, cream the butter and the sugar in a large bowl until smooth. Beat in the eggs, one at a time, and blend well.
3. Add the ground almonds, vanilla and amaretto and stir until creamy and well blended, about 5 minutes. Sift in the flour and blend into a smooth batter.
4. Remove the *pasta frolla* from the refrigerator, unwrap and place on a lightly floured work surface. With a floured rolling pin, roll into a 10-inch-diameter circle and arrange in the bottom of the prepared tart pan, pressing the excess against the sides.
5. Pour in the egg custard and top with the apples slices, arranged in overlapping concentric circles.
6. Bake until lightly golden, about 40 minutes. Remove the sides of the pan and cool to room temperature.

7. Pass the raspberries through a food mill* and spread 2 tablespoons of the purée on each serving plate. Top with a slice of pie and serve.

* The raspberries can also be puréed in a food processor. Strain before serving.

VARIATIONS: Walnuts or hazelnuts can be substituted for almonds.

MAKE AHEAD: The pie can be prepared earlier in the day as can the raspberry purée. Store the purée in a sealed container, refrigerated, until ready to serve.

Colomba Pasquale
Dove-Shaped Easter Sweet Bread

MAKES
1 DOVE-SHAPED
SWEET BREAD
(10 SLICES)

TIME: 8 TO 9
HOURS

LEVEL:
ADVANCED

When Noah saw the flood waters retreat, he realized that God had finally forgiven his earthly sinners. The final confirmation came when a white dove flew onto the deck of the Ark carrying in its beak the olive branch of peace. From that moment, doves have signified peace and forgiveness and, as such, have become the symbol of Easter.

How doves and peace came to be associated with the following dessert is another story altogether. According to legend, the eighth century Lombardian King, Alboin, was set to declare war on the northern Italian town of Pavia when one of his frightened subjects baked a dove-shaped sweet-bread and delivered it as a symbol of peace. Upon tasting the bread and witnessing first-hand the fear on the face of the humble baker, Alboin changed his mind about the war and from that day on, northern Italians have always baked this bread in the shape of a dove (colomba) on Easter to celebrate the glories of peace.

1 tablespoon fresh yeast
3 cups bread flour
1½ cups sugar
½ teaspoon salt
1 teaspoon grated lemon zest
5 eggs, at room temperature
1½ cups unsalted butter, at room temperature
⅓ cup warm milk
Vegetable oil, for oiling
3 tablespoons chopped candied orange

3 tablespoons chopped candied lime
Unsalted butter, for greasing
Flour, for dusting
1 dark raisin, for the eye
2 tablespoons blanched almonds, whole

Suggested equipment: A dove-shaped baking pan (The dove can also be shaped free form in a rectangular baking pan).

1. Dissolve the yeast in ½ cup warm water. Add enough flour, approximately 3 tablespoons, to form a soft dough.
2. Transfer the dough to a lightly floured surface and knead for 5 minutes, incorporating enough additional flour, approximately 4 tablespoons, to form a smooth and elastic dough. Place the dough in a medium-size bowl along with 2 cups warm water, cover with a kitchen towel and let sit, in a warm place, until the dough has doubled its size and floats, about 2 hours.
3. Heap the remaining approximately 2½ cups flour on a flat work surface and sift in 1 cup of the sugar, the salt and the lemon zest. Mix with a fork until the ingredients are well blended and then form a well in the center.
4. Place 4 eggs, ¾ cup butter and the warm milk in the well and, using a fork, beat the ingredients, incorporating the flour a little at a time, until a smooth, elastic dough has formed. Knead with floured hands for 5 minutes.
5. Remove the risen dough from the bowl of water and place on a cloth to drain. Place the two balls of dough (wet and dry) on a floured work surface and knead together for 5 minutes. Oil a large bowl. Transfer the dough to the oiled bowl, cover with a kitchen towel and let sit, in a warm place, for 2 hours.
6. Return the dough to the floured work surface, incorporate 6 tablespoons of the remaining butter and the chopped candied fruit. Knead until the dough is smooth and uniform.
7. Place once again in the oiled bowl, cover with a cloth and let sit in a warm place until double in size, about 1 hour. Grease the dove-shaped baking pan and dust with flour, shaking off the excess.
8. Return the dough to a floured work surface one last time, knead it gently for a minute or two and then incorporate the remaining 6 tablespoons butter. Knead for 5 minutes and arrange in the baking

pan.* Place the raisin to resemble an eye. Cover with a kitchen towel and let sit for 1 hour.

9. Preheat the oven to 400°F. Beat the remaining 1 egg. Brush the dough with the beaten egg and sprinkle with almonds and the remaining ½ cup sugar.

10. Bake for 10 minutes; lower the heat to 325°F and continue to bake until a tester inserted into center comes out clean, about 30 minutes. Cool on a rack, slice into wedges and serve.

* In you're not using a dove-shaped baking pan, cut the bread and mold it into the shape of a dove in Step 8. As it rises the final time, the shape will become somewhat distorted, but the basic outline will still be recognizable.

VARIATIONS: One-half cup golden raisins soaked in *Vin Santo* or rum to cover for ½ hour and drained can be added in Step 6.

Frittelle di pere
Pear Fritters made with Beer Batter

MAKES
APPROXIMATELY
20 FRITTERS

TIME: 2 HOURS

LEVEL:
MODERATE

When fall comes to Tuscany, pears are everywhere. Boiled, stuffed, caramelized, covered with chocolate, marinated in liqueurs, even cooked into sauces and served with roasted meats and grilled fish. Their most popular role is when paired with pecorino and served as part of a cheese course. In fact, there's an old Tuscan saying: "Al contadino non fate sapere, quanto è buono il cacio con le pere!" ("Don't tell the farmer how good pecorino tastes with pears!")

These fritters are generally served as part of a dessert course, accompanied by wedges of pecorino cheese and small glasses of Vin Santo.

2 eggs, separated, at room temperature
⅓ cup sugar
1¾ cups cake flour
½ cup beer
¼ teaspoon salt
¼ teaspoon cream of tartar
3 medium pears, peeled and cut lengthwise into ½-inch slices
Vegetable oil, for frying

Flour, for dredging
Confectioners' sugar, for dusting
Wedges of pecorino cheese

1. Using an electric mixer or a hand whisk, beat the egg yolks and the sugar and flour in a large bowl until smooth, about 5 minutes with the mixer (15 minutes by hand).
2. Slowly add the beer to form a batter, then let rest for 1 hour.
3. Using an electric mixer or a hand whisk, beat the egg whites and the salt in a large bowl until foamy. Add the cream of tartar and beat until stiff peaks form. Gently fold the egg whites into the batter.
4. Pour the oil to a depth of 1 inch in a 12-inch-diameter skillet and heat to 375°F (a small bread cube should sizzle around the edges when immersed). Dredge the pears in flour; dip into the batter to coat completely. Add the pear slices, 6 or 7 at a time, to the hot oil. Do not overcrowd the skillet, or the oil temperature will drop.
5. Fry the slices until golden, about 3 minutes, turning once.
6. Remove with a slotted spoon and drain on paper towels. Dust with sugar and serve hot with the cheese.

VARIATIONS: Apples can be used in place of or in addition to the pears.

MAKE AHEAD: The batter can be prepared 1 day in advance and refrigerated in a sealed container. If too thick, stir in 1 or 2 tablespoons of beer before using.

Zuppa lucchese o dell'Ariosto
Strawberry Custard Cake

Ludovico Ariosto, author of the epic poem Orlando Furioso, *served as Governor of Castenuovo di Garfagnana between 1522 and 1525. Known as both a competent administrator and an indefatigable epicure, his favorite foods were grilled brook trout, potatoes roasted with rosemary and his beloved* giulebbe, *the name he gave to this Tuscan version of strawberry shortcake. Tuscans use* Buccellato di Lucca (Traditional Lucchese Sweet Bread) *for the base (see recipe page 261), which they make fresh on Sundays, but the recipe works just as well with country-style raisin or other types of dense, crusty sweet bread.*

MAKES
1 SHORTCAKE
(6 SLICES)

TIME:
45 MINUTES

LEVEL: EASY

2 cups fresh strawberries, washed, hulled, drained and halved

1 cup sugar

20 slices of *Buccellato di Lucca* (see page 261) or other country-style sweet bread

1½ cups *Vin Santo* or sherry

3 cups Basic Custard (see page 34)

1. Toss the strawberries with the sugar and let sit for 30 minutes to marinate.
2. Arrange 10 bread slices in the bottom of an 11 x 7 x 2½-inch-deep serving dish.
3. Pour ¾ cup *Vin Santo* over the slices to lightly soak, spread with 1½ cups custard and top with 1 cup strawberries. Add another layer in the same order: bread, *Vin Santo,* custard and strawberries.
4. Refrigerate for 2 hours before serving.

VARIATIONS: Fresh cherries can be used in place of strawberries.

MAKE AHEAD: The *buccellato* can be prepared in advance, wrapped in plastic and stored in a cool place for 4 days before using. The entire dessert can be made earlier in the day, wrapped tightly in plastic and refrigerated until just before serving.

Mousse meringata al cioccolato
Chocolate Mousse Meringue

MAKES
ONE 10-INCH
CAKE (8 SLICES)

TIME:
1½ HOURS

LEVEL:
MODERATE

Some people buy their desserts instead of making them. The pastry shop in Stiava, where I live, claims that this baked chocolate mousse cake topped with meringue is their best seller on Sundays. People come from Viareggio and even as far as Pisa, the owner told me, adding in a cautious aside: "I'm very happy that they do and I can understand buying your Sunday dolce every now and then, but every Sunday? What kind of home do these people live in?"

This traditional Tuscan dessert combines layers of rum-soaked sponge cake spread with chocolate mousse and topped with snowy meringue.

1½ cups sugar

2 cups water

1 cup rum
3 recipes *Pasta Genovese*, or Basic Sponge Cake (see page 36)
3 eggs, separated, at room temperature
2 tablespoons milk
1 cup grated unsweetened chocolate
2 cups whipped heavy cream
¼ teaspoon salt
½ teaspoon cream of tartar
Unsalted butter, for greasing
Cocoa powder, for dusting

1. Place 1 cup sugar and 1 cup water in a large saucepan and bring to a boil, stirring constantly until thick and syrupy. Remove from heat and let cool to room temperature. Blend in the rum.
2. Preheat the oven to 400°F. Place each of the sponge cakes on a large plate and drizzle the syrup over the tops to soak.
3. In a large bowl, beat the egg yolks and the remaining ½ cup sugar until smooth and fluffy. Pour into the top of a double boiler, add the milk and cook over simmering water until a candy thermometer registers 160°F, about 10 minutes. Do not let the water touch the bottom of the pan. Stir in the grated chocolate and cook until melted. Remove from heat and let cool.
4. Gently fold the whipped cream into the cooled custard until just blended.
5. Using an electric mixer or a hand whisk, beat the egg whites and the salt in a large bowl until foamy. Add the cream of tartar and beat until soft peaks form.
6. Grease a 10-inch-diameter springform pan. Place the first circle of soaked sponge cake in the prepared pan. Spread with ½ of the mousse and level with a spatula. Cover with the second layer of sponge cake and top with the remaining mousse.
7. Cover with the third circle of sponge cake and top with the whipped egg whites, spreading them with a spatula and lifting the spatula quickly to create peaks.
8. Bake until lightly golden, about 3 minutes. Remove from oven and let cool to room temperature.
9. Refrigerate for 2 hours. Lightly dust with sifted cocoa before serving.

VARIATIONS: Cognac or brandy can be used in place of rum.

Torta di riso coi becchi
Easter Sunday Rice and Chocolate Cake

MAKES ONE
10-INCH CAKE
(8 TO 10
INCHES)

TIME: 2 HOURS

LEVEL:
ADVANCED

Becchi *in Tuscan means "scalloped edges," an image that can be equally applied to pastry crusts or the scalloped towers of ancient medieval castles. In fact, Tuscan recipes direct cooks to shape the edges of this cake "like the turrets of Malaspina Castle."*

Unfortunately, the word becchi *also means "billy-goat" as well as "to cuckold," neither of which have anything to do with this traditional Easter cake.*

THE DOUGH

2 cups bread flour
1 teaspoon baking powder
½ teaspoon of salt
½ cup unsalted butter, at room temperature
⅓ cup sugar
2 eggs, at room temperature
1 egg yolk, at room temperature
1 teaspoon grated lemon zest
1 tablespoon warm milk
1 tablespoon extra-virgin olive oil
1 tablespoon anisette or other anise-flavored liqueur
1 teaspoon vanilla extract
Unsalted butter, for greasing

THE FILLING

1 cup arborio rice
1 quart milk
Rind of 1 lemon, grated
8 ounces unsweetened chocolate, grated
½ cup cocoa powder
1 cup sugar
½ cup chopped toasted pine nuts
½ cup golden raisins, soaked in 1 cup of rum for 2 hours and then
   drained, liquid reserved

½ cup finely diced candied fruit

6 tablespoons *Amaretto di Saronno*

5 tablespoons anisette or other anise-flavored liqueur

10 tablespoons cherry or other fruit liqueur

2 eggs, at room temperature

1 egg yolk, at room temperature

1. To make the dough, place the flour, baking powder and salt in a large bowl and stir until well blended.
2. Using an electric mixer or a wooden spoon, cream the butter and the sugar until fluffy and smooth. Beat in the eggs (one at a time), egg yolk, lemon zest, milk, oil, anisette and vanilla. Sift in the flour-baking-powder mixture and beat until well blended into a smooth dough. Shape the dough into a ball, wrap in plastic and refrigerate for 1 hour.
3. Preheat the oven to 350°F and grease a 10-inch springform pan
4. To make the filling, place the rice, milk and lemon rind in a large, heavy-gauge saucepan. Cook over low heat until the rice is tender, about 20 minutes.
5. Drain the rice and place in a small bowl. Add the chocolate and cocoa powder, and using a wooden spoon, stir until all the ingredients are thoroughly blended.
6. Stir in the sugar, pine nuts, raisins (with rum liquid), candied fruit and liqueurs. Beat in the eggs (one at a time) and the yolk and mix well.
7. Divide the dough into 2 balls, one 3 times as large as the other. On a lightly floured surface, roll the larger of the balls into a 14-inch-diameter circle, ½-inch thick. Arrange the circle in the pan, pressing the excess against the sides.
8. Shape the excess crust so that the top edge is of uniform height and standing approximately 3 inches high (the edges should stand approximately ½ inch above the filling). Using a butter knife, cut the edge into a pattern resembling a series of small towers (or make pointed scallops). Pour the rice-chocolate mixture into the pan and level with a spatula.
9. Add the excess dough to the remaining dough ball. Roll into a 10-inch square, ½-inch thick. Cut into ½-inch-wide strips and arrange the strips in lattice fashion on the surface of the cake.
10. Bake for 45 minutes. Remove the sides of the pan and cool to room temperature.

VARIATIONS: The cake can also be served with whipped cream or fresh fruit purée.

MAKE AHEAD: The dough can be prepared up to 2 days in advance, wrapped in plastic and stored in the refrigerator.

⚜⚜⚜⚜

Gattò Aretino
Chocolate Roll from Arezzo

MAKES 1 CAKE ROLL (8 TO 10 SLICES)

TIME: 2 HOURS

LEVEL: MODERATE

Arezzo is known for being one of the wealthiest cities in Tuscany. Its jewelry industries and antiques firms are among the largest in Europe and, more important, it is known for the annual Giostra del Saracino *(Saracen's Joust), which takes place each year on the first Sunday of September. An ancient tournament dating back to the Crusades when Christendom dedicated itself to driving the Moors out of Europe, the Joust centers on magnificently costumed knights striking the wooden effigy of the Saracen with their lances while trying to avoid a cat-of-three-tails swinging back and unseating them. Each pair of knights represents one of the four rival* contrade, *districts that compete in this traditional event.*

The recipe for this traditional log, which is filled with a blend of gianduja, coffee, custard, grappa and Cointreau, comes from Adua Mantuetti, an Aretino housewife who rises at 4 in the morning on the day of the event to prepare two for her own household and 15 others for the local pasticcerìa. *"I have done it for 26 years," she says. "And every year, people ask for the recipe. By now I should be famous all over the world."*

3 tablespoons Cointreau
6 tablespoons sugar syrup (½ cup sugar dissolved in ¼ cup simmering water and cooled)
1 recipe *Pasta Genovese*, or Basic Sponge Cake (see page 36)
1 recipe Basic Custard (see page 34)
2 teaspoons ground espresso
1 tablespoon grated orange zest
1 cup melted unsweetened gianduia (Italian hazelnut chocolate) or bittersweet chocolate
1 tablespoon unsalted butter, melted
Confectioners' sugar

2 cups sliced strawberries marinated in grappa for 2 hours and then drained, liquid reserved

1. Pour the Cointreau and 2 tablespoons grappa (reserved from the strawberry marinade) into the sugar syrup and stir until well blended.
2. Place the sponge cake on a slightly damp towel. Drizzle the syrup over the surface and let soak for 10 minutes.
3. In a large bowl, mix the custard, the espresso, orange zest, melted chocolate and butter, and beat with a wooden spoon until smooth and glossy.
4. Spread the chocolate custard over the soaked sponge. Gently roll the dough into a log. Dust the surface with confectioners' sugar, slice and serve with strawberries.

MAKE AHEAD: The cake can be made up to 1 day in advance, wrapped in plastic and stored in the refrigerator until needed. Dust with the confectioner's sugar just before serving. The strawberries can be marinated in grappa up to 24 hours in advance.

Tartellette di cioccolata
Chocolate Hazelnut Tartlets

Chocolate is one of my very favorite things. Coming home from a trip to Switzerland two years ago, I packed the trunk of my car with every type of chocolate I could buy. But when I arrived at the Swiss Border, customs agents confiscated half my stash because they thought I had bought it for resale in Italy. I begged, I pleaded, I even offered my 93-year-old grandmother in sacrifice, but it was no use. They were immovable. So I lost my chocolate but not my addiction to it. I make these tarts on summer Sundays, when raspberries are plentiful, and I always make at least two extras, which I eat before ever presenting them at the table.

MAKES 8
TARTLETS

TIME:
60-70 MINUTES

LEVEL:
MODERATE

1 recipe Basic *Pasta Frolla* (see page 34)
3 ounces milk chocolate
3 ounces bittersweet chocolate
1 cup ground hazelnuts
1 cup unsalted butter

⅓ cup sugar

1 egg, at room temperature

1 egg yolk, at room temperature

1. Preheat oven to 350°F. Remove the *pasta frolla* from its wrapping and place on a lightly floured work surface. Roll into a 9 x 18-inch rectangle, ⅛-inch thick. Cut into eight 4½-inch-diameter circles and arrange each in the bottom of 4-inch-diameter tartlet tins with removable bottoms. Press the excess against the sides. Chill the tartlet crusts while making filling.
2. Melt the chocolates in a double boiler over simmering water and stir in the ground hazelnuts. Remove from heat and let cool slightly.
3. In a large bowl, cream the butter and the sugar until smooth. Add the egg and egg yolk and beat until the mixture is well blended and slightly thickened. Beat in the chocolate mixture until just combined.
4. Fill the tart shells with the mixture and place on a baking pan.
5. Bake until filling is set and pastry is golden, about 25 minutes. Cool to room temperature and remove the sides of the pan before serving.

VARIATIONS: Tartlets can also be served with puréed (and sieved) raspberries or a dollop of whipped cream.

Torta primaverile
Fresh Lemon Cake for Springtime

MAKES ONE 8-INCH LAYER CAKE (8 SLICES)

TIME: 1 HOUR PLUS 9 HOURS REFRIGERATION

LEVEL: ADVANCED

Although lemons are available almost year-round in Tuscany, there's something about their color and flavor that I have always associated with spring. I serve this cake on the first Sunday after Carnival, which is still technically winter, but by then the trees are starting to bud and the 40-day countdown to Easter has begun.

THE CAKE

Unsalted butter, for greasing

Flour, for dusting

½ cup plain yogurt

½ teaspoon baking soda

½ cup unsalted butter

½ cup plus 2 tablespoons sugar
4 teaspoons grated lemon zest
2 eggs, at room temperature
1 cup bread flour
1½ teaspoons baking powder
¼ teaspoon salt
3 tablespoons lemon juice
3 tablespoons orange juice

THE LEMON FILLING

1 teaspoon water
1 teaspoon unflavored gelatin
½ cup sugar
⅓ cup lemon juice
3 egg yolks, at room temperature
2 teaspoons grated lemon zest
5 tablespoons unsalted butter, melted

THE LEMON FROSTING

2 cups confectioners' sugar
2 tablespoons reserved lemon filling
4 tablespoons unsalted butter
2 to 4 tablespoons plain yogurt

THE GARNISH

Lemon twists
Sprigs of fresh mint

1. To make the cake, preheat oven to 350°F. Lightly grease two 8-inch-round cake pans. Line bottoms with circles of waxed paper and grease again. Dust sides with flour and shake out excess. Combine yogurt and baking soda; let sit for 10 minutes.
2. Using an electric mixer or wooden spoon, cream the butter, sugar and lemon zest in a large bowl until smooth. Add the eggs (one at a time) and beat well. Sift together flour, baking powder and salt.
3. Stir lemon and orange juices into the yogurt mixture. Whisk half the dry ingredients into the butter mixture, then the yogurt-juice mixture, then the remaining dry ingredients. Mix until just combined.

4. Divide batter between the prepared cake pans.

5. Bake until tester comes out clean, about 15 minutes. The layers will be quite thin. Cool for 10 minutes. Loosen edges and turn out onto waxed paper.

6. To make the lemon filling, sprinkle the gelatin over the water; stir until softened, about 1 minute. Stir until dissolved.

7. In a medium-size saucepan, whisk sugar, lemon juice, egg yolks and lemon zest until well blended. Gradually add the melted butter. Cook over low heat, stirring constantly, to a temperature of 160°F on a candy thermometer. The mixture will thicken somewhat and be quite steamy. Do not boil.

8. Remove from heat and stir in gelatin until blended. Pour into a flat dish, cover and refrigerate until set, at least 3 hours. Reserve 2 tablespoons for frosting.

9. To make the lemon frosting, combine the sugar, 2 tablespoons reserved lemon filling, the butter and yogurt. Mix until smooth, adding enough yogurt for frosting consistency. Let sit at room temperature for 30 minutes before frosting cake.

10. To assemble the cake, stir filling gently until smooth. Spread onto 1 cake round and cover with the other. Spread the frosting to cover the top and sides of the cake. Chill at least 6 hours. Serve wedges garnished with lemon twists and mint.

MAKE AHEAD: The cake layers can be made up to 2 weeks ahead and frozen. Thaw before using. The filling keeps for 3 days in the refrigerator.

Babà di cioccolata alla crema di rum
Chocolate Baba Cake with Rum Cream

MAKES
ONE 8-INCH
CAKE (8 SLICES)

TIME: 1 HOUR

LEVEL:
MODERATE

If you like rum, this is the cake for you. The cream is a dessert in itself and one that I often serve with simpler cakes to raise them to the level required for Sundays.

I'm amazed to say that this recipe comes from my ex-husband, Allesandro. I thought I'd taught him everything he knew about cooking, but I was very surprised when he arrived one Sunday for dinner bearing this cake.

THE CAKE

6 ounces bittersweet chocolate

6 tablespoons unsalted butter

¼ cup sugar

3 eggs, separated, at room temperature

½ cup plus 2 tablespoons ground almonds

¾ cup fresh unflavored bread crumbs

¼ teaspoon salt

½ teaspoon cream of tartar

THE RUM CREAM

¾ cup heavy cream

3 tablespoons sugar

¼ cup light rum

1. To make the cake, preheat oven to 375°F. Put chocolate and butter in a double boiler and melt over simmering water. Remove from heat. Stir in sugar and egg yolks and add ½ cup ground almonds and the bread crumbs.

2. Using an electric mixer or hand whisk, beat the egg whites and the salt in a large bowl until foamy. Add the cream of tartar and beat into peaks that are stiff but not dry. Fold in about a quarter of the chocolate mixture. Pour in the remaining chocolate and fold gently until just combined.

3. Grease an 8-inch-diameter springform pan and sprinkle in 2 tablespoons ground almonds. Shake pan to distribute nuts. Pour in batter.

4. Bake until set in the middle (check with a tester), about 25 minutes.

5. To make the rum cream, beat the cream until soft peaks form. Add the sugar and beat until stiff peaks form. Add the rum and whip briefly to rethicken cream. Pour into a small pastry bag with star tip. Pipe the cream around the outer rim of the cake. Pipe an additional circle onto the cake's center.

VARIATIONS: Ground hazelnuts can be used instead of almonds. Cognac or brandy can also be substituted for the rum.

MAKE AHEAD: The cake can be made through Step 4 up to 1 day in advance, wrapped in foil and stored in a cool, dry place.

Crespelle con fragole
Strawberry Crepes

MAKES
APPROXIMATELY
12 CREPES
(6 SERVINGS)

TIME:
1½ HOURS
INCLUDING
1 HOUR
REFRIGERATION

LEVEL:
MODERATE

Crepes are used as widely in Tuscany as they are in some parts of France, maybe more so since all types of vegetable and seafood crepes are routinely served in fine Tuscan restaurants as appetizers. This simple strawberry version can serve as both a dessert and as a breakfast offering on those mornings when you're feeling alive with the fervor of culinary creation. While this is not really standard Sunday fare, it has become so in my house because I serve the crespelle with strawberries flambé and the theatrics of alcoholic ignition are enough to satisfy the requirement that desserts be "special."

THE CREPES

¾ cup cake flour
1 cup milk
1 egg
2 tablespoons vegetable oil
2 tablespoons sugar

THE SAUCE

2 pints fresh strawberries, hulled and chopped (reserve 6, for garnish)
2 tablespoons Cointreau
½ teaspoon grated orange zest
¼ cup sugar
Confectioners' sugar for dusting

1. To make the crepes, mix flour, milk, egg, oil and sugar until smooth. Cover and refrigerate for 1 hour.
2. Heat a nonstick, slope-sided, 8-inch-diameter skillet or crepe pan until a drop of water placed on the surface sizzles. Pour ¼ cup batter into the pan and swirl to spread the batter evenly on the surface. Cook over low-medium heat until the underside is slightly browned, 2 to 3 minutes. Flip and cook an for additional 30 seconds. Slide onto waxed paper. Repeat the cooking process until all the batter has been used. You will have approximately 12 crepes.
3. To make the strawberry sauce, place the chopped strawberries, Cointreau, orange zest and sugar in a medium-size saucepan and cook

over low heat, stirring constantly, until the sugar has dissolved and the mixture is heated through.

4. Remove the chopped strawberries with a slotted spoon and place a few on half of each crepe. Fold into quarters and drizzle with strawberry sauce. Dust with confectioners' sugar and garnish with one strawberry.

VARIATIONS: To serve as a flambé, heat ¼ cup brandy or cognac over medium heat. Carefully ignite and pour over crepes just as you serve them.

MAKE AHEAD: *Crespelle* (crepes) can be made early in the day and briefly reheated before using

---

Torta di mele e noci
Apple Nut Cake

Walnuts are not native to Tuscany as are pignolis and hazelnuts and hence, their use signifies a special occasion. This cake—basic to some, but special to us—is made even more special when paired with freshly whipped cream scented with walnut liqueur.

MAKES
ONE 9-INCH-
SQUARE CAKE
(10 SLICES)

TIME:
1½ HOURS

LEVEL: EASY

2 cups cake flour
2 teaspoons baking soda
2 teaspoons ground cinnamon
½ teaspoon salt
2 eggs, at room temperature
2 cups sugar
1 teaspoon vanilla extract
½ cup vegetable oil
1 cup chopped walnuts
4 cups peeled and finely chopped Golden Delicious apples
1 cup heavy cream
1 tablespoon walnut liqueur, optional

1. Preheat oven to 325°F. Sift flour, baking soda, cinnamon and salt into a large bowl.
2. Using an electric mixer or a hand whisk, beat the eggs, sugar, vanilla

and oil in a large bowl until thick and creamy, about 5 minutes with the mixer (10 minutes by hand). Stir into flour mixture. Add nuts and apples and mix well.

3. Pour into an ungreased 9-inch-square baking pan.
4. Bake until tester comes out clean, about 1 hour. Transfer to a wire rack and let cool for 15 minutes.
5. Whip cream and walnut liqueur in a large bowl until it forms soft peaks. Slice the cake and serve with walnut-scented whipped cream.

MAKE AHEAD: The cake can be made through Step 4 up to 3 days in advance, wrapped in foil and stored in a cool, dry place until ready to serve.

Crostata di pere e lamponi
Bosc Pear and Raspberry Tart

MAKES
ONE 11-INCH
TART
(10 SLICES)

TIME:
70 MINUTES

LEVEL:
MODERATE

A delicate dessert for a delicate day. In Tuscany, this tart is usually made in late summer or early fall when pears and raspberries overlap into the same season.

2 recipes Basic Puff Pastry (see page 37)
1 egg white, lightly beaten, for wash
1½ cups raspberry preserves
3 tablespoons unsalted butter
2 tablespoons raspberry liqueur
3 firm bosc pears, peeled, thinly sliced and brushed with lemon juice
¼ cup sugar
½ pint fresh raspberries
Fresh mint leaves, for garnish

1. Preheat oven to 425°F.
2. Roll pastry into two 11-inch-diameter rounds on a lightly floured surface. Lift one round onto a baking sheet. From the second round, cut a 1-inch-wide ring to form a rim for the tart. Reserve the remaining pastry for another use.
3. Brush part of the egg wash on the 1-inch-wide band of the outer edge of the pastry round on the baking sheet, being careful not to drip over the edges. Place pastry ring on top and freeze for 15 minutes.

4. Melt preserves and butter over medium heat in a small saucepan. Add the raspberry liqueur and cook until the alcohol evaporates, about 3 minutes.

5. Remove the tart shell from the freezer and arrange the pear slices on top in a spiral. Coat each layer with melted preserves and sprinkle with sugar. Leave ¼ inch between fruit and the edges of the shell. Brush exposed pastry with egg wash.

6. Bake for 10 minutes. Reduce heat to 375°F and bake for 20 minutes more. Transfer to a wire rack and cool to room temperature. Garnish with fresh raspberries and mint leaves.

VARIATIONS: The reserved pastry can be rolled into a rectangle, cut into squares, topped with fruit preserves and baked on a greased baking sheet at 350° for 20 minutes. For best results, chill the pastry for 20 minutes before rolling.

MAKE AHEAD: The entire dessert can be prepared early in the day, wrapped loosely in foil and kept at room temperature until ready to bake.

Torta al caffè con salsa di nocciole
Espresso Amaretto Cheesecake with Hazelnut Espresso Sauce

I waited until the end to include the recipe for this lavish cheesecake, which is the favorite of everyone in my house except my grandmother, who thinks it is too complicated. Don't listen to her. Any complication is well worth the effort.

MAKES
ONE 9-INCH
CHEESECAKE
(10 SLICES)

TIME:
3 HOURS PLUS
OVERNIGHT
REFRIGERATION

LEVEL:
MODERATE

THE CRUST

1 cup amaretto cookie or other cookie crumbs
⅓ cup ground hazelnuts
3 tablespoons unsalted butter, melted
Unsalted butter, for greasing

THE FILLING

1½ pounds mascarpone or softened cream cheese
1¼ cups packed brown sugar

4 eggs, at room temperature
2 tablespoons brewed espresso

4 tablespoons unsalted butter, melted
½ cup packed brown sugar
½ cup heavy cream
1 tablespoon grappa
2 tablespoons brewed espresso
½ cup roughly chopped hazelnuts

1. To make the crust, combine the cookie crumbs, hazelnuts and butter in a medium-size bowl.
2. Grease a 9-inch-diameter springform pan. Press the crust onto the bottom and sides. Freeze for 10 minutes. Preheat oven to 350°F.
3. To make the filling, place the mascarpone and sugar in a large bowl and mix until combined. Add the eggs (one at a time), beating until just blended. Stir in the espresso and pour into the prepared crust.
4. Bake until center is almost set when the cheesecake is shaken, about 55 minutes.
5. Turn the oven off, partially open the door and let cheesecake cool for 1 hour. Transfer to a wire rack for 30 minutes. Refrigerate for 8 hours or overnight.
6. To make the sauce, combine the butter, sugar, cream, grappa and espresso in a medium-size saucepan. Bring to a boil, stirring constantly. Reduce heat and simmer for 5 minutes. Stir in the hazelnuts.
7. To serve, spoon a tablespoon of sauce onto each plate. Release the springform, slice the cake into wedges and center on the plates.

VARIATIONS: Ground almonds can be used in place of the hazelnuts. Cognac or brandy can be substituted for the grappa in the sauce.

CHAPTER SEVEN

Cakes, Tarts, Pies and Terrines

Living with Cacophony

I open the window and it is spring. I close the window and it is spring. Either way, the air is filled not with butterflies, not with the scent of roses, not even with the soft mist of spring rains, but with noise. Noise, defined by Treccani as "loud shouting, clamor, din, any sound that interferes with communication, talking much, talking loud, uproar, disagreeable sound or sounds, commotion, disturbance, excited protest, excited demand, hubbub, racket, discordance."

Today, in this minute, the air is filled with all of the above.

No, nothing is wrong, nothing unusual, nothing that I would not otherwise expect. "Noise," my mother says. "What noise?" She says this at a decibel level geared both toward contributing to and speaking above the general level of cacophonous noise.

Anyone who has ever been to Tuscany knows it is a noisy place. Markets filled with vendors hawking, buyers contending, children screeching, their parents pretending all is well. Restaurants packed with large families seated at large tables eating and drinking for four hours at a clip, everyone talking at once. Village streets crowded with residents running errands, taking a stroll. *"Agostino! Agostino! Come sta la tua mamma?"* An innocent query about one's mother, shouted from across the piazza. Motorbikes buzzing through the streets like warrior bees on route to battle, BRMMM, BRMMM, BRMMMMMM!!! Religious festivals processing through town, priests on loudspeakers chanting the rosary, hundreds of church faithful singing hymns. *Sagras,* feast days, holiday parades, political rallies, bands marching through town fifty times a year to lay wreaths on this site or that monument.

All routine. All part of life. All the stuff of tourist interest. "Tuscany is so *alive!*" say the Brits and the Dutch and the Aussies and the peach-skinned Californians who flock to Tuscany seeking just this level of social interaction. "It's a festival wherever you go!"

Yes it is. But sometimes, just sometimes, I want to walk out my front door and hear the soft early morning winds rustling among the boughs of the fragrant mimosas. I want to thrill to the sound of the first robin signaling the onset of spring. I want to know when the crickets have broken from their shells, when the gurgle of the stream behind my house swells to a roar following last night's rain, when the terra-cotta tiles on my roof shake loose, as they did last week, because the ivy vines had wormed their way between the joints. Is this too much to ask? Am I not entitled, just once, to the luxury of walking from my front door to the bread bakers on the market piazza embroiled purely in thoughts of my own making? Without having to be interrupted by 27 scenes, 16 of them requiring some level of interaction for the sake of maintaining intact the social fabric of small town life?

Apparently, the answer is no. Because wherever I go, I'm always engaged in at least one conversation about what has come to be mockingly referred to as the "American Invasion of Stiava." The whole thing started six years ago, when a couple from West Virginia bought a house in the center of town and, after spending a few summers, decided, last fall, to move here permanently. Nobody could figure out what their decision was based on, since they never seemed to make any attempt to meet anyone or be part of anything except for weekly forays to the produce market in Piazza Vittorio Emanuele.

There are not many outsiders in Stiava. Before this couple, the only nonlocals ever to move here were three men from Calabria who had come over thirty years ago with their families to work on the construction of the *autostrada*. The job took more than seven years and they eventually just bought one big house on the outskirts of town and stayed. As adjustments go, theirs was, initially, a somewhat difficult one given the regional prejudice against southern Italians.

But eventually, they became as much a part of the town as the new shops on Via Emilia. It's not difficult to do, just that few people seem to to make the choice, which is strange, given that Stiava lies just five miles away from the seaside resort of Viareggio. As such, it hosts more than its share of transient foreigners; most come during the beach season to rent villas or houses or rooms in houses. You see them in the market, in restaurants, in shops, in the local caffès where they come for breakfast or late afternoon tea. Everyone smiles at everyone else and the relationships are, for the most part, extremely cordial. But that's because these people don't live here and, hence, would never presume to dictate what goes on or doesn't go on. It's a very different thing when you sign your name to ownership papers.

In this case, the West Virginians (Maggy and Howell Fisher, Howell's name being virtually unpronounceable by Italians, who have a hard time with initial *H*s and thus refer to him as "Owl") got sick and tired of the noise emanating from the caffè located just across the piazza from their house. As they never fail to mention every time they see me, me being one of the few people in town who speaks English, "Those men sit there every night until at least two in the morning playing cards and shouting."

My initial mistake was to sympathize with them. "I know," I said the first time we ever talked about it. "It's terrible how they carry on." But I really did feel for them, located as I am on the other side of the same piazza and, hence, well within earshot of the exact same experience. It's just that it would never occur to me to try to do anything about it other than complain to the very few people who might sympathize.

Most people, even if they have a problem with the noise, chalk it up to village life. "Better that than the ghost villages in American suburbs," says my friend, Enrico, who spent a year in Englewood, Colorado, as an exchange student. "You could walk from one end of the town to the other all day and night without seeing anyone other than people whisking by in cars."

The older people are the worst when it comes to blithe acceptance. "It's a sign of vibrancy—of life!" beams my grandmother's friend, Milva, who lives three houses away fom the Fishers.

The first year after the Fishers moved here, they would occasionally stop by the bar to speak to Sirio, the owner, about their "problem." Speak is actually not a good term for Howell's attempts to communicate his displeasure. He would appear at the bar in late morning—when I guess he thought he had a better chance of getting Sirio's undivided attention—holding a script he'd written out using his Italian-English dictionary. As the bar customers looked on, sipping occasionally from their *caffè correttos,* Howell would read his phonetically-penned list of complaints.

At first, that's all it was, a list of complaints. "We can't sleep with everyone screaming that way until late into the night." Or "It's very difficult trying to concentrate on a book with that kind of noise." A little later, Howell began tacking on a request for behavioral change. "If you could just ask the men to lower their voices a bit."

Sirio would always smile politely and clap Howell on the shoulder.

"Dai," he would say, the Italian equivalent of "go on." Sirio's wife would always offer a cup of coffee, which was always refused, and the incident would come to an end with all parties feeling resolved.

But then last fall, Howell apparently lost it, and one night, around 2:30 in the morning, he came running across the piazza holding his dictionary and a prepared speech and, to everyone's astonishment, yelled out an order for everyone to stop screaming immediately.

As Sirio later told it, "The American looked like madman. He was wearing his pajamas with a trench coat tied at the waist and his hair spiked out around his head like a halo. I tried to get him to sit down, Mariella made him a cup of coffee, but we could not calm him. He read from his paper like always in his dreadful imitation of the Italian language, but this time he was screaming as if his mother had just died. We didn't know what to do."

They did not know what to do. When I heard Sirio utter those words, I almost lost it myself. "What do you mean, you didn't know what to do?" I wanted to scream at him. "The man was asking you all to quiet down— obviously that would have been the thing to do."

But quieting down would never have occurred to any man present on that momentous occasion. As a matter of fact, I am here to tell you that never once in the entire year of this travesty has it even remotely occurred to them that they might simply refrain from screaming like banshees after midnight. To them, this is simply a case of someone having a bad day— not of the person actually *believing* what they're saying. A case of venting, as in "Oh, you know that Howell. Sometimes his stock broker tells him he's lost a few thousand in the market and then he comes over here screaming for us to be quiet. It will pass, it always does."

Howell, however, seems to be quite serious in his campaign to reform Stiava's late night etiquette. So far, he has spoken to a few lawyers (all of whom have apparently told him to forget it), the mayor (who later reported the incident to the men in the caffè. *"Che shemo,"* he said of Howell ["What a jerk"]), the real estate agent from whom he bought the house, and the pastor of San Lorenzo. Nowhere was he given even a modicum of hope, although, as Maggie told me the other morning at the market, "My husband is a tiger. Once he catches the scent, he doesn't quickly lose sight of his prey." What a choice of words, I thought to myself. I hope he uses more diplomatic phrasing in his various appeals.

"It's not so much whether he's right or wrong," said the real estate agent, a friend of my brother's. "It's that no one wants to hear an outsider, specifically an American, complaining about a culture that has existed this way for centuries without any problem other than the one created by the very nature of the complaint itself."

He's right, although certain things cannot be excused simply by virtue of the fact that they've always been done that way.

Theoretically, I'm on Howell's side. The fact that six or seven men can commandeer the central piazza every night from 9:30 until 2:30—that we all have to listen to them screaming about politics and soccer and whatever else riles them in that moment—is just not right. It is a lack of consideration of the highest order, not to mention the sexism implicit in such patriarchal behavior.

But the real estate agent does have a point in saying that's the way it's been done for centuries and if you take away even one foundation stone, what you're ultimately left with is a crumbling building. What the men are really saying with their behavior is "This is MY town and I'm a big man here." Take away their right to do as they please, which in this case means screaming when they so choose, and next thing you know, they'll be home watching television instead of playing cards in the local caffè. While that in itself might not be the end of civilization, a few similar transformations and good-bye village life. One would think there'd be a happy medium, but rarely do things work out so rationally.

Furthermore, there's the fact of Howell and Maggie's Americanness. Even if the men agreed with them about the lack of consideration implicit in their actions, they'd refuse to make modifications for fear of appearing spineless. Especially now, with the almighty Americans seeming to dictate just about everything from who will join NATO to which of the world's economies will be bailed out and which left to rot.

Dislike of American power simmers beneath the surface of any American-Italian interaction, so much so that the only thing that prevented an even greater outpouring of national grief when Gianni Versace died is that he had gone to live in Miami. Headlines veered from "They Even Co-Opted Versace" to "Versace Should Have Known Better."

And so even though I agree with the Fishers in theory—wouldn't I just love to lean out my window one night without having to listen to old Maurizio screeching about the Socialists—I can't help but feel glad that they're headed for an interpersonal collision. Right now, nobody even takes them seriously, a fact that makes Howell purple.

"What do I have to do to convince them I'm serious?" he pleaded when I met him at Stiava's weekly market. "It's like I'm invisible. I ask them nicely to just lower their voices a little and they pat me on the back and go back to their card playing. Are they playing a cunning game of spite or are they just dumb?"

Neither, I wanted to say. So far, they think you've just got a bad case of nerves. It hasn't occurred to them yet that you might be serious. When it does, I wouldn't want to be in your shoes.

Tuscans are not nice people, I want to warn him. On the surface, they're all bubbly and open and effusive and kind and generous to the point of helping you build your house within three days of knowing you. But under the surface of all that manipulative charm is a land of rogues who spit in the face of the mighty, who laugh in the face of those who would oppress and humiliate, who make themselves respected without fearing to run afoul of the law's enforcers, who reply to villainy with low blows, to suspicion with teeth in the jugular, to kisses on the cheek with claws in the eyes.

It has been said about Tuscans that they have never warred against other Italians. This is true but I have always wondered why? Is it because they are so peaceful and filled with reason? Or because they believe that a dead Italian, unlike a dead Tuscan, is worth nothing more than the dust from which he was created?

I want to tell the Fishers all these things—not only because I fear for their states of mind, but because they would be so much happier letting go of their myths and joining the actual reality. I'm sure they bought this house because of visions having to do with ebullient Tuscans milling about their quaint little villages in peace and harmony. What they saw when they first came was what everyone sees initially: beautiful panoramas, relaxed lifestyle, good food, great wines. All those things are true, but they do not even begin to define what life here is all about. And yet, can anyone ever truly become part of a culture not their own?

But I say nothing. Because ultimately the Fishers will learn that tradition, not reason, is what motivates this culture. Or they won't. In either case, nothing I say is going to make the difference. And besides, he thinks the men in the bar are dumb? What does he think *he* looks like, standing there at 2:30 in the morning in his pajamas, reading ultimatums from a phonetically-composed script!

Cakes, Tarts, Pies and Terrines

Wherever you go in Tuscany, from the largest city to the smallest village, you are never far from a *pasticcerìa* (bake shop). You might miss the bank, you will definitely miss the post office, but if your nose follows that sweet fragrance wafting through the *viali,* you will most definitely find the town's dessert center. The reason is that desserts are as central to Italian life as are pasta and Parmesan cheese. So devilish is this addiction that Gabriele d'Annunzio, the great twentieth century poet, routinely referred to chocolate cakes and almond tarts as his "Mephistopheles" and Giacomo Puccini, wrote many of his most famous operas at the huge grand piano in the corner of his studio while sipping Hibiscus tea and eating hefty slices of hazelnut cake (this despite his diabetes).

Being able to make good cakes and tarts is easier than most people think. The hardest part is the pastry itself, which, contrary to making bread, requires a light, delicate touch. A few tips before you begin:

- Handle pastry dough as little as possible to inhibit the development of gluten which would otherwise toughen it.
- Fat protects flour from mixing with water and becoming a soggy mess. When cutting fat (butter) into flour, use a large bowl and cut in the butter with a pastry blender or two knives used in scissors fashion. For a flaky crust, cut in the butter until the mixture resembles coarse cornmeal. For uniform tenderness, cut until the particles are approximately the same size, but remember that too much cutting makes the mixture pasty and then it becomes almost impossible to incorporate the liquid.
- Avoid too much flour, which can toughen the dough.
- Avoid too much liquid, which can result in soggy pastry. Toss the dough with a fork, simultaneously pouring in only as much liquid as necessary to dampen the fat-flour clumps so they hold together. Add liquid gradually, and only to the dry portions, because the moistened clumps will continue to absorb liquid.
- Avoid too much fat, which makes dough greasy and crumbly.
- Chilling pastry dough after mixing tenderizes it, keeps it from shrinking during baking and makes it easy to handle.
- Always preheat the oven. The contrast between the coolness of the dough and the heat of the oven causes rapid air expansion and contributes to a light texture.

Cakes, Tarts, Pies and Terrines

Crostatina di pasta di mandorle
Lacy Almond Tart

Terrina ai tre cioccolati
Three-Chocolate Terrine

Mattoni di gianduia
Chocolate-Hazelnut Nutella Cake

Delizie di montagna con nocciole e zabaione
Hazelnut Zabaione Cake

Torta di pistacchio
Pistacchio Tart

Torta di stracchino e cioccolata
Chocolate Marbled Cheesecake

Terrina ai tre frutti
Three-Fruit Pastry Terrine

Torta di farro e ricotta
Farro and Ricotta Cake

Zuppa Inglese
Rum Refrigerator Cake

Ciambella di polenta
Polenta Ring Cake

Torta di noci con crema al caffè
Walnut Coffee Tart with Espresso Cream

Torta di cioccolata caramellata
Chocolate Truffle Loaf with Caramel Sauce

Torta della mamma con fragole
Mom's Almond Tart with Raspberry Sauce

Torta alla crema di amaretto con pesche fresche
Amaretto Cream Cake with Fresh Peaches

Crostatina di pasta di mandorle
Lacy Almond Tart

MAKES
ONE 10-INCH
TART
(10 SLICES)

TIME: 2 HOURS

LEVEL:
MODERATE

Tuscan pastry is defined by its frequent dependence on three or four ingredients, chief among them, almonds. Used in every form from whole to slivered to paste, their pointed flavor pairs well with two other regional dessert mainstays: fruits and custard. The following tart uses a Basic Pasta Frolla crust (see page 34 for a description of this butter and egg pastry) topped with a light, delicate orange-flavored custard.

1 recipe Basic *Pasta Frolla* (see page 34)
Unsalted butter, for greasing
1 cup Basic Custard (see page 34)
2 teaspoons orange extract
2 cups lightly toasted and finely ground almonds
2 cups confectioners' sugar
2 tablespoons amaretto
4 egg whites, at room temperature
½ teaspoon salt
½ teaspoon cream of tartar
1 egg, lightly beaten with 1 tablespoon water, for wash
¼ cup almond slivers, for garnish
Tangerine segments, for garnish*

1. Remove the *pasta frolla* from the refrigerator, unwrap it and transfer to a lightly floured working surface.
2. Using a floured rolling pin, roll the dough into a 10-inch-diameter circle about ¼ inch thick.
3. Grease a 9-inch-diameter springform pan and line it with the circle of dough, pressing the excess against the sides. Preheat the oven to 375°F.
4. In a medium-size bowl and using a wooden spoon, mix the custard with orange extract until well blended. Pour the custard over the crust and tap the pan lightly to level the surface.
5. In another medium-size bowl and using a wooden spoon, mix the ground almonds with confectioners' sugar and amaretto. Stir until well blended.
6. Using an electric mixer or hand whisk, beat the egg whites in a large

bowl until foamy. Add the salt and cream of tartar and beat into peaks that are stiff but not dry. Fold the whites into the almond mixture until just blended.

7. Pour the mixture into a large pastry bag fitted with a star tip and pipe the top of the tart with a lattice pattern of small stars. Brush the lattice lightly with the egg wash.

8. Bake the tart for 15 minutes then reduce the heat to 325°F and bake until lightly golden, about 30 minutes. Remove the sides of the pan, let cool to room temperature, slice and garnish with tangerine segments.

* To prepare the tangerines for garnish, peel completely, making sure to remove all the pith. Separate into neat segments, cutting between each of the membranes. Place in pairs and arrange a few slivers of sliced almond on each.

MAKE AHEAD: The tangerines can be peeled and separated early in the day.

Terrina ai tre cioccolati
Three-Chocolate Terrine

The first time I had this terrine was in Staffoli at the famous restaurant Da Beppe. At the end of a glorious meal consisting of more than nine courses, Luca, the chef and owner, came out of the kitchen holding a beautiful plate decorated with curls of orange peel, fresh mint leaves, and this mysterious chocolate rectangle sitting on a bed of blood-orange syrup. As soon as he presented it, I knew I had to have the recipe. Thank you, Luca.

MAKES ONE
10 X 5-INCH
TERRINE
(10 SLICES)

TIME:
3 HOURS PLUS
3 HOURS
REFRIGERATION

LEVEL:
ADVANCED

THE CHOCOLATE MOUSSE

4 ounces unsweetened chocolate, cut into small chunks
2 tablespoons unsalted butter, at room temperature
4 egg yolks, at room temperature
4 tablespoons sugar
2 tablespoons milk
2 tablespoons Grand Marnier
5 egg whites, at room temperature
¼ teaspoon salt
½ teaspoon cream of tartar

THE WHITE MOUSSE

4 ounces white chocolate, cut into small chunks
3 tablespoons unsalted butter, at room temperature
3 egg yolks, at room temperature
4 tablespoons sugar
2 tablespoons milk
1 teaspoon vanilla extract
¾ cup heavy cream

THE COFFEE MOUSSE

1½ cups milk
1 cup sugar
5 egg yolks, at room temperature
1 teaspoon vanilla extract
1½ tablespoons cake flour
5 tablespoons brewed espresso
3 tablespoons ground espresso
1 cup heavy cream

THE ORANGE SYRUP

Juice of 4 medium oranges
1 cup confectioners' sugar
2 tablespoons Cointreau
Fresh mint leaves, for garnish

1. To make the chocolate mousse, melt the chocolate and butter in a double boiler over simmering water. Keep warm.

2. Using an electric mixer or a hand whisk, beat the egg yolks, sugar and milk vigorously, until smooth, fluffy, pale and tripled in volume, about 5 minutes with the mixer (15 minutes by hand). Pour into another double boiler. (If only one double boiler is available, pour the chocolate into a heated bowl and keep warm.) Cook over simmering water, stirring constantly, until the mixture reaches 160°F as measured on an instant read thermometer, about 5 minutes.

3. Stir the Grand Marnier into the egg mixture and then gradually add the melted chocolate, stirring constantly until the consistency is smooth and well blended. Remove from heat and let cool to room temperature.

4. Using an electric mixer or hand whisk, beat the egg whites and the salt and cream of tartar in a large bowl until stiff peaks form. Gently fold the whites into the chocolate mixture until just blended. Cover and refrigerate for 2 hours.

5. To make the white mousse, melt the white chocolate and butter in a double boiler over simmering water, stirring frequently. Keep warm.

6. Using an electric mixer or hand whisk, beat the egg yolks with the sugar and milk until smooth, fluffy, pale and tripled in volume, about 5 minutes with the mixer (15 minutes by hand). Pour the mixture into another double boiler, and cook over simmering water until the temperature reaches 160°F as measured with an instant read thermometer, about 5 minutes. Stir constantly. (If only one double boiler is available, pour the chocolate into a heated bowl and keep warm.)

7. Stir the vanilla into the eggs and then gradually pour in the melted chocolate, stirring constantly until the consistency is smooth and well blended. Let cool to room temperature.

8. Using an electric mixer or hand whisk, beat the cream in a large bowl into stiff peaks. Gently fold the cream into the chocolate mixture until just blended. Cover and refrigerate for 2 hours.

9. To make the coffee mousse, place the milk and sugar in a large saucepan and boil over very low heat, stirring constantly.

10. Using an electric mixer or hand whisk, beat the egg yolks with the vanilla until smooth, fluffy, pale and tripled in volume, about 5 minutes with the mixer (15 minutes by hand). Stir in the flour until the batter is creamy and smooth. Pour in the brewed espresso and stir until well blended.

11. Slowly pour ½ cup of the hot milk-sugar mixture into the yolks, whisking constantly. Gradually pour in the remaining ½ cup milk-sugar mixture, whisking until smooth. Transfer the mixture to a saucepan and cook over very low heat, stirring constantly. Cook until a heavy ribbon forms when the spoon is lifted, about 8 minutes. Do not boil. Let cool to room temperature.

12. Using an electric mixer, beat the ground espresso with the cream in a large bowl until stiff peaks form. Fold the cream into the cooled custard until just blended. Cover and refrigerate for 2 hours.

13. To assemble the terrine, line a 9 x 5 x 3-inch loaf pan with aluminum foil. Pour in the chocolate mousse and level with a spatula. Cover with foil and freeze for 10 minutes.

14. Pour the white chocolate over the dark chocolate. Level with a spatula, cover with foil and freeze for 10 minutes.
15. Pour in the coffee mousse, level with a spatula, cover with foil and refrigerate for 3 hours.
16. To make the orange syrup, place the orange juice, sugar and Cointreau in a double boiler and cook, stirring constantly, until thickened, about 10 minutes.
17. Unmold the terrine onto a serving plate and remove the aluminum foil. Cut into ½ inch thick slices.
18. Swirl 1 tablespoon orange syrup onto individual plates, top with a slice of terrine and garnish with fresh mint.

MAKE AHEAD: The syrup can be prepared 1 day before and refrigerated in a sealed container until needed. The terrine can be made one day in advance, wrapped in plastic and stored in the refrigerator until needed

---

Mattoni di gianduia
Chocolate-Hazelnut Nutella Cake

MAKES
ONE 9-INCH
CAKE (8 SLICES)

TIME: 1 HOUR

LEVEL:
MODERATE

Gianduia is the nickname of Giovanni del Boccale, a mythical farmer figure whose loyalty, work ethic and understated wit represent the people of Italy's Piedmont region. For reasons I have never understood, gianduia is also the name of Italy's beloved chocolate, made with finely ground hazelnuts.

Right after World War II, an Italian chocolate maker decided to capitalize on the national craze for gianduia and created a chocolate hazelnut cream called "Nutella" that looks like a darker version of peanut butter and is sold in similar-size jars in supermarkets everywhere. Today, Italians consume approximately 3 million pounds of Nutella every year and when the huge floods of 1994 almost destroyed the Piedmont-situated producer, Italians were desperate. Thank God the factory was up and running in less than a month!

½ cup bread flour
½ teaspoon salt
½ teaspoon baking powder
4 ounces bittersweet chocolate, cut into small chunks
3 ounces milk chocolate, cut into small chunks
1 teaspoon orange extract

½ cup *Nutella** or other chocolate spread
½ cup unsalted butter, at room temperature
½ cup sugar
2 eggs, at room temperature
7 ounces hazelnuts, lightly toasted and coarsely ground
½ cup frozen raspberries
Fresh raspberries, for garnish

1. Preheat the oven to 350°F. Line a 9-inch-square baking pan with parchment paper.
2. In a medium-size bowl, sift together the flour, salt and baking powder.
3. Place both types of chocolate in a double boiler and melt over simmering water. Add the orange extract, *Nutella* and butter and stir until smooth. Remove from heat.
4. Whisk in the sugar and eggs (one at a time) until glossy and smooth. Sift in the dry ingredients and mix until well blended. Stir in the ground hazelnuts.
5. Pour the batter into the prepared baking pan.
6. Bake for 40 minutes. Remove from oven and let cool in the baking pan. Purée the frozen raspberries. If the raspberries contain seeds, strain the purée through a fine sieve.
7. Cut into individual portions, drizzle with the raspberry sauce and garnish with fresh raspberries.

* *Nutella* is available in specialty stores.

MAKE AHEAD: The cake can be made up to 1 day in advance, wrapped loosely in foil and stored in a cool, dry place.

Delizie di montagna
con nocciole e zabaione
Hazelnut Zabaione Cake

MAKES
ONE 8-INCH
CAKE (6 SLICES)

TIME:
1½ HOURS

LEVEL:
MODERATE

Dante Alighieri has always been my favorite writer. Recently, however, I re-read Inferno and was quite surprised to find that he had relegated all dessert gluttons to Hell since he was apparently convinced that sugar was dangerous to the soul. Poor man, I thought to myself. Better he should have listened to the ancients—to Apicus, for example, whose pre-Christian culinary epic, De Re Coquinaria, *advised adding ridiculous amounts of honey to just about everything.*

Following is a wonderful lemony layer cake spread with zabaione *and drizzled with fresh strawberry purée.*

4½ tablespoons potato starch, sifted
1 cup cake flour, sifted
6 eggs, separated, at room temperature
1 cup sugar
1 teaspoon grated lemon zest
1 teaspoon vanilla extract
¼ teaspoon salt
¾ teaspoon cream of tartar
1 cup Basic *Zabaione* (see page 35)
1 cup ground raw hazelnuts
1½ cups whipped heavy cream
8 ounces strawberries, hulled and puréed

1. Preheat the oven to 350°F. Line an 8-inch-square baking pan with parchment paper. In a medium-size bowl sift the potato starch with the flour.
2. Using an electric mixer or hand whisk, beat the egg yolks and the sugar in a large bowl until smooth, pale and tripled in volume, about 5 minutes with the mixer (15 minutes by hand). Stir in the grated lemon zest and vanilla.
3. Sift in half of the dry mixture, stirring until well blended.
4. Using an electric mixer or hand whisk, beat the egg whites and the salt in a large bowl until foamy. Add the cream of tartar and beat until stiff peaks form. Fold half the whites into the egg mixture.

5. Fold in the remaining half of the dry mixture and gently stir until blended.
6. Fold in the remaining whites until just blended.
7. Pour the mixture into the prepared baking pan, tap against a counter to level the surface.
8. Bake until lightly golden, about 40 minutes. Remove from the pan, transfer to a wire rack and cool to room temperature. Cut the cooled cake in half horizontally.
9. In a medium-size bowl, gently stir ½ cup hazelnuts into the *zabaione*. Fold in the whipped cream until just blended.
10. Spread the cream over the bottom half of the cut cake. Cover with the second half and dust with the remaining hazelnuts. Slice and serve with strawberry purée.

VARIATIONS: Basic Custard (see page 34) or fruit purée can be used in place of the *zabaione*.

MAKE AHEAD: The cake can be prepared through Step 8 up to 1 day in advance. Cut the cake in half just before serving.

Torta di pistacchio
Pistacchio Tart

This wonderful tart recipe comes from my friend, Umberto, who is the chef at one of Viareggio's oldest restaurants, Caffè Margherita. The pastry is made with marsala wine and topped with a unique combination of chopped pistacchios, nutmeg and milk. Umberto claims it is an old family recipe but I have never tasted anything like it anywhere in else Italy.

MAKES
ONE 10-INCH
TART (8 SLICES)

TIME: 1 HOUR

LEVEL:
MODERATE

THE CRUST

2 cups cake flour, sifted
1 egg, at room temperature
¼ teaspoon salt
½ cup unsalted butter, at room temperature
½ cup sugar
2 tablespoons marsala or sherry
Unsalted butter, for greasing

2 cups milk

2 eggs, lightly beaten, at room temperature

1 cup pistachios, finely chopped

¼ cup sugar

¾ cup cake flour

¼ teaspoon ground nutmeg

1 tablespoon confectioners' sugar

⅛ teaspoon salt

1. To make the crust, place the flour, egg, salt, butter, sugar and the marsala in a large bowl and mix until a dense dough has formed.

2. Pinch off ⅓ of the dough and set aside. Roll the remaining dough on a lightly floured work surface to a 12-inch-diameter circle, ⅛-inch thick. Grease a 10-inch-diameter tart pan with removable bottom and transfer the dough to the pan, pressing the edges against the sides. Roll a rolling pin over the top to level the edges.

3. Preheat the oven to 350°F.

4. To make the filling, blend together the milk, eggs, pistachios, sugar, flour, nutmeg, confectioners' sugar and salt, and pour into the prepared tart pan.

5. Roll the remaining dough into a 10-inch square and cut into 1-inch-wide strips. Arrange the strips in lattice fashion over the filling.

6. Bake until the dough is golden, about 40 minutes. Let cool to room temperature, remove the sides of the pan and serve.

MAKE AHEAD: The dough can be prepared up to 2 days in advance and refrigerated in a sealed container. It can also be frozen for up to 3 weeks; thaw in the refrigerator before using.

Torta di stracchino e cioccolata
Chocolate Marbled Cheesecake

Whenever my relatives go to visit my cousin Anna in New York, they always go down the street from her apartment to Eileen's cheesecake store and bring back what's called a "Marble Cheesecake." They like it well enough (as well as any Tuscan can like food not prepared by Tuscans in Tuscany), but the real lure is that it reminds them of a similar cake made in their hometown of Stiava. I suppose the ingredients are very similar, but there is a big difference between using stracchino, a soft farmer's cheese, and packaged cream cheese, which is how I think Eileen makes all her cakes. Try to find fresh farmer's cheese at a cheese store rather than settling for a supermarket variety.

MAKES
ONE 10-INCH
CHEESECAKE
(10 TO 12
SLICES)

TIME: 2½
HOURS PLUS
8 HOURS
REFRIGERATION

LEVEL:
MODERATE

THE CRUST

¾ cup cake flour
2 tablespoons sugar
¼ teaspoon salt
¼ cup unsalted butter, at room temperature
1 cup semisweet chocolate, melted

THE FILLING

1½ pounds *stracchino* or other fresh Farmer's cheese
1 cup sugar
¼ cup cake flour
2 teaspoons vanilla extract
6 eggs, at room temperature
1 cup plain yogurt

1. Preheat the oven to 400°F. To make the crust, sift together the flour, sugar and salt. Using a pastry blender, cut in the butter until the dough resembles coarse crumbs. Add 4 tablespoons melted chocolate and stir until a ball of dough has been created.
2. Press the dough into the bottom of a 10-inch-diameter springform pan. Cover the dough with aluminum foil, top with raw rice, dried beans or commercial pie weights and bake for 10 minutes. Remove the weights and foil and bake for 5 more minutes.
3. To make the filling, meanwhile, using an electric mixer or a hand

whisk, beat the cheese with the sugar until creamy. Blend in the flour and vanilla.

4. Add the eggs (one at a time) beating well after each. Blend in the yogurt.

5. Remove 1¾ cups filling and blend with the remaining ¾ cup chocolate. Pour the rest of the filling over the cooled crust and top with spoonfuls of the chocolate mixture. Drag a knife through the filling to create a marbled effect. Place in oven and immediately reduce heat to 300°F.

6. Bake 1 hour, turn oven off and leave cake in oven for 1 hour. Cool to room temperature and refrigerate for at least 8 hours. Remove the sides of the pan and serve.

VARIATIONS: One-quarter cup raspberry or strawberry purée can be added in Step 4.

MAKE AHEAD: The cheese cake can be prepared up to 3 days in advance, wrapped in plastic or foil and stored in the refrigerator until ready to serve.

Terrina ai tre frutti
Three-Fruit Pastry Terrine

MAKES 1 PASTRY
TERRINE
(10 SLICES)

TIME:
1¾ HOURS

LEVEL:
MODERATE

This very unusual recipe was developed by my brother, Paolo, when he went to cooking school in Lucca. The assignment was designed to teach how to layer pastry with fruit toppings and each student was supposed to practice with a recipe of his own making. I remember Paolo standing in front of our kitchen table, which was covered with dozens of jars of fruit preserves. He had about 25 little bowls and each contained various combinations of fruit. "Taste this," he would say from time to time. Eventually, I realized that he was getting closer and closer to the time when he would have to leave for school, and the kitchen was getting messier by the second. "Okay," I said at one point. "It's time to bake the terrine." His stare withered me. "How can I become a great cook," he scolded, "if all your thoughts are on pragmatism?"

Following is Paolo's masterpiece.

Unsalted butter for greasing
1 cup unsalted butter, at room temperature
¾ cup sugar

½ teaspoon salt
5 eggs, at room temperature
4 cups bread flour
3 teaspoons baking powder
⅓ cup orange juice
1 cup cherry preserves
1 cup orange marmalade
1 cup fig or apricot preserves
1½ cups golden raisins
1 cup coconut flakes
1 cup chopped hazelnuts
2 tablespoons grated lemon zest
2 tablespoons lemon juice

1. Preheat oven to 325°F and lightly butter a 14 x 10-inch baking pan.
2. Whisk together the butter, ½ cup of the sugar and the salt. Add the eggs (one at a time), beating after each addition. Add 1 cup flour, the baking powder and the orange juice and mix well. Gradually add the remaining 3 cups flour and mix until all ingredients are well blended.
3. Place the dough on a lightly floured work surface and divide into 3 equal portions. Roll out 1 portion and fit into the bottom of the prepared pan, pressing the excess against the sides.
4. Spread the dough with the cherry preserves and ½ cup orange marmalade. Top with ¾ cup raisins, ½ cup coconut and ⅓ cup hazelnuts. Sprinkle with 1 tablespoon grated zest and 1 tablespoon lemon juice.
5. Roll out the second portion of dough and place over fillings. Repeat the process in Step 4, except substitute fig preserves for the cherry preserves.
6. Roll out the last portion of dough and place over the fillings. Sprinkle with the remaining ⅓ cup hazelnuts and dust with the remaining ¼ cup of sugar. Carefully cut the top layer only into diagonal slices (to avoid having the filling leak out when slicing after the terrine is baked).
7. Bake for 1 hour. Cool to room temperature and serve.

VARIATIONS: Other types of preserves can be used; try raspberry or strawberry or peach or even lemon curd.

MAKE AHEAD: The dough can be prepared up to 3 days in advance, sealed in plastic and stored in the refrigerator. It can also be frozen for up to 3 weeks. Thaw in the refrigerator before using.

Torta di farro e ricotta
Farro and Ricotta Cake

MAKES
ONE 10-INCH
CAKE (8 TO 10
SLICES)

TIME: 2 HOURS

LEVEL:
MODERATE

Farro is a barley-like grain that belongs to the wheat family. Often confused with spelt (triticum spelta), *farro* (triticum dicoccum) *has two distinct spikes and a fuller flavor. Today most farro is cultivated in Umbria, Latium and Tuscany although the one grown in the Tuscan Garfagnana is the most famous for its pure, nutty flavor. In the United States, it can be purchased at specialty stores in a variety of forms: whole kernels (used in soups, stews and the following recipe), cracked kernels (same uses but less nutty flavor) and ground into flour for pasta and bread.*

8 ounces *farro* or wheat berries*
6 to 8 cups milk
3 tablespoons sugar
1 teaspoon cinnamon
1 tablespoon vanilla extract
4 eggs, separated
1 cup *farro* or cake flour
¾ pound fresh sheep's milk ricotta or other fresh ricotta
¾ cup raisins, soaked in ½ cup Cointreau for 20 minutes
1 teaspoon grated lemon zest
½ teaspoon salt
Unsalted butter or cooking spray, for greasing
½ teaspoon cream of tartar

1. Place the *farro* in a large, heavy-gauge saucepan. Add 6 cups milk, the sugar, cinnamon and vanilla, cover and cook over low heat for 45 minutes. Add the remaining 2 cups milk if necessary to keep the grains from drying out. The cooked *farro* should be tender but dry. Cool to room temperature.
2. Preheat the oven to 350°F. Beat the egg yolks, flour, ricotta, raisins and Cointreau, lemon zest and ¼ teaspoon of the salt until creamy and smooth.
3. Grease a 10-inch-diameter springform pan. Stir the eggs into the cooled *farro*.
4. Using an electric mixer or a hand whisk, beat the egg whites and the

remaining ¼ teaspoon of salt and cream of tartar in a large bowl until stiff peaks form. Gently fold the egg whites into the *farro* mixture. Pour the batter into the prepared pan.

5. Bake for 40 minutes and let cool to room temperature before serving.

* Wheat berries can be found in specialty grocers.

VARIATIONS: The cake can be served on a blood orange sauce. To make the sauce, squeeze 4 blood oranges into a saucepan, add 1 teaspoon grated blood orange zest, and cook over low heat until reduced by half, about 10 to 15 minutes.

MAKE AHEAD: The farro can be cooked the day before, stored in a sealed container, and refrigerated until needed. Bring to room temperature before using.

Zuppa Inglese
Rum Refrigerator Cake

One of Tuscany's most outstanding cakes is this version of the legendary Zuppa Inglese. While the name suggests an English pedigree, this is the most Tuscan of cakes, incorporating egg custard, marsala wine and rum. A guaranteed delight!

½ cup marsala or sherry
1 recipe Basic Custard (see page 34)
1 recipe *Pasta Genovese,* or Basic Sponge Cake (see page 36)
1 cup light rum
1 cup heavy cream
½ cup finely chopped hazelnuts

1. Stir the marsala into the custard.
2. Carefully slice the sponge cake into 3 very thin horizontal layers. Put 1 layer in the bottom of a deep serving bowl. Soak with ⅓ cup rum and cover with ⅓ of the marsala-custard mixture. Top with the second layer of sponge cake and repeat the process, dousing with another ⅓ cup rum and topping with another ⅓ of the custard. Do the same with the third layer and then refrigerate the cake for at least 3 hours.

MAKES 1 LAYER
CAKE (8 SLICES)

TIME:
30 MINUTES
PLUS 3 HOURS
REFRIGERATION

LEVEL:
MODERATE

3. Just before serving, beat the cream in a large bowl into stiff peaks. Spread the cream over the top of the cake, sprinkle with nuts and serve.

VARIATIONS: Sliced fruit such as strawberries or other berries can be layered on top of the marsala-custard mixture.

Ciambella di polenta
Polenta Ring Cake

Polenta (cornmeal) is used in many Tuscan recipes, but one of the more un-usual is this wonderful ring cake that is somewhat similar to the Torta di semolino *(Baked Semolina Tart) on page 127 but lighter and fluffier. The recipe comes from Gianluca Podesti of Ristorante Giambelli in Massa.*

MAKES 1 RING
CAKE (8 SLICES)

TIME:
1½ HOURS

LEVEL:
MODERATE

Unsalted butter, for greasing
Flour, for dusting
1 teaspoon dry yeast
2 tablespoons lukewarm water
1 cup unsalted butter, at room temperature
5 eggs, separated, at room temperature
¼ cup sugar
5 tablespoons coarsely ground polenta
½ teaspoon salt
½ teaspoon grated lemon zest
½ teaspoon cream of tartar
2 cups blackberries or other berries, for garnish

1. Preheat the oven to 375°F. Grease and flour a 2-quart-tube baking pan.
2. Dissolve the yeast in the water and let stand until foamy, about 10 minutes.
3. Using an electric mixer or a hand whisk, cream the butter in a large bowl and add the egg yolks (one at a time) until well blended. Add the sugar, mixing well.
4. Stir the yeast and the polenta into the butter-egg mixture, add ¼ teaspoon salt and the lemon zest and stir until all ingredients are thoroughly blended.
5. Using an electric mixer or hand whisk, beat the egg whites with the re-

maining ¼ teaspoon salt and the cream of tartar in a large bowl until stiff peaks have formed. Gently fold the whites into the egg batter. Pour the mixture into the prepared pan.

6. Bake for 45 minutes. Remove from pan and invert onto a cooling rack and let cool to room temperature. Top with blackberries and serve.

VARIATIONS: For a less coarse texture, use finely ground polenta (cornmeal).

MAKE AHEAD: This cake can be prepared 1 day before, wrapped in plastic or foil and stored in the refrigerator. Bring to room temperature before serving.

Torta di noci con crema al caffè
Walnut Coffee Tart with Espresso Cream

Tuscans love coffee, and what better dessert to accompany a steaming cup of espresso than a coffee tart with coffee cream? With all that caffeine, it's a wonder anyone sleeps at night here.

MAKES
ONE 10-INCH
TART (8 SLICES)

TIME: 1 HOUR
PLUS 1½ HOURS
COOLING AND
REFRIGERATION

LEVEL:
MODERATE

THE TART

1 recipe Basic *Pasta Frolla* (see page 34)
½ cup sugar
¼ cup brewed espresso
3 eggs, at room temperature
½ cup honey
4 tablespoons unsalted butter, melted and cooled
1½ cups chopped walnuts

THE CREAM

½ cup heavy cream
2 tablespoons confectioners' sugar
1 tablespoon brewed espresso
Coffee ice cream as an accompaniment
Ground espresso, for dusting

1. To make the tart, preheat oven to 400°F. Roll the *pasta frolla* into a 12-inch-diameter circle and arrange in a 10-inch-diameter tart pan with

removable bottom, pressing the excess against the sides. Line with foil, fill with raw rice, dried beans or commercial pie weights and bake for 10 minutes. Remove foil and weights and let cool.

2. Stir the sugar into the coffee until dissolved. Whisk in the eggs (one at a time); whisk in the honey and butter.

3. Toast the walnuts in a 350°F oven for 7 minutes. Stir them into the egg-honey mixture. Pour into the cooled crust.

4. Bake until set, about 30 minutes. Cool to room temperature, then refrigerate for 1 hour.

5. To make the cream, whip the cream and the sugar in a large bowl into soft peaks. Add the brewed coffee and beat to stiff peaks.

6. Remove the sides of the tart pan and cut into slices. Serve with a scoop of coffee ice cream dusted with espresso.

VARIATIONS: For less of a caffeine fix, use decaffeinated espresso.

MAKE AHEAD: The tart can be made the day before, covered with foil and refrigerated until ready to use.

Torta di cioccolata caramellata
Chocolate Truffle Loaf with Caramel Sauce

MAKES ONE
8½-INCH LOAF
(8 SLICES)

TIME:
1 HOUR PLUS
OVERNIGHT
REFRIGERATION

LEVEL:
MODERATE

This recipe comes from Donatella Masotti, who runs a wedding catering service in Stiava. I met her at the wedding of my friends, Silvia and Claudio, and asked to have this heavenly recipe.

Since both cake and sauce need to be refrigerated before serving (the sauce for one hour; the cake overnight) it is an ideal dessert for the chronically short of time. The entire confection can be prepared the day before.

THE LOAF

1 pound unsweetened chocolate, chopped
¼ cup sugar dissolved in ½ cup boiling water
½ cup unsalted butter, at room temperature
2 cups heavy cream
3 egg yolks, at room temperature
¼ cup confectioners' sugar
1 teaspoon vanilla extract

THE SAUCE

⅔ cup sugar

2 tablespoons heavy cream

1 tablespoon unsalted butter

1 teaspoon grated lemon zest

2 teaspoons lemon zest, for garnish

1. To make the loaf, line an 8½ x 4½ x 2½-inch loaf pan with plastic wrap (dampen pan so wrap sticks better).
2. Place the chocolate, sugar-water mixture, and butter in the top of a double boiler and cook over simmering water until melted.
3. Using a fork, beat ½ cup of the cream and egg yolks until smooth, and add to the chocolate mixture. Cook, stirring constantly, until the temperature reaches 160°F on a candy thermometer. Remove from heat and set in a shallow pan of ice water. Stir until mixture cools to room temperature.
4. Beat remaining 1½ cups cream, the sugar and vanilla in a large bowl until soft peaks form. Fold into cooled chocolate mixture and pour into prepared loaf pan. Cover and refrigerate overnight.
5. To make sauce, cook the sugar, cream, butter and grated zest in a medium-size saucepan over low heat until the sugar is dissolved and mixture is smooth. Cool, cover and refrigerate 1 hour.
6. Unmold loaf and peel off the plastic wrap. Cut into slices and serve with a ribbon of sauce. Garnish with the zest.

MAKE AHEAD: The sauce can be made the day before and refrigerated in a sealed container until ready to use.

Torta della mamma con fragole
Mom's Almond Tart with Raspberry Sauce

MAKES
ONE 9-INCH
TART (8 SLICES)

TIME:
1¼ HOURS

LEVEL:
MODERATE

I'm not sure how this tart came to be called della mamma *(Mamma's Tart). Undoubtedly, the name was assigned by a man and, where Tuscan men are concerned, everything belongs to Mamma. A delicate, flaky creation, this almond and raspberry-flavored tart pairs especially well with vanilla ice cream.*

Unsalted butter or cooking spray, for greasing
½ cup unsalted butter, at room temperature
1¼ cups sugar
1 cup almond paste
3 eggs, at room temperature
¼ teaspoon almond extract
1 tablespoon kirsch
⅓ teaspoon baking powder
¼ cup cake flour
Confectioners' sugar, for dusting
2 cups fresh or frozen raspberries
2 tablespoons kirsch

1. Preheat the oven to 350°F. Grease a 9-inch-round cake pan and line with waxed paper.
2. Place butter, ¾ cup sugar and almond paste in the bowl of a food processor and pulse until well blended. Add eggs (one at a time), the almond extract and the kirsch, pulsing until just smooth.
3. Transfer to a bowl and sift in the baking powder and flour, and mix until well blended. Scrape into prepared pan.
4. Bake for 45 minutes. Remove from oven, cool and invert onto a platter. Dust with sugar.
5. Reserve ½ cup raspberries. Purée the remaining 1½ cups raspberries and remaining ½ cup sugar in a food processor. Strain, add the kirsch, chill and drizzle over slices of the tart. Garnish with the reserved berries.

MAKE AHEAD: The sauce can be made the day before and stored, refrigerated, in a sealed container. Add the kirsch just before using.

Torta alla crema di amaretto con pesche fresche
Amaretto Cream Cake with Fresh Peaches

What better flavor combination that almonds and fresh peaches! My brother and I invented this tart one night when his cooking-school friends were coming over, and we found, at the last minute, that the fresh figs we needed for our intended dessert were not to be had. We quickly checked the larder and found what every dessert-focused household always has on hand: amaretto, almonds, and heavy cream. Fortunately, we also had a crate of fresh peaches that Paolo was planning on turning into preserves the next day.

SERVES 8

TIME: 2 HOURS

LEVEL: MODERATE

THE CAKE

Unsalted butter, for greasing
Flour, for dusting
6 tablespoons unsalted butter, at room temperature
¼ cup sugar
¼ cup packed brown sugar
1 teaspoon grated orange zest
1 egg, at room temperature
¼ cup fresh-squeezed orange juice
¼ cup honey
¼ cup milk
2 tablespoons amaretto
½ cup ground almonds
1 cup cake flour
1 teaspoon baking powder
½ teaspoon salt

THE GLAZE

4 tablespoons orange juice
3 tablespoons honey
2 tablespoons amaretto

THE TOPPINGS

2 tablespoons lightly toasted sliced almonds
3–4 large peaches, pealed, pitted and thinly sliced

3 tablespoons sugar
2 teaspoons lemon juice

THE AMARETTO CREAM

1 cup heavy cream
2 tablespoons sugar
2 tablespoons amaretto

1. To make the cake, preheat the oven to 350°F. Grease and flour a 9-inch round cake pan.
2. Cream the butter, sugars and orange zest in a large bowl until smooth and fluffy. Blend in the egg, and stirring, add the orange juice, honey, milk and amaretto. Beat until all ingredients are well blended. Add the almonds, flour, baking powder and salt and mix well. Spoon into prepared cake pan.
3. Bake until tester comes out clean, 30 to 40 minutes.
4. To make the glaze, combine the orange juice, honey and amaretto in a small saucepan. Boil, then simmer until reduced to ¼ cup. Cool to room temperature.
5. Remove the cake from the oven, transfer to a wire rack and let cool for 15 minutes and turn out onto a plate. Spoon glaze over warm cake. Sprinkle the almonds over the glazed cake and let sit 30 minutes.
6. Meanwhile, combine peaches with the sugar and lemon juice. Set aside.
7. To make the amaretto cream, whip the heavy cream, the sugar and amaretto to stiff peaks. Serve wedges of warm cake with peaches and the amaretto cream.

VARIATIONS: The recipe can be doubled, baked in a tube pan and served with the peaches mounded in the center.

MAKE AHEAD: The glaze can be prepared the day before and stored, refrigerated, in a sealed container. Bring to room temperature before using.

CHAPTER EIGHT

Fruit Desserts, Fruit Preserves and Cordials

One Swallow Does Not Spring Make

Tuscan life is dictated by the seasons. Apart from what appears on the table, which adheres strictly to dictums such as when certain fish swim by, when olives are ripe enough to pick and when the ground breaks forth with new spring onions, seasons dictate which types of lights to place on cemetery tombs, which types of card games to play at night in the local caffè, and which types of songs are heard on the radio.

Spring is the season for wild asparagus, new cheeses, music festivals, short bouncy hair cuts and picnics. In fact, Easter Monday is official picnic day in Tuscany. Wherever you go, you see families eating at tables set upon the grass of lush olive groves, surrounded by mountains of food ranging from homemade lasagne to grilled steaks to crispy potatoes roasted in olive oil. Children play on makeshift swings hung on tree branches, women sit in shady alcoves smoking and playing cards, men lie in hammocks listening to soccer games.

I still remember my grandfather spending the week before Easter preparing for picnic season, making the swings out of old wooden planks that would then be hung by the braided cords he had made from skeins of hemp. Nonno would get so excited, choosing special flasks of wine and cleaning the rattan baskets we used to carry what amounted to the greater part of our kitchen and dining room supplies.

The women of the family took care of the cooking, and what a lot of cooking it was. Culinarily speaking, the Easter season comprises Good Friday, Holy Saturday, Easter Sunday and—since the Monday after Easter is a holiday—Monday picnic, which goes by the name *merendino* even though *merendino* means "snack" and this meal is anything but.

My grandmother (one of the world's foremost carnivores) would spend two or three days in the hen house, observing and assessing each of the hens and roosters in preparation for deciding which ones to kill. I would always accompany her on these evaluative jaunts, tears streaming down my face for "my dearest Fernanda," or "my beloved Agata." But that was only the beginning because then we would move on to the poor rabbits.

My mother made the cakes—a week's worth of melting chocolate, sifting flour and sieving ricotta. Easter cake recipes are dictated by tradition: There's the dove-shaped sweetbreads, the chocolate and rice cakes with edges scalloped to resemble medieval castles, and the delicate almond tarts. By the time she was finished, our larder looked like a pastry shop, with cake after cake arranged side by side on the shelves.

Papa was in charge of assembling the necessary ingredients, of strolling up and down the garden rows to pick the most perfect of vegetables, of climbing up to the orchard and bringing back the most succulent plums, of buying the cheeses from the village shepherd, of selecting the salamis and prosciuttos. Papa's job was to make sure we had enough food to make it through the weekend without starving.

All that remains of this original group is my mother and grandmother. The rest of the duties have been assumed by me and my lazy brother, whose only real area of expertise lies in packing the car. "Let's just buy the food from Malva," he says every year as we get ready for the marathon cooking fest. Malva owns the village rosticcerìa, where you can buy freshly made lasagne, roast pork, sautéed greens, stuffed vegetables and other fairly well prepared foods. "I have better things to do than spend all this time making chocolate rice cakes." What things exactly have never been demonstrated.

This Easter, Nonna Angelina has invited Don Romiro, the village priest, to join us for Monday *merendino*. Having been transferred here only seven months ago from his home in northern Italy (in a small village just outside Turin), Don Romiro is anxious to learn about our local traditions. He is very young, however, and his command of the social graces is somewhat lacking, so much of the conversation between him and my grandmother involves saying the rosary, which is more than fine as far as Nonna is concerned.

Yesterday, before anyone had even opened their eyes, she was marching through the house, getting everyone ready for Easter Mass. "*Vergognati*," I heard her yelling at my son, who was out in back practicing his soccer kicks. "It's Easter Sunday. You should be in Church, giving thanks for the wonderful miracle of Jesus' resurrection."

Eventually, she managed to get us all properly dressed ("a hat," she always tells me, "you should be wearing a hat") and over to the church, where the local chorus had prepared a rousing version of Vivaldi's *Missa Solemnis*. After the celebration was over, Don Romiro accompanied us to the local pastry shop for coffee. *"Allora,* Angelina," he said eagerly over a particularly creamy *babà* (I waited to see whether she would tell him he had spilled a dollop on his cassock, but nothing). *"Siamo pronti per la merenda?"* ("So, Angelina, are we ready for the picnic?")

The picnic site is in the upper part of my village of Stiava, on a gently rounded hill where my family continues to maintain an olive grove consisting of 230 trees. As olive groves go, this one is rather new. In fact, around 1000 A.D., Stiava was surrounded by the Mediterranean sea. When the waters receded, a fertile gulf remained and eventually olive trees and vineyards were planted on the hillsides. The oil produced by these trees is among the best in the region; dusty green in color and with a distinctive taste rendered by the salt sea air.

To get here takes about fifteen minutes from church steps to unloading the car. When I was young and the road up the hill had yet to be created, we came in a horse and buggy, the graying horse routinely reluctant to haul us up the last few hundred yards of steep climb. The groves are terraced in a series of wide, well-maintained steps. On days like today, the steps are private restaurants, each olive grove hosting one large family.

As soon as we arrive, my grandmother arranges the plaid throws on the two long tables set head to head. After more than twenty years of use, the tables are in severe need of repair, and I can't help thinking of my father and grandfather, neither of whom would ever have allowed such a display of negligence.

Today's menu consists of an appetizer of prosciutto, salami, various cheeses, olives and marinated vegetables. Then will come Nonna's *tordelli* (large meat ravioli), which she got up at 4 in the morning to prepare. Having abstained from meat for the entire 40 days of Lent (one of the few remaining people to do so), she has still not made up for the deficit, even given yesterday—Easter Sunday's—*bacchanalia*. My cousins have brought a roasted pork filet with balsamic-onion sauce, and I have made chicken cooked *al mattone,* which means "under a brick" and refers to the weight placed on the split halves to flatten them for grilling. My sister-in-law, Giada, comes from Sicily and has prepared two typical Sicilian tarts. When Nonna first saw them, she was not pleased.

"Ombretta," she whispered rather loudly to my mother. "This *merendino* is a Tuscan tradition. What are Sicilian tarts doing here? I thought you were making the desserts.

Delicious as they are, the tarts have little to do with Nonna's reaction. Fact is, poor Giada can do nothing right where Nonna is concerned. That she is perfectly lovely with a warm and giving personality does nothing to counter her having come from Sicily and, hence, not a good match for my brother, who Nonna describes as *"un fusto"* ("a fine figure of a man") a description with which my modest brother heartily concurs.

"We have four chocolate and rice tarts," my mother reassured her. "But you should at least taste a small slice of Giada's. Otherwise, she is going to be very upset."

I don't think so. Giada is remarkably resilient when it comes to fending off Tuscan prejudices regarding her heritage. But then again, she would have to be, given the frequency of their demonstration.

As we make our way through the excellent appetizer (the prosciutto comes from a local Stiavese who raises one pig each year and always gives us half a prosciutto as well as a few salamis), the talk is fast, loud and plenty. Anyone observing us would be forced to conclude that this was a reunion of people who had not seen each other in quite some time. The reality is that my immediate family eats together twice every day, and our cousins join us at least every other Sunday.

At one point, Don Romiro reaches deep into his mantle of shyness and addresses the table-at-large. "Did everyone read about the results at San Remo?" he says hesitantly. It is a good topic for a debut performance. The Festival of San Remo is Italy's most popular music festival and takes place one week each year in early spring. Its defining moment comes on the last day, when festival organizers choose the "Musical Performance of the Year." This year's winner was Annalisa Minetti, a beautiful blind model-turned-singer whose popularity soared after a recent set of appearances on national television.

"I am so happy that poor girl won," Don Romiro says.

"Me too," adds my grandmother, tossing the *tordelli* with cheese. "She really deserved it."

"I don't agree," says my contentious cousin Giovanni. "I think the contest has turned into a ridiculous battle for who has the most effective gimmick."

My grandmother gives him a sharp look. The intent is clear: You are talking to a Man of God. Be more respectful.

Giovanni is oblivious. "Minetti won purely because she is blind," he continues. "Being blind is apparently all the rage."

"Giovanni!"

"That's a fairly heartless thing to say," I tell him. "But there's no question you have a point."

"Giovanni definitely has a point," my brother comes to his rescue. "Last year the winner was Andrea Bocelli, another blind man who, as far as I'm concerned, really didn't deserve it—not because he's not a great singer. The winning singer is supposed to perform a popular, accessible piece of music that, as festival organizers put it, 'can be sung by everyone from housewives to carpenters.' The only person who can sing Bocelli's songs is Luciano Pavarotti."

Truth be told, Bocelli's music is quite difficult, although that hasn't stopped millions of people all over the world from straining their vocal cords in imitation of him.

"*Io Partirò,*" is the beautiful and now internationally famous love song for which he won the award and later recorded with Sarah Brightman. In fact, one might even say that Bocelli's performance forever changed the face of the San Remo from a festival focusing on music to one revolving around the personality of the performers, especially those who demonstrate the promise of international marketability.

Giovanni's next comment makes me realize how true that point of view may be. "Did you hear the interview with Minetti on RAI 2 the day before her performance? It went on for 45 minutes, during which she laboriously told the story of how she started to lose her sight two years ago, and the illness progressed until one morning when she woke up she was completely blind. The only problem was, she wrenched more emotion from that story than Hollywood did from the Titanic."

"The part I liked," says my brother, "is when they showed how she has been able to continue her modeling career. Designers fit her ears with special microphones through which they give her detailed directions about where to walk. That's how she was able to take part in last year's Miss Italia competition."

I hadn't known any of this, but it's clear from the enthusiastic discussion of Minetti's trials and tribulations that she is a worthy successor to

Bocelli, whose own courageous story won over last year's festival audience. The problem is, there's more discussion of the story than the performance.

"What about Giampiero Bertoli?" Giovanni continues, referring to the 1993 winner. "I don't care what anybody says. Bertoli won because he came out in a wheelchair."

"Not true," says my grandmother. "Bertoli is one of Italy's best singers." She makes a motion for everyone to pass down their plates.

Giovanni is not to be silenced. "Well, then how about Aleandro Baldi, the blind man who won in 1992?" He signals my grandmother to give him a heftier portion of *tordelli*.

"And," says my brother, "let's not forget Padre Cionfoli, who thwarted the Church's dictum about friars participating in music festivals and won because everyone was so caught up in the melodrama." He pokes my grandmother in the ribs. "When they threatened to divest him, he got married and left Italy."

"*Ora basta!*" roars my grandmother on Don Romiro's behalf. ("Enough now!")

But Don Romiro seems to be having the time of his life. "I'm sooo glad you invited me," he says, dusting his plate with grated Parmigiano. "*Complimenti,* Angelina. These *tordelli* are the best I've ever tasted."

As the meal proceeds, the shy, quiet priest decides to make yet another foray into conversational boldness. "Did you hear about the Duchess of York?" he says between enthusiastic bites of roast pork. "The priest from Castagneto Carducci told me she has moved to the Gherardesca Castle in Bolgheri near Livorno. Apparently, she has fallen in love with Tuscany and spends more and more time here."

"That will keep her slim," says my grandmother. "As long as she lived in England, she had no chance, what with all those fried meats and cream-soaked vegetables."

We make our way through four more courses, and then finally, it's time for everyone to get up from the table and stretch. Giovanni goes back to the car for his accordian, and before long, he is playing songs from this year's festival with Don Romiro serving as lead singer and enjoying his newfound position of social blade. My grandmother does not completely approve; a priest should behave like a priest, *per Dio.*

But later, the two of them can be seen sitting under the shade of the large fig tree, saying the rosary. "Five," my brother whispers into my ear.

On outings like this, he always keeps track of how many times Nonna recites the rosary. I think he missed the one she and Don Romiro recited together in the back seat of the car on route here, but I am too full even to talk.

Full or not, however, I soon hear my mother banging a spoon on the back of a pot, which means it's time for dessert. Everyone zooms back to the table like bees seeking honey. My sister-in-law, Giada, stands on one side, ready to slice her *cassata* made with ricotta and dried fruit.

"*Niente per me, grazie,*" says my grandmother when Giada asks for her plate. ("Nothing for me, thank you.")

"Believe me, Giada, if this were a Tuscan tart, I would surely include it in my book," I say to cover Nonna's rudeness. "It is delicious."

My mother exhibits her usual degree of diplomacy, holding back her rice and chocolate cake until Giada's dessert has received its share of applause. It is very difficult to live the way we do in Tuscany, I think to myself, thick in the embrace of family whose members are not chosen, like friends, for their pleasing personalities. "Family is like the seasons," an old proverb maintains. "There's abundance and harvest and darkness and renewal."

And then the unthinkable happens. Don Romiro takes charge of the situation and places half of his *cassata* on my grandmother's plate. "Taste some Angelina," he says exuberantly. "You won't believe your palate."

We all turn toward the head of the table—Giada included—none of us having any idea what will happen next. If Nonna acts true to form, she will not only push the plate away and refuse to take even the smallest bite, but will say something terribly dismissive in the process. But then again, we all know how she feels about the Church, and, on this day, in this minute, Don Romiro is the Church's personal emissary.

"*Allora,*" she says, picking up her fork. "I suppose I will take a small bite."

It is the smallest bite any of us have ever seen this 93-year-old gourmand take of anything, but finally, it makes its way successfully into her mouth. "Ummmm," she says, looking straight at Giada. "Good!" We all breathe a sigh of relief.

"You see?" Don Romiro beams, "I told you."

But the moment is short-lived. "What kind of ricotta did you use," she says to Giada and everyone turns once again to stare. She's going to blow it, I think to myself. "Was it from here? Tuscan? The good sheep's milk variety? Or was it that half and half cow's milk mixture used by Southerners?"

Giada puts down her plate and smiles broadly. "I used ricotta from your shepherd, Leando," she says, patting Nonna's hand. "Everyone says it is the best ricotta in the world. Is that the one you mean?"

Thank God for Giada, I think. Someone else might have smashed the cake in my grandmother's face.

"Yes, *cara,* that is the right one to use." She takes another bite. And then another one. And then she asks for another slice. "Very good," she says. "I would not have thought Southerners knew how to make such good desserts," she says.

Everyone laughs. Both from relief and amazement at her incredible arrogance. "What were you expecting," said Don Romiro when he and I later laughed about this incident. "Your grandmother is 93, and though she might make small changes here and there, we should not delude ourselves that anything grand will come of it. After all, the presence of a swallow does mean it is spring!"

<hr/>

Fruit Desserts, Fruit Preserves and Cordials

Tuscans agree on very little, but all would concur with the concept of seasonality—that vegetables and especially fruits should be grown locally and, hence, only used in certain seasons. It is simply not a good idea to make a strawberry tart in winter, not because strawberries are unavailable (because we do, in fact, import them from other countries), but because they are out of season and the flavor is just not right.

Apart from the logistics of traveling great distances, which necessitates their being picked green, strawberries consumed when you are bundled into a woolen sweater taste completely different from those enjoyed under the hot summer sun. Not to mention differences in flavor between strawberries grown in native soil as opposed to those grown in Chile or Tunisia. Not to mention even further how compromised one's enjoyment of strawberries becomes when they cost three dollars per pint because they came from Greece in February as opposed to the seventy-five cents per pint charged by Maurizio at the local market come July.

To Tuscan cooks, seasonality is second only to the freshness that has, from time immemorial, served as the cuisine's defining factor. Tuscans buy their produce much the same way as they have always done: at the peak of freshness and from the market in their town's central piazza. *"Chi lascia la strada vecchia per quella nuova, sa quello che lascia ma non sa quel che trova!"* ("He who leaves the old road for the new, knows what he leaves but has no idea what he will find.")

All of which, of course, explains why every single dish is just so incredibly wonderful.

Fruit Desserts, Fruit Preserves and Cordials

Sformato di fiori di lavanda e salsa tiepida di fichi
Lavender Custard with Warm Fig Sauce

Composta di albicocche e ciliege
Apricot and Cherry Compote

Torta di mele sfondata
Fig-Glazed Apple Tart

Savoiardi e pesche bianche
White Peach Custard Mold

Uvaspina e rabarbaro croccante
Gooseberry and Rhubarb Crunch

Nidi di pere caramellate al cioccolato
Chocolate Pears with Caramelized Sugar Nests

Elisir all' albicocca
Apricot Elixir

Marmellata di carote, pere e miele
Carrot, Pear and Honey Preserves

Pere candite
Candied Pears

Frittata alle fragole
Strawberry Frittata

Aranci fritti
Batter-Fried Orange Segments

Zuppa di fragole
Cold Strawberry Soup

Torta di lamponi e crema
Raspberry and Custard Tart

Sformato di fiori di lavanda e salsa tiepida di fichi
Lavender Custard with Warm Fig Sauce

SERVES 6

TIME: 45
MINUTES PLUS
2 HOURS
INFUSION AND
3 HOURS
REFRIGERATION

LEVEL:
MODERATE

With its brilliant blue color and sensual, heady scent, lavender carpets the fields of Tuscany. Its name was coined during the Middle Age and derives from the Latin verb lavare, *which means "to wash," a reference to the fact that ancient cultures routinely used the scented flowers to scent their baths. In my grandmother's day, sprigs of lavender were routinely folded between the bed linens to impart a sense of freshness and purity.*

Lavender is not very well known in culinary circles, and this is a great shame. Since lavender belongs to the same family as mint, thyme, sage and oregano, it pairs well with tender meats such as lamb and veal and enhances the sweet flavor of vanilla ice cream and almond cantucci, *among other dessert preparations. In the following recipe, its flavor is folded into a custard mold and enhanced by the sweetness of warm figs.*

THE CUSTARD

2 cups heavy cream
3 tablespoons crushed lavender flowers
6 eggs, separated, at room temperature
1 cup sugar
1 envelope (2¼ teaspoons) unflavored gelatin
¼ cup cold water
½ teaspoon salt
½ teaspoon cream of tartar

THE SAUCE

12 fresh figs, stemmed, peeled and halved
⅔ cup sugar

1. Place the heavy cream in a large, heavy-gauge saucepan and bring to a boil over a very low heat.
2. Stir in the lavender flowers, remove from heat and steep the infusion for 2 hours. Strain the cream through a fine sieve and discard the flowers.
3. Using an electric mixer or a wooden spoon, beat the egg yolks and the

sugar in a large bowl until smooth and pale, about 5 minutes with the mixer (15 minutes by hand). Gradually pour in the cream and stir to blend. Transfer the mixture to a sauce pan.

4. Sprinkle the gelatin over the water in a small bowl and let sit for 1 minute to soften. Stir the gelatin until completely dissolved and then add to the saucepan. Cook over very low heat, stirring constantly, until thickened, about 10 minutes. Do not let the mixture boil. Remove from heat and let cool to room temperature.

5. Using an electric mixer or hand whisk, beat the egg whites and the salt in a large bowl until foamy. Add the cream of tartar and beat until stiff peaks form. Fold the whites into the cream until just blended. Pour the mixture into 6 ramekins and refrigerate for 3 hours.

6. Meanwhile make the sauce. Place 16 fig halves and the sugar in a saucepan and cook over medium heat for 15 minutes, stirring occasionally. Pass through a food mill and return to the pot. Heat through.

7. Just before serving, drizzle a tablespoonful of warm fig sauce onto each plate. Using a spatula remove the custards from the ramekins and center on the sauce. Drizzle 1 teaspoon sauce over the custard and garnish with the remaining slices of fresh figs.

MAKE AHEAD: The cream sauce can be infused early in the day and stored in a sealed container in the refrigerator until ready to use. The fig sauce can be prepared 1 day before and stored, refrigerated, in a sealed container.

Composta di albicocche e ciliege
Apricot and Cherry Compote

Apricots were cited by Apicus in ancient culinary texts as "gifts from the gods." Throughout Tuscany, they are used in both savory recipes such as pork with apricot sauce, apricot focaccia, and desserts such as this simple compote, which works very well on its own or can be served as an accompaniment to ice cream or custards.

SERVES 4

TIME:
30 MINUTES

LEVEL: EASY

½ cup sugar
¼ cup confectioners' sugar
½ teaspoon vanilla extract

1 cup water
1 cup dry white wine
2 tablespoons grated orange zest
2 pounds apricots, halved and thinly sliced
1 pound dark cherries, washed and pitted
3 tablespoons cognac plus 4 tablespoons, for drizzling
Fresh mint sprigs, for garnish

1. In a large, heavy-gauge saucepan, combine the sugars, vanilla, water, wine and orange zest, and cook over very low heat for 10 minutes, stirring constantly.
2. Add the apricots, cherries and cognac, and simmer until fruits are tender, about 10 minutes. Remove from heat and transfer to a bowl. Cool to room temperature. Serve with a drizzle of cognac. Garnish with the mint.

VARIATIONS: Other combinations of fruit can be used instead of the apricots and cherries.

MAKE AHEAD: The entire compote can be made early in the day and left at room temperature in a covered bowl until ready to use. Drizzle with cognac just before serving.

Torta di mele sfondata
Fig-Glazed Apple Tart

MAKES
ONE 12-INCH
TART
(10 SLICES)

TIME:
1½ HOURS

LEVEL:
MODERATE

If you are ever in Marina di Massa (a coastal village in Lucca province) and craving extraordinary food, head directly for Da Ricca, a gorgeous restaurant right on the water with views of the Ligurian Islands, Palmaria and Il Tino. Every aspect of this very upscale dining experience reflects attention of the owner Riccardo to the most minute detail—especially the menu, which is his personal approach to pairing classic Tuscan dishes with an artist's sense of presentation. My favorite is this simple apple tart, made with both red and yellow apples and expertly glazed with fig preserves. Ask to be served by Franco, an extremely funny waiter who is a dead ringer for Dustin Hoffmann.

Unsalted butter, for greasing
3 medium red apples, peeled, halved and thinly sliced

2 medium yellow apples, peeled, halved and thinly sliced
4 tablespoons lemon juice
3 eggs
1 cup sugar
½ cup unsalted butter, melted
1 tablespoon grated lemon zest
2 tablespoons cognac
7 tablespoons bread flour
1 tablespoon baking powder
3 tablespoons fig or apricot preserves
Fresh mint sprigs, for garnish

1. Preheat the oven to 350°F. Grease a 12-inch-diameter springform pan.
2. Place the red apples in a large bowl of water acidated with 2 tablespoons lemon juice. (The water should just cover the apple slices.) Place the yellow apples in another bowl of water acidated with the remaining 2 tablespoons lemon juice. Drain before using.
3. Using an electric mixer or hand whisk, beat the eggs and sugar in a large bowl until smooth, creamy and pale, about 5 minutes with the mixer (15 minutes by hand). Stir in the melted butter and lemon zest. Pour in the cognac and stir until well blended.
4. Sift in the flour and baking powder and stir until a thick batter has formed.
5. Add the red apples and stir until completely coated. Transfer to the prepared baking pan and arrange the yellow apples on top in overlapping spirals.
6. Bake for 45 minutes.
7. Meanwhile melt the fig preserves in a saucepan over very low heat.
8. When the tart is baked, remove from the oven, and immediately brush with the melted preserves. Remove the sides of the pan, let cool to room temperature and serve, garnished with mint.

VARIATIONS: Pears can be used in place of the apples. If possible, combine a sweet pear such as a Williams and a tarter variety such as bosc.

MAKE AHEAD: The tart can be made early in the day and covered with a cloth until ready to serve.

Savoiardi e pesche bianche
White Peach Custard Mold

MAKES 1 QUART

TIME:
30 MINUTES
PLUS CHILLING

LEVEL:
MODERATE

Throughout Tuscany, peaches are one of the most beloved summer fruits—especially white peaches, tinged with a blushing red color emanating from the pit. Their flavor mixes sweetness with musk, their scent is reminiscent of freshly picked roses. White-peach season is about one month long, from the end of July to the beginning of September, during which time this extraordinary fruit is sliced and diced into every possible form—from peach-steeped liqueurs to fried peach rings to peach sauces for grilled fish. This white peach and custard mold is one of my very favorites.

2 pounds ripe white or yellow peaches, peeled and thinly sliced
2 tablespoons lemon juice
1 cup light rum
1 cup peach or apricot nectar
30 ladyfingers
Unsalted butter, for greasing
1 envelope (2¼ teaspoons) unflavored gelatin
¼ cup plus 2 tablespoons water
4 tablespoons unsalted butter, at room temperature
4 tablespoons sugar
1 teaspoon vanilla extract
2 tablespoons apricot preserve
1 cup Basic Custard (see page 34)
1 cup whipped heavy cream
16–20 white peach slices, for garnish

1. Place the peaches in a large bowl of water aciduated with the lemon juice. (The water should just cover the peaches.) Drain before using.
2. In a medium bowl, blend the rum and peach nectar. Briefly dip the ladyfingers into the juice, turning to coat both sides.
3. Grease a 1-quart pudding mold. Stand the ladyfingers vertically around the edge of the mold, sides touching. Reserve the rest.
4. Sprinkle the gelatin over ¼ cup water to soften for 1 minute. Stir until completely dissolved.
5. Melt the butter in a large saucepan over low heat. Add the sliced peaches, sugar, vanilla, the remaining 2 tablespoons water, the pre-

serves and the gelatin. Cover with a lid and cook until the peaches are completely softened, about 10 minutes. Remove from heat and let cool to room temperature.

6. Pass the cooled peaches through a food mill and place in a bowl.
7. Fold the whipped cream into the custard.
8. Pour ⅓ of the peach mixture into the prepared mold. Top with ⅓ of the custard and a layer of ladyfingers. Repeat the layers until all the ingredients have been used. Top with the remaining ladyfingers and refrigerate for 3 hours before serving.
9. Dip bottom of the mold for 30 seconds into a bowl of hot water. Place a large plate over the top of the mold, and holding one hand over the plate, turn both the mold and plate upside down and unmold over a round serving platter. Serve, garnished with fresh sliced peaches.

VARIATIONS: Apricots or apples can be substituted for the peaches.

MAKE AHEAD: The peaches can be cooked 1 day before and stored, refrigerated, in a sealed container until ready to purée.

<hr>

Uvaspina e rabarbaro croccante
Gooseberry and Rhubarb Crunch

While gooseberries have grown in various parts of Tuscany for years, their thorny stems have kept them out of the culinary spotlight. Only lately have chefs discovered their similarity to white grapes (in fact, the word uvaspina *means "thorny grapes") and begun positioning these unusual fruits in salads and desserts. Following is the Tuscan version of a fruit cobbler with a twist: The crust is spiced with ginger and made especially crunchy with sliced almonds.*

SERVES 4

TIME: 1 HOUR

LEVEL: MODERATE

Unsalted butter, for greasing
1 cup gooseberries, stemmed, washed and drained
1 cup sliced rhubarb
½ cup sugar
3 tablespoons water
½ cup cake flour
4 tablespoons unsalted butter, chilled
2 tablespoons rolled oats, lightly toasted

2 tablespoons thinly sliced almonds, lightly toasted
½ teaspoon powdered ginger
2 tablespoons brown sugar
1 pint vanilla gelato or ice cream

1. Preheat the oven to 400°F. Grease an approximately 11 x 7-inch glass or porcelain baking dish.
2. Place the gooseberries, rhubarb, sugar and water in a medium-size enamel or stainless steel saucepan and cook, over medium heat until the fruit has softened, about 10 minutes. Remove from heat.
3. Remove the fruit with a slotted spoon and arrange on the bottom of the prepared baking dish.
4. Place the flour in a small bowl and using a pastry blender cut in the butter until a crumbly mixture has formed. Blend in the oatmeal, sliced almonds, ginger and brown sugar and pour the crumbly mixture over the fruit.
5. Bake until the crust is lightly golden in color, about 25 minutes. Remove from heat and spoon the mixture to individual plates. Serve with vanilla gelato.

VARIATIONS: White grapes can be substituted for the gooseberries.

Nidi di pere caramellate al cioccolato
Chocolate Pears with Caramelized Sugar Nests

SERVES 6

TIME: 1 HOUR

LEVEL: ADVANCED

This is a favorite dessert among our cooking school students. Yes, they love the flavor, but they love the preparation even more. They hover around the stove waiting for the sugar to reach the right degree of caramelization and then immediately whisk the pot to their work station. And there they stand, spinning their intricate webs of sugar. The finished desserts are all so beautiful that, when we finally get to the table, no one ever wants to eat.

Caramel cages are very easy to prepare once you get the hang of making them. Don't be afraid to try creating them. And make sure to have a candy thermometer on hand. When purchasing the pears, make sure to choose those that are equally sized and shaped.

6 medium pears, peeled, do not remove the stem
3 tablespoons sugar
1 pound bittersweet chocolate, cut into chunks
2 tablespoons Grand Marnier
5 tablespoons sugar
1 teaspoon water

1. Preheat the oven to 375°F. Arrange the pears vertically in 1 inch water in a 9-inch-round baking pan. If necessary to enable them to stand, cut a small slice from the bottom. Dust with sugar and cover tightly with aluminum foil. Bake until the pears are soft, about 30 minutes.
2. Meanwhile, place the chocolate in a medium double boiler and melt over very low heat. Stir in the Grand Marnier and remove from heat.
3. Using a slotted spoon, gently lift the pears from the cooking liquid and arrange them on a large platter. Spoon the cooking liquid over the pears and set aside to cool.
4. Transfer the cooled pears to individual plates. Discard the liquid.
5. Pour the warm melted chocolate randomly over the pears to create a partial coating.
6. To make the nests, place the sugar and water in a small, heavy-gauge skillet and melt over very low heat, stirring occasionally.
7. When the sugar turns into a clear syrup, turn the heat to medium and begin to cook down the syrup. Boil gently until the syrup turns pale yellow and the thermometer reads 300°F (hard crack stage), about 10 minutes. At this point a drop of syrup will form a brittle ball when dropped into ice water. Continue to cook until the syrup turns a dark amber color and the thermometer reads 340°F.
8. Remove the pan immediately from the heat and cool to 225°F at which point it will make long threads when dripped from a spoon.
9. Dip a wooden spoon into the syrup and raise it over your head. Working quickly, pinch off a piece of cooking syrup and begin pulling it down in threads. Wrap the thread around the pear and pull down another thread. Continue until each pear is surrounded by a free-form cage. Let the threads make wide circles around the pears for a more artistic effect. Serve immediately.

MAKE AHEAD: Caramel sugar can be made 1 to 2 months in advance and stored, refrigerated, in sealed containers. When ready to use, rewarm over low heat to pouring consistency.

Elisir all' albicocca
Apricot Elixir

MAKES 1 QUART
APRICOT ELIXIR

TIME: 1 HOUR

LEVEL: EASY

Tuscan monks (certosini) have always experimented with making potions and elixirs designed to cure illnesses and lengthen human life. To them we owe an extraordinary number of bitters, routinely consumed by Italians everywhere as after-dinner digestives. Elixirs are a completely different category of curative, sweet not bitter. They are employed for complaints ranging from migraines to arthritis. While I cannot guarantee the validity of any of these claims, I can assure you that for years to come, you will enjoy carting out this easy-to-make liqueur at the end of a satisfying meal.

2 pounds apricots, washed, drained and halved, pits reserved
1 pound sugar
1 inch of stick cinnamon, crumbled
2 cups grappa or vodka
1-quart jar with cap
1-quart glass bottle with cork

1. Place the halved apricots in the jar. Using a small hammer, crush the pits and remove the seeds.
2. Add the seeds to the jar along with sugar, cinnamon and alcohol. Seal with the cap and shake for 5 minutes until completely blended.
3. Let sit in a dark, cool place for 1 month, shaking the jar frequently during that period.
4. Pour the liqueur through a cheesecloth-lined funnel into the glass bottle. Seal with the cork and let age for 8 months.*

* The marinated apricots are wonderful as a topping for ice creams or custards. Once separated from the elixir, they will keep for 2 weeks in a tightly sealed container in the refrigerator.

MAKE AHEAD: The elixir will keep for 9 months in a cool, dark place.

Marmellata di carote, pere e miele
Carrot, Pear and Honey Preserves

The beauty of preserves is that they do exactly what their name suggests: preserve the past season. Our grandmothers used to make preserves year round to save the flavors of fruit and vegetables in beautifully decorated jars whose caps were "dressed" with rustic little pieces of cloth and tied with ribbons. The following recipe is for an unusual winter preserve that is delicious when spread on bread, especially over a slathering of fresh ricotta. It also works well as a pie filling, paired with grilled or roasted chicken or, as it is often used in Tuscany, an accompaniment for almond biscuits (cantucci).

MAKES 5 CUPS
PRESERVES

TIME:
1½ HOURS

LEVEL: EASY

1 pound carrots, scraped and finely chopped
1 pound ripe pears, peeled and cubed
Juice of 1 lemon, filtered
Five 1-cup jars with lids
1 cup water
1 cup sugar
1 cup honey
½ teaspoon ground coriander
8-quart soup pot, filled with boiling water

1. Place the carrots, pears, lemon juice and water in a 4-quart, heavy-gauge pot. Cook uncovered until the carrots are soft, about 20 minutes. Stir occasionally.
2. Meanwhile, sterilize the jars and caps in boiling water for 10 minutes.
3. Add the sugar, honey and coriander to the fruit and stir until the sugar is completely dissolved. Cook, stirring frequently, until all the liquid has evaporated, about 20 minutes.
4. Using tongs, remove the jars from the water and fill with preserves. Cap loosely and place in enough boiling water to cover the tops by 1 inch. Boil for 15 minutes. Remove with tongs and let cool to room temperature. Tighten the caps.

VARIATION: The recipe can be scaled up in direct proportion.

MAKE AHEAD: Stored in a cool, dry, dark place, this preserve will keep for up to 6 months.

Pere candite
Candied Pears

MAKES 1 POUND
CANDIED PEARS

TIME: 11 DAYS

LEVEL:
ADVANCED

Candied fruit is used throughout Tuscany as an ingredient, a garnish or a decoration on cakes and custards. It can also make a wonderful present when placed in decorative petit fours cups, layered between sheets of tissue and placed in an unusual gift box. I prefer eating them one after the other, quickly, and without having to share.

1 pound small pears, peeled and cored
Approximately 1 pound sugar
1 cup corn syrup

1. Place the pears in a large, heavy-gauge pot, and add enough hot water to cover by 2 inches. Cook over medium heat for 15 minutes. Using a slotted spoon, transfer the cooked pears to a shallow, 12-inch-round platter.
2. In a medium-size, heavy-gauge pot, simmer 7 tablespoons sugar and the corn syrup in 2½ cups water, stirring constantly until the sugar is completely dissolved, about 5 minutes.
3. Bring the sugar syrup to a boil, remove from the heat and immediately pour over the pears, immersing them completely. Let sit for 24 hours.
4. Using a slotted spoon, remove the pears and pour the syrup into a pot along with another 7 tablespoons sugar. Bring to a boil over very low heat, stirring constantly for 5 minutes. Place the pears back on the platter and pour the syrup over the pears until coated. Let sit for 24 hours.
5. Repeat Step 4 five more times.
6. Drain the syrup from the pears, place it in a large heavy gauge pot and add another 7 tablespoons sugar. Bring to a boil stirring constantly. Add the pears and cook for 5 minutes.
7. Remove from heat, cover and let sit for 48 hours.
8. Transfer the candied pears onto a cooling rack in a cool, dry place and let sit for 3 days, turning them several times during the process.

VARIATIONS: Spices such as nutmeg or cinnamon or allspice can be added in Step 2.

MAKE AHEAD: Store the candied pears in a sealed glass container layered between sheets of waxed paper. They will keep for up to 3 months.

Frittata alle fragole
Strawberry Frittata

Frittatas have always solved the age-old Tuscan question: What to make tonight? There are so many types of frittatas, in fact, that whole books could be written about them. Why not ? I ask myself. From savory to sweet, frittatas can be served hot, warm, cold or skewered along with vegetables and fruits. If cut into small strips and tossed with sauce it can pass for the famous trippa falsa (false tripe); if mixed with vegetables in a soup, nobody would think other than that it was a meat soup. This is one of the recipes I will include in that frittata book when I get around to it. It's a wonderful dessert confection that introduces frittata as not just a breakfast item.

MAKES 4 SMALL FRITTATAS

TIME: 1 HOUR

LEVEL: MODERATE

8 eggs, at room temperature
4 tablespoons sugar
½ teaspoon salt
4 tablespoons kirsch
1 tablespoon unsalted butter, at room temperature
2 cups strawberries, hulled and thinly sliced
1 cup whipped heavy cream
Confectioners' sugar, for dusting
4 skewers threaded with cut fruit, such as melons, apricots, peaches, kiwifruit

1. Beat the eggs, the sugar and salt in a medium-size bowl until well blended. Stir in the kirsch and let sit for 5 minutes.
2. Warm a small (approximately 7 inches) nonstick skillet over low heat. Add the butter and swirl to coat the pan.
3. When the butter begins to foam, pour in a ladleful of the egg batter and shake the skillet to coat the bottom. Cook until golden on one side, about 3 minutes.

4. Flip the frittata (or cover it with a plate, turn the skillet upside down and slide the frittata back into the skillet). Cook until the frittata is set and both sides are golden brown, about 3 minutes. Transfer to a heated plate and keep warm. Repeat three more times until the mixture has all been used.

5. Fill the warm frittatas with sliced strawberries and 1 or 2 tablespoons whipped cream. Fold in half, dust with confectioners' sugar and serve with fruit skewers.

VARIATIONS: Any type of fruit can be used in place of strawberries.

Aranci fritti
Batter-Fried Orange Segments

MAKES
15 TO18 SLICES

TIME: 45
MINUTES PLUS
MARINATING
AND
REFRIGERATING

LEVEL:
MODERATE

Fried fruit is very popular throughout Tuscany. Almost any type of fruit can be used, from apples to bananas to fresh pineapple to peaches. It is important that the fruit be ripe but not mushy and that the batter be allowed to rest at least 1 hour after mixing. The following recipe uses orange slices that have been marinated overnight in cognac. Fruit for frying can also be marinated in rum, brandy, kirsch or wine. But remember to drain the fruit well and dust with a little confectioners' sugar before dipping it into the batter.

3 oranges, peeled, pith removed and cut horizontally into ½-inch slices
2 cups cognac
2 eggs, separated, at room temperature
1 tablespoon unsalted butter, at room temperature
1 cup cake flour
½ teaspoon salt
1 tablespoon sugar
Confectioners' sugar
Vegetable oil, for frying

1. Marinate the oranges in the cognac in a covered medium-size bowl for 4 hours or overnight. Drain, reserving the liquid.

2. Beat the egg yolks with ⅔ cup of the reserved cognac and the butter in a large bowl. Sift in the flour, ¼ teaspoon salt and the sugar, and beat until well blended. Place in a sealed container and refrigerate at least 1 hour.

3. Remove from refrigerator and beat again until smooth and creamy.
4. Using an electric mixer or a hand whisk, beat the egg whites and the remaining ¼ teaspoon salt in a large bowl until stiff peaks form. Fold the whites into the yolk batter until just blended.
5. Pour oil until 1 inch deep in a large, heavy-gauge skillet. Heat until hot enough to immediately crisp a tiny sliver of bread. Dust the drained orange slices in confectioners' sugar, dip in batter and immerse six or seven at a time in the oil. Do not add more fruit, or the oil will cool. Fry until lightly browned, turning once, about 3 minutes. Drain on paper towels, dust again with sugar and serve.

MAKE AHEAD: The batter can be prepared the day before through Step 2 and stored, refrigerated, in a sealed container. Bring to room temperature before using. The oranges can remain in the marinade for up to 2 days.

Zuppa di fragole
Cold Strawberry Soup

In Scandinavia, chilled fruit soups are served as first courses. In Tuscany, they are desserts and this one (recipe from Gianmarco Sfini of Viareggio's La Bettola) is absolutely delicious.

1 quart strawberries, washed and hulled
1 cup orange juice
1 tablespoon instant tapioca
½ cup sugar
¼ teaspoon cinnamon
1 teaspoon grated lemon zest
1 tablespoon lemon juice
1 cup heavy cream
4 apricots, peeled and thinly sliced
1 tablespoon cognac or grappa

SERVES 6

TIME:
45 MINUTES
PLUS
OVERNIGHT
REFRIGERATION

LEVEL: EASY

1. Reserve 6 strawberries for garnish, place the rest in a food processor and purée.
2. Reserving ¼ cup purée, combine the purée and orange juice in a large saucepan. Dissolve the tapioca in the reserved ¼ cup purée. Stir into the saucepan. Heat the mixture slowly over low heat, stirring con-

stantly, until it comes to a boil and thickens, about 5 minutes. Remove from heat and add sugar, cinnamon, zest and lemon juice and mix until all ingredients are well blended. Transfer to a large bowl and let cool to room temperature. Stir in the cream, cover and refrigerate overnight.

3. Just before serving, stir in the apricots and cognac and divide among 6 bowls, garnishing each with a reserved berry.

VARIATIONS: Other kinds of berries work just as well. Thinly sliced melons can be substituted for the apricots.

Torta di lamponi e crema
Raspberry and Custard Tart

MAKES
ONE 10-INCH
TART (8 SLICES)

TIME: 1 HOUR
PLUS 2 HOURS
REFRIGERATION

LEVEL:
MODERATE

In good years (just enough rain, just enough sunshine), Tuscany crawls with raspberries, which is a fine time for making this tart. In lean times, cut the quart to a pint and pray for future abundance.

1 recipe Basic *Pasta Frolla* (see page 34)
4 eggs, at room temperature
2½ cups milk
1 cup sugar
2 tablespoons cognac
¼ teaspoon freshly grated nutmeg
1 quart raspberries
½ teaspoon lemon juice

1. Preheat the oven to 375°F. On a lightly floured surface and using a floured rolling pin, roll the *pasta frolla* into a 10-inch-diameter circle and arrange in a 9-inch-diameter tart pan with removable bottom. Press the excess against the sides. Line with foil, weight with raw rice, dried beans or commercial pie weights and bake for 10 minutes. Remove the weights and foil and bake for 5 minutes longer.

2. Place the eggs, milk, ½ cup sugar, cognac and nutmeg in a medium-size, heavy-gauge saucepan and cook over very low heat, whisking constantly until the custard begins to thicken. Cool slightly, pour into the tart pan.

3. Bake until firm, about 20 minutes. Remove and let cool to room temperature.
4. Place the raspberries and remaining ½ cup sugar in a heavy saucepan. Sprinkle with the lemon juice and cook over very low heat for 2 or 3 minutes, stirring occasionally. Let cool to room temperature. Spread gently over the surface of the cooled tart. Chill for 2 hours, remove the sides of the tart pan and serve.

VARIATIONS: The tart can also be served with whipped cream.

CHAPTER NINE

Traditional Tuscan Desserts

Carnival in Viareggio

"Fa piu male una notte di Carnevale che un digiuno quaresimale." ("One night of Carnival is worse for you than an entire Lenten fast.")

Anyone who studies Tuscany history would have to presume that the average Tuscan is a very serious, very sober person whose life is largely centered around foolproof actions and the nobility of sacrifice. One would be wrong—although it's hard to understand where exactly the error lies. Certainly, if one looks at the society's history and underlying structure, everything points to the supposition that Tuscans should be modest, humble people striving for nothing more grandiose than comfortable, anonymous lives with boundaries.

For one thing, they have lived through centuries of wars, earthquakes, foreign rulers and the kind of general disorder and unpredictability that batters people into the ground, that makes them unable to lift their heads and stretch toward anything more lofty than a simple tin roof. Their greatest age of factional strife began in 1215, when a Tuscan nobleman, Buondelmonte del Buondelmonti, was assassinated by his enemies while crossing Florence's Ponte Vecchio. The entire region was subsequently thrown into a 300-year battle that pitted merchant against nobleman, common people against the newly-rich bourgeois and city-state against fiefdom.

The quarrel polarized the region into two contentious camps: on one side were the free-city, free-trade, papist Guelphs and on the other, the Ghibellines, the party of the same German emperors who had been trying to assert their dominance over the area since the days of Charlemagne. Political symbolism permeated every aspect of life from architectural construction (simple, squared crenellations were Guelph, ornate, swallow-tail crenellations, Ghibelline) to the colors of one's clothes (black, Ghibelline, white, Guelph). With that kind of historical background, Tuscans are lucky they survived as a regional group.

Add to that the Church, with its continuous steam of homilies espousing humility, modesty and self-effacement. My favorite has to do with the proverbial Flavia, a peasant woman on route to the market to sell the tin of ricotta that she carried on her head. "With the money I get, I'll buy a chicken," she dreamed. "And the chicken will lay 4 eggs a day and I'll sell the eggs and keep the money until I have enough to buy a cow. And then I'll sell the cow's milk and eventually have enough to buy a fine house. And then I'll stand out in front of my fine house and everyone passing by will say 'Buongiorno, Signora Flavia'." And with that, Flavia bowed her head to simulate the respectful greeting she would be accorded and the tin of ricotta fell into the gutter and was ruined. Motto: Never inflate your head with dreams.

As if the influences were not already overwhelming, throw in the regional obsession with putting things in order (*sistemare*), which leads Tuscans to dictate even the roof color of any new structure or organize the countryside as if it were a simple garden plot. And let's not forget the extreme sensitivity to making a *bella figura* (a good showing) which permeates every action, every thought, every desire. Put it all together and the result should be a group of people so rigid, so lifeless, so squelched, so devoid of any creative or revolutionary impulse as to lull you into a long, bored sleep immediately upon crossing into the region.

But again I say, you would be very wrong. Because Tuscans are quintessential party people. Take for example, carnival in Viareggio.

The word *carnevale* is a modern distillation of the ancient *carnemlevare*—*carnem* for "meat" and *levare* for "take away." It is the perfect explanation for a no-holds-barred period of revelry that ends one day before this Lenten denial begins. Until about 20 years ago, eating meat during the forty days of Lent was a sin against Jesus Christ, who committed the ultimate act of sacrifice by dying on the cross. Moral: The least we can do as Christians is to refrain from eating meat for five and a half weeks. Carnival theoretically prepares us for this somber ritual by providing an excessive journey of music, dance, colors, food and costumes that delivers you to the somber doorstep of Lenten abstinence.

The first clue to the anything-but-sober aspect of the Tuscan character is the fact that Carnival lasts four weeks. Its bounty is somewhat reminiscent of the Roman festivals that are its legitimate precursors: *Saturnalia,* the great free-for-all celebration of life itself where men dressed as women and vice versa; *Bacchanalia,* the drunken orgies and unlimited eating feasts dedicated to the god, Bacchus; and *Lupercalia,* the libertine fertility rites that encompassed live sacrifices and naked dancing through the streets. Viareggio's Carnival has none of these but, at the same time, it has elements of all three.

The King of the Carnival is a huge plaster mascot whose name, Burlamacco, comes from Buffalmacco, one of the funnier of Bocaccio's narrators in his epic *Decameron.* Burlamacco's costume consists of a red and white diamond-shaped suit, a long black mantle and a large red tri-corner hat like Napoleon's. His placement is a constant source of contention, although never more so than in 1994, when he could be found on the edge of the beach waving a symbolic good-bye to the joys of the flesh as represented by the setting sun. That of course meant his back was to Lucca, the eleventh century walled city that lies 12 miles east of Viareggio and serves as its provincial seat. Every newspaper carried the story: "The Final Insult!" "Last Straw From the Arrogant Viareggini!", "Now They Give Us Burlamacco's Backside!"

In the end, Viareggio's *Comitato Carnevale* (Carnival Committee) was forced to move Burlamacco from his sojourn on the sand and place him safely in Piazza Mazzini with his back toward the sea. So now, we say he is waving an actual good-bye to all those who visited Viareggio for Carnival. Not quite as lyrical but much less likely to provoke a boycott.

The floats are begun in June and take nine months to complete— Viareggio's pregnancy, albeit a pregnancy whose entire gestation must remain secret for fear that the designs will be copied. There are generally 10 to 20 floats in the Carnival parade; each is approximately 20 feet high, 30 feet long and made completely by hand out of plaster of paris. Most of the floats have political themes—the President of the country depicted as a wild boar; a certain parliamentarian shown jutting his hand in and out of the till.

In order to qualify, each float must have a significant number of moving parts and all must be operated by actual people installed in the bowels of the float. The designs themselves must first be approved by the Carnival Committee which then grants the necessary money to fund the construction and support the workers for each individual *rione* or crew.

The first of Viareggio's Carnivals was held in 1873 after the publication of Jules Verne's "Around the World in Eighty Days," which gave millions of readers a sense of magic and adventure that, for the most part, was severely lacking in their everyday lives. The drawings in Verne's original edition sparked the idea for the Carnival floats—the first of which were simple horse drawn carts topped with live action dramas. Although most people were too poor to afford Carnival costumes, they took a cue from their Roman ancestors and swapped clothes with their spouses. Men became women, women became men, and both dusted their faces with flour or chimney ashes for added cachet.

I am sitting at an outdoor cafe along the Carnival route, the Viale Margherita, waiting for both my friend Cinzia and the roar of the 3:00 cannons that will jump-start the final day of the festivities. The sun is shining brilliantly, the air scented with the flowering mimosa trees that form a hedge along the boulevard. Behind me, the Apuan Alps are a necklace of white-capped peaks, marble, not snow.

A woman and her two children occupy the next table. The woman is dressed as a slim, fashionable bear with a large furry jumpsuit and an elaborate headpiece with moving parts for the mouth. The young boy is an alien ala *Independence Day* and the girl is Agent Scully from the *X Files*.

"I want a *bombolone*," Agent Scully is demanding. (A cream-filled doughnut.)

"No, *cara*, a *bombolone* is too much. You already had gelato at home. Have a pizzetta instead."

"No. I want a *bombolone*."

"It's either the *pizzetta* or nothing, Andrea. You decide."

I'm not sure why she bothers. We all know, her included, that, in the end, Andrea is going to have a *bombolone*. Tuscans are not great disciplinarians, as anyone who has ever visited the area will testify. There is something about the concept of discipline itself that strikes Tuscans as both unpleasant and unnecessary.

"What is the point?" asks Alberto Moravia, one of Italy's great modern writers. "Are we not already disciplined enough by virtue of being encased in the physical body and sentenced to live in a physical world with distinct geographic barriers? Are not the grim circumstances of twentieth century existence enough of a disciplinarian without overlaying yet more limitations?"

Some, Moravia continues, think discipline is good for the soul. That to force oneself into questionable behaviors for questionable end-results leads to the development of willpower and that willpower is an undeniable good. "I could not disagree with any greater fervor," he says. "The only possible end product of forced behavior is the gradual distancing of the soul from anything having to do with beauty and majesty and the ability to imagine what the brain can never comprehend."

As Andrea takes her first bite of the *bombolone*, the cream squirts all over her secret agent jacket. Her mother leaps out of her chair.

"*E ora?*" she says. "*Come si puo andare al Carnevale in questo stato?*" ("How are we supposed to go to Carnival in this state? What will people think of us?")

She turns to me because she knows I have been eavesdropping. "I'm so incredibly tired," she says. "For the last four weeks, my family and friends have done nothing but celebrate. It's been one party after another. The food, the dancing, the costumes, the late nights. Thank God for Lent."

Just at that moment, the first BOOM rips through the air and as people jump up from their cappuccinos, the second and third shots are fired. Everyone crowds the entrance, pushing and pulling to be the first to enter the gates on this final and most frenetic Sunday. For the past four weeks, Viareggio has been routinely flooded with hundreds of thousands of people who come here to shed their rough winter skins. There were dozens of masked balls, many held on the streets of the city, and concerts every night.

The stores and restaurants were open nonstop, and the main thoroughfares were routinely lined with stalls selling nut brittles, *brigidini* (a type of aniseed waffle), doughnuts and *cenci fritti* (fried pieces of dough powdered with sugar). We had song contests and theater performances and dinner parties enough to fill everyone's schedule from morning till night. As my mother always says, "*Per Carnevale, tutti impazziscono.*" ("Everyone goes a little crazy during Carnival.")

The judging of the floats took place this morning, the Sunday before Ash Wednesday. This year the competitors included *Manca il Pastore* (The Shepherd Is Missing), an assemblage of political "sheep," chief among them the current Prime Minister, Romano Prodi, who despite his inclusion in this dismal line-up, has admirably succeeded in tempering Italy's frightening drive toward debtor's oblivion. Each one of the "sheep" was dressed in a white wool coat and shown aimlessly veering off the perimeter of the flatbed. The soundtrack was a wonderful chorus of bleats laid over a famous Italian song called "*Tutte Pecore*" ("All Sheep").

"The Monster Factory" depicted the evils of the paparazzi, who were shown filming actual spectators, with the films instantly viewable on the huge monitor that formed the float's center. In recent weeks, this has been the most talked about of the floats; its creator, Palo Lazzari, was interviewed by just about all of Europe's famous newspaper and television reporters. Every time I've seen him, I've been amazed at his hostility, although it is clearly a self-defensive reaction, given his unyielding demonization of the press.

"You are all criminals," he has repeated to every reporter who journeyed to his home just outside Viareggio. "All for the news. Never wondering about the effect of your fascist tactics on the lives of ordinary people. Look at Marchetti."

The reference is to the mayor of nearby Massarosa, who was initially hounded for his revolutionary insistence that public figures both be on time and limit their midday meal breaks to one hour. In the process of following him around, however, reporters discovered that his secretary, who was also his mistress, was on the public payroll but never showed up for work. The barrage of stories and the number of reporters flocking to this small village from all over Europe led to a nervous breakdown on the part of his wife and the Mayor's ultimate suicide.

"You killed him just as surely as if you'd plunged in the knife yourselves," Lazzari accused reporters in one interview.

"Our job is to report the news and this was definitely news," reporters countered although all agreed they had been too aggressive.

"That is your point of view. Mine is represented by this float."

The winning float represented Italian Nobel Prize Winner, Dario Fo, and was entitled "*Ridendo e cantando, che male ti fo?*", which translates roughly to "laughing and singing, what harm can I do?" It was a reference to the fact that when Fo won the coveted prize last January, Italians were not very happy. "The Nobel committee chose not a scholar, not a philosopher, not even a serious writer. They gave the prize to a comedian!" the papers trumpeted. "One million dollars for what?"

Dario Fo is a satirist (a very funny satirist; hence, he is often referred to as "a comedian"). Until he won the prize, he had been a very popular figure, both in his own country and internationally. Generally, his works parody Italy's social and political climate, which he refers to as "not yet ready for civilized viewing." Where he came under fire, however, was not in his criticism, but in the constant revision to which he subjects every one of his works.

"Plays, or for that matter, poems and books, are not static entities," he maintains. "Just like we change our clothes or change our minds, plays are constantly changing."

"The problem," said *La Nazione,* one of Italy's most respected newspapers, "is that Fo won the prize precisely for works that he considers to be in a state of evolution. Unlike Montale (Eugenio Montale, Italy's Nobel prize-winning poet) whose poetry can forever be read in the form that garnered him world acclaim, Fo's body of work is, so to speak, nonexistant. If we attempt to read one of his plays in the form that so moved the Nobel committee, we are bound to hear the author's voice cheeping in our ears that it no longer has any value."

"What did you think of the winning float?" Cinzia asks as we leave the parade route and make our way toward Fappani's, Viareggio's oldest and most famous caffè.

"I thought it was completely appropriate in the way it satirized a satirist. Can you imagine what Fo must have felt when Italians turned on him for winning the prize? Italians, the most anarchistic of peoples, going completely to pieces because their Nobel laureate doesn't play by the rules."

"Do you think that's what was going on? To me it is equally plausible that Italians thought Fo was wonderful when he was our own local jokester, but on the international stage, his 'laughing and singing' as he puts it, just doesn't seem so very accomplished."

"Well, what do you think?" I signal the waiter for two bowls of hot chocolate. "IS he accomplished?"

"I've always loved his work," she says settling back against the silk pillows. "I think the problem is that people generally don't value comedy as much as they do drama."

"Obviously, not here, though the float about him won first prize after all."

"Tuscans are somewhat more comfortable with laughing and singing. I just came back from Venice's Carnival, for example, and, while it was extraordinary and wonderful and beautiful and all those things you always hear about it, there was also an air of melancholy that, to me, negated the spirit of Carnival."

Cinzia is not the first to describe Venice's Carnival using words like "sober" and "austere." This dark, baroque city celebrates Carnival primarily by donning ancient mantles and historic hats (many handed down from ancestors dead hundreds of years) and parading through the piazzas as if on Giorgio Armani's runway. No floats for the Venetians; *they* are the Carnival; *they* are the parade. No music, no dancing, no revelry, parties are private and centered on great banquets.

"Would you go again?" I ask her taking a bite of an oversized carnival cookie dusted with sugar and vanilla powder. Having been to Venice's carnivals a number of times, I find them fascinating from a historical perspective but not in the same league as Viareggio's

"*Certo,*" she responds. "You know me. A party is a party, even if it's really not very festive. Fact is, when you're in Venice, you feel as though that's the way Carnival should be. Any other type of observance would seem out of place in such an austere city."

I think about her answer as the waiter arrives with our steaming bowls of hot melted chocolate topped with a mountain of freshly whipped orange-infused cream. She's right. Venice is as Venice does, or in this case, it does as it is.

"Thank God we live here," I say gratefully taking the first decadent sip.

⚬⚬⚬⚬

Traditional Tuscan Desserts

Tuscany lives by its traditions. Whether related to religious holidays, seasonal harvests, nostalgia for grandparents or even the nation's unification, Tuscans enjoy having a full calendar of celebrations dedicated to "the way it has always been." And, of course, there is no tradition in Tuscany that does not have its related foods. Generally, traditional foods run the gamut from appetizers to fish courses to wines to after-dinner liqueurs. This chapter is devoted to a few of the great many desserts prepared by home cooks and professional bakers alike to celebrate some of Tuscany's most heartfelt traditions.

Traditional Tuscan Desserts

Frittelle di San Giuseppe
St. Joseph's Day Rice Fritters

Cenci fritti
Carnival Fritters

Dolce di Natale
Christmas Eve Fruit and Nut Cake

Crostata di ricotta
Carnival Pine Nut Tart Made with Fresh Sheep's Milk Ricotta

Ricciarelli di Siena
Christmas Almond Cookies

Castagnaccio
Harvest Chestnut Cake

Torta della nonna di Lisa Contini Bonacossi
Lisa Contini Bonacossi's Ricotta Cake

Buccellato di Lucca
Traditional Lucchese Sweet Bread

Frittelle di neccio
Harvest Chestnut Fritters

Monte bianco
Harvest Chestnut Mousse with Puréed Raspberries

Pasimata
Good Friday Sweet Bread

Panforte
Christmas Fruit and Nut Cake

Befanini
Epiphany Cookies

Frittelle di San Giuseppe
Saint Joseph's Day Rice Fritters

MAKES
APPROXIMATELY
20 FRITTERS

TIME: 1 HOUR

LEVEL:
MODERATE

Before Joseph became a saint, he was a father, which is why Father's Day is celebrated here on his feast day, March 19th. I'm not sure about the connection between rice and St. Joseph, but I am grateful to him for whatever part he played in the creation of this wonderfully crunchy recipe.

1 cup arborio rice
4 cups milk
1 teaspoon grated lemon zest
1 teaspoon vanilla extract
½ cup sugar
4 tablespoons confectioners' sugar
2 tablespoons anisette
3 eggs, lightly beaten, at room temperature
5 tablespoons cake flour
Vegetable oil, for frying
Confectioners' sugar, for dusting

1. Place the rice, milk and lemon zest in a saucepan and cook over medium heat until the rice is tender, about 20 minutes. Drain the rice and place it in a large bowl.
2. Add the vanilla, sugar, confectioners' sugar, anisette, eggs and flour and stir until well blended.
3. Pour oil 2 inches deep into a 12-inch-diameter skillet and heat to 375°F.
4. Form the fritters by pouring the batter by the tablespoonful into the hot oil and frying until golden. Do not overcrowd the skillet or the oil will begin to cool. Drain on paper towels, dust with sugar and serve immediately.

MAKE AHEAD: The rice can be cooked 1 day before and stored, refrigerated, in a sealed container until ready to use.

Cenci fritti
Carnival Fritters

Cenci fritti *means "fried clothes." Its name originates in the Tuscan province of Prato, where fabrics are produced and also recycled. "We can do anything with used clothes, even fry them!" the Pratesi used to say jokingly. The name varies according to the region where they are made:* chiacchere *in Milan,* galani *in Venice,* frappe *in Rome; and although enjoyed during every month of the year, they are most visible during Carnival when they appear in every shape from pinwheels to knots to stripes to diamonds. Among the oldest desserts in history,* cenci fritti *were routinely prepared by ancient Roman street vendors in 500 B.C. for festivals dedicated to the god Bacchus.*

MAKES
APPROXIMATELY
30 *CENCI*

TIME: 2 HOURS

LEVEL: EASY

2½ cups cake flour, sifted
⅓ cup sugar
2 eggs, at room temperature
1 egg yolk, at room temperature
Pinch of salt
2 tablespoons rum or grappa
1 tablespoon unsalted butter, at room temperature
1 tablespoon grated lemon zest
½ teaspoon baking powder
Vegetable oil, for frying
Confectioners' sugar, for dusting

1. Heap the flour onto a flat work surface and make a well in the center. Place the sugar, the eggs, egg yolk, salt, rum, butter, lemon zest and baking powder in the well.

2. Using a fork, mix the ingredients, incorporating the flour a little at a time until a smooth dough has formed. With floured hands knead for 5 minutes, form the dough into a ball, wrap in plastic and refrigerate for 1 hour.

3. On a lightly floured work surface and using a rolling pin, roll the chilled dough into a 1-inch-thick sheet. Cut the sheet into 3 x 2-inch rectangles.

4. Pour the oil to 1½ inches deep in a 12-inch skillet. Heat over high heat to 375°F. Fry 5 or 6 dough rectangles at a time until lightly golden on

both sides, about 3 minutes. Drain on paper towels and let cool to room temperature. Dust with confectioners' sugar and serve.

MAKE AHEAD: The dough can be prepared up to 2 days in advance, wrapped with plastic and refrigerated. Bring to room temperature before using.

Dolce di Natale
Christmas Eve Fruit and Nut Cake

MAKES
ONE 10-INCH
CAKE

TIME:
1½ HOURS

LEVEL:
MODERATE

Traditional Italian Christmas cakes include panettone, panforte, ricciarelli and an amalgam of all three referred to simply as Christmas Eve Cake. The preparation of this fruit and nut sweet dates back many hundreds of years, when poor people were limited to very few ingredients and used lard in place of butter.

Unsalted butter, for greasing
Flour, for dusting
½ cup raisins, soaked in hot water for 10 minutes
½ cup stemmed and chopped dried figs
1 cup lightly toasted, coarsely chopped walnuts
⅔ cup toasted chopped pine nuts
1 tablespoon grated orange zest
6 tablespoons grappa
3⅔ cups bread flour
2 teaspoons baking powder
¼ teaspoon salt
½ cup unsalted butter, at room temperature
¾ cup sugar
3 eggs, at room temperature
¼ cup milk

1. Preheat the oven to 375°F. Grease and lightly flour a 10-inch-round cake pan. Drain the raisins and place in a large bowl along with the figs, walnuts, pine nuts, orange zest and grappa. Cover and let sit for 30 minutes to marinate.
2. In another large bowl, sift together the flour, baking powder and salt.
3. Cream the butter and the sugar in a large bowl. Add the eggs (one at a

time) and beat them in. Stir in half the dry ingredients; add the milk. Stir in the remaining dry ingredients. Fold in the fig-nut mixture. Transfer the batter to the prepared pan.

4. Bake until a tester inserted into center comes out clean, about 1 hour. Remove from the pan and cool on a rack. Serve at room temperature.

VARIATIONS: Other fruits, nuts and liquors can be substituted. Another combination is dried apples and apricots, pecans and cognac or apple brandy.

⚜ ⚜ ⚜ ⚜

Crostata di ricotta

Carnival Pine Nut Tart Made with Fresh Sheep's Milk Ricotta

Tuscans use ricotta in recipes ranging from butternut squash ravioli to vegetable terrines to cakes such as this delicate blend of nuts, chocolate, lemon zest and rum. In most cases, the preferred ricotta is made with sheep's milk, which is just beginning to be imported into the United States. At the cooking school, we use ricotta prepared by a colorful shepherd, who lives at the bottom of the hill, in Stiava, and delivers it on Tuesdays and Thursdays, still warm. Generally, we subject every group of students to a taste comparison between the shepherd's cheese and a commercial brand, but for the sake of diplomacy, we will say nothing further about their ecstatic comments. If you like, however, we can give you his phone number and you can judge for yourself.

The following tart is generally served around Carnival time, when grass is reborn and the ricotta is made from sheep who have eaten the new green shoots. The difference between this early spring ricotta and its later or earlier counterparts is noticeable even to those who have never before tasted fresh ricotta.

MAKES
ONE 9-INCH PIE
(8 SLICES)

TIME: 3 HOURS

LEVEL:
ADVANCED

THE CRUST

2 cups plus 2 tablespoons cake flour
1 teaspoon baking powder
¼ teaspoon salt
½ cup plus 2 tablespoons unsalted butter, at room temperature

¾ cup sugar

2 eggs, at room temperature

1 teaspoon vanilla extract

Unsalted butter, for greasing

THE FILLING

12 ounces fresh sheep's or cow's milk ricotta

½ cup sugar

2 eggs, at room temperature

2 egg yolks, at room temperature

¾ cup raisins soaked in 1 cup rum for 30 minutes

3 tablespoons chopped toasted pine nuts

3 tablespoons chocolate chips

1 tablespoon grated lemon zest

1. To make the crust, mix together the flour, baking powder and salt in a medium-size bowl.
2. In another medium-size bowl, cream the butter and the sugar. Beat in the eggs and vanilla.
3. Add the flour mixture and beat until all ingredients are well blended into a smooth and elastic dough.
4. Turn the dough out onto a floured work surface and divide in half. Using a floured rolling pin, flatten each half into a ½-inch-thick disk, wrap in plastic and refrigerate for 1 hour. Preheat the oven to 375° and grease a 9-inch-diameter glass pie pan.
5. To make the filling, using a spatula, press the ricotta through a strainer into a large bowl. Stir in the sugar, eggs, egg yolks, raisins with the rum, pine nuts, chocolate chips and lemon zest.
6. Remove the dough from the refrigerator and, on a lightly floured work surface, roll each half into a 10-inch-diameter circle. Transfer one of the two dough circles to the prepared pan and press the excess against the sides.
7. Pour the filling into the pie pan, level the surface with a spatula and moisten the edges of the crust with a little water. Top with the remaining dough. Toll the edges, and pierce the crust with a fork in several places and then cover the pie with foil.
8. Bake the pie for 30 minutes, remove the foil and continue to bake until the top crust is lightly golden, about 10 minutes. Let cool to room temperature before serving.

VARIATIONS: Other types of nuts, such as pecans or walnuts, can be added to the ricotta mixture along with various dried fruits. Dried cherries are especially good with this recipe.

MAKE AHEAD: The dough can be prepared up to 2 days in advance, wrapped with plastic and stored in the refrigerator.

Ricciarelli di Siena
Christmas Almond Cookies

Immediately upon arriving in Siena, you are plunged into ancient memories, beautiful medieval piazzas, romantic narrow streets and gothic churches. The past is in the architecture, the circular grid of the streets, the frescoes fading from interior courtyards, the judgmental looks on the faces of the people. But it is also in the fragrance of ricciarelli, a Christmas cookie whose preparation dates back to the Medicis. The fragrance fills the air wherever you are, hypnotizing you, forcing you to buy a dozen and swallow them immediately.

At one time, women made the almond paste with a mortar and pestle. I still use the same method today, not because I haven't moved into the modern age of food processors, but for the connection the old way offers to a moment in time when Siena's cobblestones were brushed by the feet of the immortals.

MAKES
APPROXIMATELY
20 *RICCIARELLI*

TIME: 8 HOURS

LEVEL:
MODERATE

Unsalted butter, for greasing
Flour, for dusting
1 pound toasted almonds
8 ounces toasted pine nuts
2 cups sugar
½ cup confectioners' sugar
1 teaspoon grated orange zest
3 egg whites, at room temperature
½ teaspoon salt
½ teaspoon cream of tartar
Confectioners' sugar, for dusting

1. Preheat the oven to 350°F. Grease and flour a 12 x 15-inch baking sheet. Place the almonds and pine nuts in a food processor (or mortar) and process until finely ground.

Traditional Tuscan Desserts　257

2. Transfer the mixture to a large bowl, add the sugar, confectioners' sugar and orange zest and stir until well blended.

3. Using an electric mixer or hand whisk, beat the egg whites and the salt in a large bowl until foamy. Add the cream of tartar and beat until stiff peaks form. Gently fold the whites into the nut mixture.

4. Drop the batter by spoonfuls onto the prepared baking sheet.

5. Bake the cookies for 15 minutes and then transfer to a cooling rack. Serve at room temperature dusted with confectioners' sugar and accompanied by *Vin Santo* (Tuscan dessert wine).

MAKE AHEAD: The pine nuts and almonds can be ground up to 1 week in advance, sealed in an airtight container and stored in the refrigerator. The cookies themselves can be stored in an airtight container for up to 1 week.

Castagnaccio
Harvest Chestnut Cake

MAKES
ONE 9-INCH
CAKE (8 TO 10
SLICES)

TIME: 1 HOUR

LEVEL: EASY

When harvest time arrives in early autumn, castagnaccio or chestnut cake is the most popular Tuscan cake, whether in the humblest home or the most famous restaurant. Its name varies according to the Tuscan province in which it is sampled; in Massa Carrara, for example, it is called pattona; *in Versilia,* Torta di neccio. *Aside from its incomparable flavor,* castagnaccio's *chief claim to fame is the ease with which it is prepared.*

4 cups chestnut flour*
Approximately 1 cup water
4 tablespoons chopped toasted pine nuts
1 teaspoon fresh chopped rosemary
3 tablespoons extra-virgin olive oil
1 tablespoon grated orange zest
2 cups fresh sheep's or cow's milk ricotta

1. Preheat the oven to 350°F. Place the flour in a large bowl. Whisk in the water, one tablespoon at a time, until the consistency is creamy and smooth.

2. Add the pine nuts, rosemary, 2 tablespoons oil and the orange zest and blend well.

3. Grease a 9-inch-diameter baking pan with the remaining 1 tablespoon oil. Pour in the chestnut mixture and tap the pan against a countertop to level the surface.

4. Bake until a crispy crust has formed, about 45 minutes. This is a rather flat cake with a dense consistency. Remove from pan with a spatula and cool on a rack. Serve at room temperature topped with a dollop of fresh ricotta.

* Chestnut flour can be found at most specialty food stores.

VARIATIONS: Walnuts and chocolate chips can be added to the mixture in Step 2.

MAKE AHEAD: The mixture can be prepared through Step 2 one day in advance and stored, refrigerated, in a sealed container.

Torta della nonna di Lisa Contini Bonacossi
Lisa Contini Bonacossi's Ricotta Cake

Lisa Contini Bonacossi is a somewhat different style of grandmother. For one thing, she is a trained chemist whose scientific knowledge contributes to the excellent wines made on her estate, called Capezzana. She is also the wife of Ugo Contini Bonacossi, and thus, a Countess. But despite her employment of a personal chef who undoubtedly prepares delicious cakes of his own, she herself chooses to make this traditional grandmother's tart for her fourteen grandchildren. The recipe, she says, has been in her family for centuries.

MAKES
ONE 10-INCH
TART (8 TO 10
SLICES)

TIME:
2½ HOURS

LEVEL:
MODERATE

THE CRUST

Unsalted butter, for greasing
2 recipes Basic *Pasta Frolla* (see page 34)

THE FILLING

3 egg yolks, at room temperature
4 tablespoons sugar
1 tablespoon grated lemon zest
1 tablespoon cake flour, sifted

1 teaspoon confectioners' sugar
2 cups warm milk
1 cup fresh sheep's milk ricotta
2 tablespoons ground lightly toasted almonds
Confectioners' sugar, for dusting

1. To make the crust, preheat the oven to 375° and grease a 10-inch-diameter spring form pan.
2. Using an electric mixer or hand whisk, beat the egg yolks and sugar in a large bowl until smooth, fluffy and pale in color, about 5 minutes with the mixer (15 minutes by hand). Stir in the grated lemon zest, flour and confectioners' sugar. Gradually whisk in the warm milk.
3. Transfer the mixture to a stainless steel saucepan. Cook the custard over low heat stirring constantly with a wooden spoon. When the consistency is thick enough to spread, remove from heat and let cool to room temperature.
4. Using a spatula, press ricotta through a strainer into a large bowl. Stir in the custard and ground almonds, and mix until well blended.
5. On a lightly floured work surface, roll one ball of *pasta frolla* into a 12-inch-diameter circle and the other into an 11-inch-diameter circle. Arrange the larger one in the bottom of the prepared pan, pressing the excess against the sides. Pour in the custard filling, tapping the pan against a countertop to level the surface.
6. Cover with the second circle of dough and create a crimped edge crust with the excess. Press lightly to seal. Using a fork, pierce top crust in several places. Cover with foil.
7. Bake for 35 minutes. Remove the foil and continue to bake until the top crust is lightly golden, about 10 minutes.
8. Cool for 20 minutes and remove the sides of the pan. Dust the cake with confectioners' sugar and serve.

VARIATIONS: The cake can also be drizzled with a fruit purée before serving or accompanied by whipped cream.

MAKE AHEAD: The dough can be prepared up to 2 days in advance, wrapped in plastic and stored in the refrigerator.

Buccellato di Lucca
Traditional Lucchese Sweet Bread

The Treccani Dictionary *of the Italian language offers these facts about Lucchese Sweet Bread: 1.* "Buccellato *is derived from the Latin* buccellatum, *meaning 'crown-shaped bread'; 2.* Buccella *in Latin also means* boccone *or 'bite;' 3. The ancient Romans fed this bread to their soldiers because its sweetness supposedly heightened their warrior energies; and 4. From 1578 until the end of 1606, Lucca levied a tax on every* buccellato *to pay for the banks that enclosed the Serchio River."*

As the Lucchesía's most famous cake, buccellato *can be found in almost any bakery throughout the province and can be prepared in any of a hundred different variations. The definitive version, however, belongs to Taddeucci's in Lucca's Piazza San Michele. A sign in the window makes joking reference to the cake's simple ingredients: "No wonder the Lucchese have adopted the* buccellato *as their traditional cake; what a perfect pair—both stingy!"*

MAKES 1 SWEET
BREAD (8 TO 10
SLICES)

TIME: 4 HOURS

LEVEL:
ADVANCED

THE CAKE

1 tablespoon fresh yeast
Approximately 1 cup warm water
4 cups bread flour, sifted
3 tablespoons sugar
3 tablespoons unsalted butter, at room temperature
3 tablespoons golden raisins, soaked in 1 cup rum for 30 minutes and
    drained
1 teaspoon vanilla extract
1 egg white, lightly beaten, for wash
Vegetable oil, for oiling
Unsalted butter, for greasing

THE SYRUP

½ cup sugar
2 tablespoons confectioners' sugar
1 cup water
1 quart strawberries, hulled and thinly sliced

1. To make the cake, dissolve the yeast in the warm water, add 1 table-spoon flour and set aside until foamy, about 10 minutes.
2. Heap the remaining flour onto a flat work surface and make a well in the center, add the water-yeast mixture and mix by hand, incorporating a little of the flour wall at a time. Add more water as necessary to incorporate all the flour into a smooth, elastic ball of dough.
3. Oil a large bowl. Place the dough into it, cover and let sit for 2 hours in a warm place until doubled in size, about 1 hour.
4. Transfer the risen dough to a lightly floured work surface, and add the sugar, butter, raisins and vanilla, kneading until well blended, about 10 minutes. Return to the bowl, cover and let sit for 1 hour. Preheat the oven to 350°F and grease a 12 x 15-inch baking sheet.
5. Stretch the dough into a long oval shaped log about 10 inches long and let rise for 30 minutes.
6. Place the risen dough into the prepared pan, brush with the egg wash.
7. Bake until a tester inserted into the center comes out clean, 40 minutes. Transfer to a cooling rack and brush with syrup. Slice into wedges and serve at room temperature with fresh strawberries.
8. To make the syrup, blend the sugar, confectioners' sugar and water in a medium saucepan and cook for 1 minute over very low heat, stirring constantly. When the mixture is smooth and liquid, remove from heat and set aside.

VARIATIONS: The sweet bread can also be served warm, with rum-raisin ice cream.

Frittelle di neccio
Harvest Chestnut Fritters

MAKES
APPROXIMATELY
30 FRITTERS

TIME: 1 HOUR

LEVEL:
MODERATE

Of the many chestnut desserts native to Tuscany, this is probably everyone's favorite in spite of the fact that its ingredients are among the humblest. Typically made throughout the Garfagnana and the mountain regions of Massa Carrara, chestnut fritters are traditionally served in late autumn, after the chestnut harvest with a scoop of fresh sheep's milk ricotta.

2 cups chestnut flour*
½ to ¾ cups warm water

½ teaspoon salt
2 tablespoons grated orange zest
1 tablespoon extra-virgin olive oil
1 tablespoon fresh chopped rosemary
Vegetable oil, for frying
2 cups fresh sheep's milk ricotta, optional

1. In a medium-size bowl, blend together the chestnut flour and salt. Whisk in ½ cup warm water and continue adding water, 1 tablespoon at a time until a smooth, creamy mixture has formed.
2. Stir in the grated orange zest, olive oil and rosemary, and mix until well blended. The consistency should be like thick pancake batter.
3. Pour the oil to 1 inch deep in a 9-inch skillet. Heat over high heat to 375°F. Drop the mixture by the tablespoonfuls into the hot oil and cook until the fritters are golden on both sides, turning once. Remove with a slotted spoon and drain on paper towels. To serve, place three or four on a plate with a small scoop of ricotta.

* Chestnut flour can be found in most specialty stores.

VARIATIONS: The fritters can also be sprinkled with confectioners' sugar before serving.

MAKE AHEAD: The chestnut mixture can be prepared early in the day and stored, refrigerated, in a sealed container. If too dense, thin with water before using.

Monte bianco
Harvest Chestnut Mousse with Puréed Raspberries

La castagna in acqua cotta
prende il nome di ballotta
se la macini è farina
deliziosa e sopraffina
se l'impasto, cosa faccio?
un gustoso castagnaccio!

SERVES 6 TO 8

TIME: 2 HOURS

LEVEL:
MODERATE

Cooked in boiling water
the chestnut takes the name ballotta
If you grind it, you wind up with delicious, superfine flour
If you knead it, what do you make?
A delicious chestnut cake!

Tuscans have almost as many uses for chestnuts as they do for their beloved beans. Two types of chestnuts grow in the forests of northern Tuscany: marrone, *which are the large, meaty types used for eating whole (especially marinated in syrup), and* comune, *a smaller, less sweet variety perfect for puréeing or adding to stuffing mixes. Boiled, baked, roasted or ground into flour, chestnuts form the base for a wide variety of delicious dishes that include soups, stuffing mixes, vegetable side dishes, and, of course, desserts, including this delicious harvest confection shaped like the mountains where chestnut trees grow.*

2 pounds chestnuts
2 bay leaves
1 teaspoon salt
1 quart milk
1 teaspoon vanilla extract
1 cup sugar
2 tablespoons cognac
2 cups heavy cream, whipped into stiff peaks
1 cup puréed raspberries or strawberries

1. Place the chestnuts, bay leaves and salt in a large pot, along with enough water to cover by 2 inches. Cover and cook until tender, about 30 minutes. Drain and peel.
2. Place the milk, peeled chestnuts and vanilla in a heavy-gauge soup pot and cook for 15 minutes over very low heat.
3. Using a slotted spoon, remove the chestnuts from the milk and pass through a food mill. Discard the milk.
4. Stir the sugar into the chestnut mash, transfer the mixture to a nonstick sauce pan, pour in the cognac and cook over low heat for 5 minutes. Let cool to room temperature.
5. Place on a platter and shape into a round ball representing a mountain. Refrigerate for 1 hour and then frost with the cream. Cut into wedges and serve immediately on a pool of puréed berries.

VARIATIONS: Fresh ricotta (preferably sheep's milk) can be used in place of the heavy cream. Before spreading, whip the ricotta with 1 tablespoon sugar until the mixture is smooth and creamy.

MAKE AHEAD: Chestnuts can be boiled 1 day in advance and stored, refrigerated, in a sealed container until needed.

Pasimata
Good Friday Sweet Bread

Pasimata is an Easter bread whose preparation begins on Good Friday (possibly as penance for one's sins). Throughout Tuscany, one can smell the dough yeasting, and upon entering any traditional home, see the covered bowls tucked away in warm corners. On Easter Sunday, the baked breads are brought to the church and blessed by the priest during High Mass along with boiled eggs (signifying purity) and an olive branch (signifying peace).

The recipe for this bread differs according to the province where it is made: lard may be used in place of butter, rosewater in place of Vin Santo. *Its long preparation is justified by at least one person: Adua Manfredi of Torre del Lago, who says: "Yes, it takes two days, but then again,* pasimata *is a religious bread so a little sacrifice is called for."*

MAKES 1 LOAF
(6 SLICES)

TIME: 3 DAYS

LEVEL:
MODERATE

2 tablespoons fresh yeast
1 cup sugar plus ½ teaspoon
1 cup warm milk
Vegetable oil, for oiling
4 cups bread flour
4 eggs, at room temperature
1 teaspoon rose water or *Vin Santo*
2 cups unsalted butter, at room temperature
Unsalted butter, for greasing
½ cup golden raisins, soaked for 2 hours in 1 cup of *Vin Santo* and
     squeezed dry
2 tablespoons anise seeds
1 teaspoon grated lemon zest
1 egg yolk, beaten, for wash

1. Dissolve the yeast along with ½ teaspoon sugar in the warm milk.
2. Heap 2 cups flour onto a flat work surface and make a well in the center. Pour the yeast-milk mixture into the center and, working with both hands, incorporate the flour a little at a time until a smooth elastic dough has formed. Knead for 5 minutes to activate the yeast and the gluten.
3. Oil a large bowl, place the dough in it, cover with a cloth and let sit for 12 hours in a warm place.

ONE DAY BEFORE EASTER

1. Transfer the risen dough to a floured work surface, knead for 5 minutes and set aside.
2. Heap the remaining 2 cups flour onto a flat work surface, make a well in the center and add the eggs, the remaining 1 cup sugar, rose water and butter. Using a fork, blend all the ingredients incorporating a little of the flour wall at a time until a ball of dough has formed.
3. Top with the risen dough and knead the two into one smooth elastic ball. Place the dough in a large bowl, cover and let sit until it has doubled its size, approximately 2 hours. Grease a 12 x 15-inch baking sheet.
4. Transfer the dough to a floured work surface and add the raisins, anise seeds and the grated lemon zest. Knead for 10 minutes, then form a ball and using the blade of a knife, draw a cross in the center. Place the bread on the center of the greased baking sheet, brush with the egg wash and let sit for 1 hour. Preheat the oven to 375°.
5. Bake until a tester inserted into the center, comes out clean and dry, about 40 minutes. Let cool on a rack.
6. Cut the cooled bread into thick wedges and serve.

MAKE AHEAD: Wrapped tightly in plastic, the sweet bread will keep for up to 1 week.

Panforte
Christmas Fruit and Nut Cake

You cannot say you have truly been to Siena unless you have tasted two of its most distinctive desserts: Ricciarelli di Siena (Christmas Almond Cookies), recipe on page 257, and panforte, a traditional Christmas fruit cake (the recipe follows). Produced year round, panforte is nonetheless associated specifically with Christmas, when it is dressed to the nines in lustrous foils and beautiful gift boxes. Sapori and Nannini are the two most important producers, and I'd be lying if I chose one over the other. While both use precisely the same ingredients, the hands that make them are completely different and, to me, the difference screams its identity. The original recipe is still one of Tuscany's best kept secrets but the one that follows is as close as you can come.

MAKES
ONE 10-INCH
CAKE
(12 SLICES)

LEVEL:
MODERATE

TIME: 2 HOURS

2 cups chestnut honey*
1 cup sugar
1 pound dried cantaloupe or other dried or candied fruits, chopped
1 pound candied orange, chopped
1 pound candied lime, chopped
6 tablespoons cake flour, sifted
Pinch of ground coriander
½ teaspoon ground cinnamon
¼ teaspoon ground nutmeg
¼ teaspoon ground ginger
Pinch of ground cloves
½ teaspoon vanilla extract
1½ cups toasted almonds
1½ cups toasted hazelnuts
Unsalted butter, for greasing
Flour, for dusting
Confectioners' sugar, for dusting

1. In a large nonreactive (enamel, stainless steel, or nonstick) saucepan, blend the honey and the sugar. Bring to a boil over low heat and cook for 5 minutes, stirring constantly.
2. Remove from heat and stir in the chopped candied fruits. Sift in the flour and mix until well blended.
3. Stir in the spices, vanilla and nuts and set aside for 10 minutes.

4. Preheat the oven to 375°F. Grease and flour a 10-inch-diameter tart pan with removable bottom.
5. Pour in the mixture, tap against a countertop to level the surface.
6. Bake for 30 minutes. Remove from oven and let cool to room temperature. Remove the sides of the pan, dust with confectioners' sugar and serve.

* Chestnut honey can be found at specialty stores. Another strongly flavored variety of honey, such as loose strife, sage, thyme, can be substituted.

VARIATIONS: Walnuts, pine nuts and freshly ground black pepper can be added to the cake mixture.

MAKE AHEAD: Like other fruitcakes, *panforte* lasts for 2 weeks if wrapped tightly in foil after each use.

Befanini
Epiphany Cookies

MAKES
APPROXIMATELY
20 LARGE
COOKIES

TIME: 2 HOURS

LEVEL:
MODERATE

Oh Befana,
Sei la mia sposa,
Sei la mia Dama,
Tirami giù
Qualche cosa
Un arancin,
Un mandarin,
O un pezzetto di Befanin!

Oh Befana,
You are my bride
You are my Lady
Throw me something
A little orange
A mandarin
Or a piece of a Befanino!

Epiphany is celebrated January sixth throughout Italy in memory of the three Kings who brought gifts to the Christ child. In place of three lavishly outfitted kings, Italians have settled on the good witch Befana who arrives on a straw broom dressed in black rags and a tattered head scarf. Befana delivers gifts to "good" children and arrives via the chimney, hence her dusty dirty appearance. What about bad children? Italians have no patience with denial; bad children get their gifts anyway, but they also get carbone (coal) or caccori di miccio (mule droppings), both of which, in modern times, come in the form of shiny black candy.

The following cookies are left by the hearth for Befana and presumably eaten before dawn by good mothers and fathers throughout Italy.

4 eggs, at room temperature
1 cup sugar
2 cups unsalted butter, at room temperature
5 tablespoons confectioners' sugar
½ teaspoon salt
4 cups bread flour, sifted
1 tablespoon grated lemon zest
½ cup milk warmed to 110°F
5 tablespoons anisette
2 tablespoons *Vin Santo*
1 tablespoon baking powder, sifted
Unsalted butter or cooking spray, for greasing
1 egg yolk, beaten, for wash

1. Using an electric mixer or a wooden spoon, beat the eggs and sugar in a large bowl until fluffy, smooth and pale, about 5 minutes with the mixer (15 minutes by hand). Stir in the butter, confectioners' sugar, salt, sifted flour and the grated lemon zest. Blend until creamy.
2. Pour in the warm milk, the 2 liqueurs and baking powder, and stir until a smooth dough has formed.
3. Shape into a ball, wrap in plastic and refrigerate for 30 minutes. Preheat the oven to 375°F.
4. Transfer the chilled dough to a flat work surface. Using a floured rolling pin, roll out the dough to ½ inch thick and, using cookie cutters, cut into shapes such as stars, animals or witches.
5. Grease a 12 x 15-inch baking sheet. Place the shapes on the prepared sheet, brush with the egg wash.

6. Bake until lightly golden, about 20 minutes. Transfer to cooling racks. Serve at room temperature with hot chocolate, champagne or *Vin Santo*.

MAKE AHEAD: The dough can be prepared up to 2 days in advance, wrapped in plastic and refrigerated. It can also be frozen for up to 3 weeks. Thaw in the refrigerator before using.

CHAPTER TEN

Low-Fat Desserts

Before the Beach

Going to the beach in Tuscany is like auditioning for the elite modeling agency. You must wear the right suit (which means this year's cut and yes, everyone will know the difference), and you must have the right sandals and hair clips and sunglasses and beach bag and watch and towel (also adhering to the very latest fashion). You must arrive at the proper time (9:30 in the morning) and be off the beach by the fashionably late 1:30 lunch hour. And most importantly, your belly must be absolutely flat and your legs long, taut, tanned and striated with just the proper hint of muscle.

What happens if you are found lacking in any of these areas? Well, let's just say that you might rather not have gone in the first place. Understand that Tuscan beaches are as formally laid out as the region's houses and gardens. Chairs are organized in straight rows, each with its own personal table and umbrella (opened by the caretaker as soon as he sees you exiting your changing room or, if you are an annual client, 10 minutes before your scheduled arrival).

Since all beaches are private, you must rent one of these umbrellas and its accompanying changing room for a minimum of a week (some bathhouse concerns also rent by the day but only in the less crowded beginning and end of the season) although most people rent by the month or the season. So wherever you choose to take the sun, your immediate neighbors will be the same exact people for at least a week. In most cases, people rent from the same bath house year after year, so the people in the chairs next to you are as familiar as family.

This arrangement could create a loving, intimate atmosphere of comfort and familiarity. But this is Tuscany after all. And so what it *really* means is that every inch of you becomes fodder for analysis and judgment—and nobody judges more harshly than Tuscans. "What happened, *cara?*" you will undoubtedly hear one woman crowing to the next. "You look so different from last year. Ah, perhaps because *now* (spoken with exaggerated emphasis) you are wearing a one piece instead of the tiny bikini you were always known for."

This cattiness is not restricted to women, mind you. Men have the same requirements when it comes to fashionable bathing attire and accessories. Their bodies are also subject to the same analysis and critique: Are they slim enough? Tanned enough? Sporting the proper hair style? Walking the proper walk? Are their muscles developed enough to look natural or are they the obvious product of thousands of hours of grueling work (either of these options can be good or bad depending on the group doing the judging). And as if this wasn't already bad enough, men must also perform: They must swim or run or sail or play soccer or volleyball, and they must do it well; if not, their audience will let them know. *"Ehi Samuel, meglio se ti sdrai al sole"* ("Better just lie in the sun, Sam.")

So March presents a bit of a crisis where Tuscans are concerned—the month when news anchors begin featuring that year's *"dieta rivolvzionaria"* and health clubs cut back on advertising budgets because the impending beach season is all the advertising they need.

My friend Marzia is even more frenzied than usual this year. Not only does she look terrible (her description) in every bathing suit she tries on, but she has a wedding to go to in May, and the slinky black dress she bought in October for her husband's business dinner no longer fits. "What can I do?" she moans in an annual ritual I have come to dread.

My answer is not going to matter regardless of what it entails. Marzia is Marzia and as such will always gravitate toward the same solution, consisting of throwing herself headlong into two or three diets at once, sometimes with disastrous results. Every now and then she also adds a new strategy. Last year she arrived at my house encased in plastic wrap beneath her pullover. Every step she took, you heard this distinct crackling. "It will help me sweat more," she explained. The "plastic plan," as her husband came to call it, backfired the day she had to be taken home from the market, where she had fainted while waiting for the fishmonger to clean her squid.

Marzia is not fat, far from it. Fellini would have loved her bountiful curves—De Sica, too. But I have put in more than a few hours shopping with her for bathing suits and no matter what her weight is in any given year, the cry from behind the dressing room door is always the same. *"Oh Dio Sandra, muoio!"* ("Oh my God Sandra, I'm about to die!")

This year, she is going to try the *brassica* diet—no food crosses the lips unless it's part of that specific botanical family: broccoli, cauliflower, cabbage, brussels sprouts, kohlrabi, kale. Her friend apparently lost 14 pounds in two weeks following this diet. I'm not even going to bother asking how much the friend gained after she stopped. Fact is, Marzia will never even last the two weeks. Whichever regimen she chooses, we always call it the Monday diet because she starts it on Monday morning and ends it by Monday dinner.

Her mother-in-law, Teresa, is no help. Whenever Marzia talks about going on a diet, Teresa always questions who she is trying to attract. "When a woman marries, she should no longer be wearing bikinis anyway. *Ci vuole un pó di modestia* (You need a little modesty after all). Piero (Marzia's husband) loves you the way you are. That should be enough for you."

Marzia has come up with a new plan. "Come with me to Saturnia," she pleads. "We'll drive down on Monday morning and spend four days enrolled in their thermal spa program. It will be great fun."

"I'll go on one condition," I tell her. "That you stick to the regimen for the entire four days. I don't want to be driving around the countryside at 10:00 at night looking for a *gelaterìa*."

Saturnia is an ancient Etruscan thermal city located in southern Tuscany in a largely undiscovered agricultural area known as the *Maremma* (Moorlands). The three-hour trip provides a stunning infinity of gentle, curved hillsides blanketed with the green spires of newly planted wheat and pencil-thin cypresses. Some fields are still barren, the red clay earth framed in stark contrast against a brilliant blue sky. Others are awash in poppies and sunflowers, a primary palette of such visual resonance as to prompt this verse from poet Robert Penn Warren: "I will bring you to a place of ancient stones and scalloped marinas; to a place of castles and falcons streaking across the sky, to a land coated with reds and yellows, flowers and seeds, to the top of a hillside once dominated by the warrior Phillip, the one with the dark eyebrows from Spain, the Tormenter and on the precipice lined with thorny boughs of juniper, we will wait together for the gales of the scirocco." (from "Promises").

As we drive, Marzia plans our week. We will rise at 7:00, walk from our hotel in town to the hillside thermal baths (about three miles, she thinks), where we will lie in repose for two hours or so, soaking in the minerals and calming our psyches and digestive systems (Marzia's current theory is that stress is causing her excess poundage). I love the way she describes what we'll look like "sitting haunch to haunch in the steaming pools—damned creatures in Dante's *Inferno*."

Then we will walk back and have lunch—nothing excessive, she says. The afternoons will be spent at the health club, working with weight machines and sitting in the sauna. Then we will shower, tour the town, have dinner ("again, a very simple meal") and go to bed. By the end of the four days, by her calculations, she will have lost eight pounds and taken on a new glow. I give the plan twelve hours.

"I don't know why you bother," I tell her at the causeway leading to the spectacular beaches of Orbetello. "You are a beautiful woman and eight pounds more or less is not going to make that much of a difference. Just buy a bigger bathing suit."

"I wish it were that simple," she says. "But you know the problem, despite all this talk about being happy with myself as is. You go through the same things and don't bother to deny it."

She is right, much as I would like to disagree. Living in Tuscany is not about making decisions for yourself and forming personal opinions about what's important and what's not.

Tuscan existence is a communal experience, much like anyplace where people are more or less of the same nationality and economic class. If it seems so much more all-encompassing here, perhaps it's because of the lack of large cities and industrial bases that might otherwise distract the attention from the personal.

For the most part, Tuscany is a region of small villages, where everyone has known everyone else for generations. Even if you don't know the person walking toward you down the street, you undoubtedly have a few common acquaintances. Furthermore, the two of you live more or less the same kind of life. You eat the same foods at breakfast, work the same morning hours, rush home to large midday meals, work some more in the afternoon and sit around the table at night, eating pasta and roast chicken, after which you watch television or take a walk in the piazza. Your points of reference are identical: family, community and tradition. Likewise the way you go about things: you scheme and plot and plan and manipulate your way through all the same scenarios: avoiding taxes, building that extra room without a permit, claiming sickness when in fact you want an extra day of vacation. You have to, you claim. What else can one do after five hundred years of governmental deception? And in the defensiveness and me-firstness of your approach, you are like every other Tuscan and hence plastered to each other's psyches like moss to a stone.

And so there is no individuality. No personal decisions about matters such as what makes a woman attractive. The answer is decided en masse. And once decided, it is adhered to by everybody. Such is the social contract that allows Tuscans to live on top of each other in tiny villages whose streets are too narrow for even the smallest Fiat.

To an outsider, the effect is charming. Tuscans themselves consider their lives charmed. But there is also that aspect that leads to precisely the situation in which Marzia and I find ourselves this March and every other March—this continuous straining to deal with a set of circumstances that values the perception of others more than—and to the exclusion of—one's personal point of view. And so here we are, in Saturnia, about to embark on Marzia's great-weight-loss marathon.

Our first day is more or less what she envisioned. We are up at 8:00 (an hour later than planned, but we're not Germans after all). We have a quick espresso (Sweet-n'-Low for Marzia), a small *brioscia*, and off to Le Cascate del Gorello, the thermal falls, where for a little more than two hours, we sit in the splendor of the beaming sun and let the grey green water of the falls cascade over our grateful bodies.

"Simply having a tan before the beginning of the beach season will help," Marzia tells me as she flips over onto her stomach in the most businesslike of fashions. "I actually think I read somewhere that tanned skin is more taut than untanned."

We are new women as we walk back to town: rested, tanned, and filled with a sense of unparalleled virtue. True to her plan, we have a simple lunch (pasta with parsley and garlic and grilled salmon with baby string beans), a quick nap and an hour and a half of weight work at Saturnia's state-of-the-art health club. We dither around town in late afternoon, have dinner and are in bed by 11:00.

"This feels sooooo good," Marzia says as she turns off her reading lamp. "We should really do this a few times a year."

The next day starts well. Same routine, breakfast, walk, soak, walk and lunch. But by early afternoon, Marzia is saying she wants to take a drive to Scansano to shop for wine. "Piero (her husband) asked me to pick up some Morellino, and I don't think we'll have time on Friday if we want to be home in time for dinner."

"What about going to the gym?" I ask her.

"We still have tomorrow," she says, an attitude I know to be the beginning of the end.

In Scansano, we go from one winery to the other, tasting and comparing. Naturally, they all serve a little something to clean the palate—an olive oil bruschetta, a wedge of cheese, a hunk of sausage.

"Hmmm," says Marzia, cleaning her palate two or three times between tastings. "It feels like a hundred years since I've enjoyed something this much."

When we get back to town, it is, naturally, time to get ready for dinner. "Let's go to Michele and Bianca's," she suggests, referring to I Due Cippi, Saturnia's most famous restaurant, not known for its skimpy portions.

"Fine," I yell out from the shower. "But I don't want to hear you moaning when we get back to Stiava that you haven't lost any weight." Silence. "Okay Marzia? No complaining." Again, silence. I step out of the shower, wondering whether she is still in the room.

She is, in fact, very much in the room. Lounging on the divan with her legs crossed, her hair spilling out from its tortoise clip and lavishly draped across the stark white pillows. She is wearing her black dress, the skirt pulled up above her knees, the top buttons opened to reveal a proud tanned bosom.

"It fits," she says between sips of vermouth. "I told you all I needed was a tan."

She looks fabulous and what's more, she knows she looks fabulous and fabulous in a way that nobody could possibly deny. But of course, it won't be real until somebody confirms it—until someone says "Oh Marzia, you look wonderful," which is much more likely given the fact that she obviously feels that way, at least in this minute. Once on the beach, under review by the ubiquitous Tuscan judges, she might feel differently, which of course, will turn out to be a self-fulfilling prophecy. But enough circles. Now is now and I need a glass of champagne.

"Does that mean we can drive to the falls tomorrow?" I say, toasting the perfection of the moment.

"No, let's walk. The walk is gorgeous and it only takes a half hour." She looks at me and laughs, "And then maybe let's go shopping for bathing suits. There's that great shop we saw in town."

Low-Fat Desserts

When the two of us began working on this book, we collected, tested and created hundreds of recipes, pored over enough information on ingredients to fill a book in itself and agonized over how to present a set of techniques that would be easy and clear enough to follow. For the most part, there was no problem with the collaboration; after all, we own a cooking school together and are used to the push and pull of colliding points of view.

But eventually we came up against a certain issue that is so ever-present in our interaction as to be considered a virtual third partner: whether the food we teach and prepare should be strictly traditional or whether it should be more or less traditional as interpreted through the filter of the ever-new and ever-changing. The corollary to this issue, especially when talking about desserts, is, of course, traditional cream and butter preparations versus desserts that are lower in fat and rely more on fresh fruit.

There are two things I (Anne) want to say about Sandra here. One is a story that highlights her overwhelming preference for the traditional; the other (which goes hand in hand with the first) is a statement defining her dessert preferences and the reasons why she feels that way.

First the story: One day early in the life of the cooking school, she and I were teaching a group how to make *cacciucco,* a traditional Tuscan fish soup. Just as we were getting ready to assemble the ingredients, Sandra was called away to the phone for an emergency regarding her son. I carried on, explaining why cuttlefish needed to be added first and what spicing produced the best *cacciucco.*

When Sandra came back (understand here that Sandra is a veritable expert when it comes to cooking fish), she looked in the pot and said to me in Italian, "What's that?" To which I replied: *cacciucco.*

"That's not *cacciucco,*" she said, still in Italian. "*Cacciucco* isn't made with chili peppers."

"I thought it would spice up the flavor some," I responded. "Micky (one of our students) said she likes spicy foods."

"Well, it's okay to eat it that way tonight, but we'll just have to tell the class that it's not *cacciucco,*" she persisted.

Feeling very much like the Stanley Tucci character in "Big Night," I said, "Look, I don't care how *cacciucco* is made in this one square acre of

Tuscany. Somewhere, somebody makes it with chili pepper." With that, I looked her straight in the eye and delivered what we now refer to as The Ultimatum. "I don't care what you *think* is in this pot. Tonight, it's *cacci-ucco.*"

The other thing I want to say about Sandra is that she has had a life-long love affair with butter, cream, cheese, chocolate, caramel, gelato, pastry...well, you get the idea. Actually, I think the best thing here is to cut to the quick and let her tell you, herself, how this book brought us head to head with our quintessential differences:

We spent an entire summer testing the recipes, Anna insisting at every turn that we try using 'a little less sugar, a cup of yogurt instead of all that cream.' Each time she would try changing some of the traditional recipes, I would remind her that they were called traditional because that's the way they've always been made. 'Not only that,' I said more of-ten than I want to remember, 'but it tastes *good* this way. Let the readers make the decision to substitute lower-fat ingredients if they want.'

'Well, how about listing substitutions in the "variations" section?' Anna persisted. To which I responded that this was a book on desserts, not on losing weight. If somebody wants to lose weight, I told her, they're not going to be buying a book like this in the first place. Besides, when lower-fat substitutes are listed, people feel immediately guilty that they chose the higher fat version, and I don't want my readers feeling guilty about having prepared one of these wonderful desserts."

And that's when she (Anna) came up with the idea of an entire chap-ter on "Low-Fat Desserts." To tell you the truth, I was initially skeptical, es-pecially when she said she'd work on it herself if I didn't want to have anything to do with it. Anna is a wonderful cook, but her idea of dessert is a bowl of cooked fruit with some grappa poured over the top. How can a dessert be good if there is no sugar in it? That was my attitude going into this chapter.

But I have lived long enough to change my mind. Not that I would will-ingly choose *gelatina* over *zabaione.* Just that I have now realized that low-fat dessert means more than simply making the same thing with no fat and no sugar. 'It's not about negatives, about leaving stuff out,' Anna would say in our many arguments over the subject. 'Low-fat means work-ing with different kinds of ingredients altogether.'

And so once again we compromised, traveling far and wide to talk with chefs, especially in Tuscany's many wonderful spas. We collected, tested and experimented with more than 80 low-fat recipes to arrive at what you see on the following pages. And yes, they're good. In fact, they're very good. But don't tell Anna I said that.

ABOUT LOW-FAT DESSERTS

The trick to making low-fat desserts is, obviously, to include as little fat as possible. This can be done either by using naturally low-fat ingredients such as fruit or by substituting reduced fat ingredients for high fat ones. Following is a list of workable substitutions:

- Yogurt cheese can be used in place of cream cheese. To make yogurt cheese, start with low-fat yogurt (many nonfat varieties have food starches and vegetable gums that prevent them from draining). Place the yogurt in a colander lined with cheesecloth, set over a bowl, cover and refrigerate for eight hours or overnight. Save the whey collected in the bowl for use in muffin or cake recipes in place of whole milk. Yogurt cheese can be used cup for cup in place of cream cheese with the addition of one tablespoon, flour per cup for thickening. Avoid placing the cheese in food processors or blenders which will cause it to thin.

- Cocoa powder can be used in place of baking chocolate. Use three tablespoons cocoa powder plus one tablespoon water or fruit juice for every ounce baking chocolate required by the recipe.

- Cakes require the use of fats to prevent the development of gluten, which causes a tough texture and is perfect for breads but not desirable in cakes. In place of fat, use lower gluten flours such as oat or whole wheat pastry in place of white. For best results, substitute only half the flour required with the lower gluten variety.

- Use fruit purées in place of fat. Applesauce and mashed banana are perfect substitutes for butter or oil. For best results, substitute half the required butter with an equal amount of purée; replace half the oil with three-fourths as much purée.

- Avoid chemical compositions such as nonfat dairy products and saturated butter substitutes such as margarine. While such substitutes reduce fat, they are both nutritionally unsound and unnecessary for the purpose of low-fat cooking. Use other substitutions as listed above.

- Two egg whites can replace one whole egg.

- Raisins and chopped fruit can replace chocolate chips.
- Grease pans with cooking spray instead of butter.
- Make your own mock whipped cream. Put a can of evaporated skim milk in the refrigerator, and place a stainless steel bowl and the beaters from an electric mixer in the freezer for an hour. Put the milk in the chilled bowl, add one teaspoon each vanilla extract and brandy and beat at high speed until peaks have formed. Use immediately. This tip comes from *In The Kitchen With Rosie* (Knopf, 1994). Thanks Rosie, this has long been one of my favorite low fat strategies.
- Top cakes, tarts and pastries with a dusting of powdered sugar or cocoa instead of frosting. Thick fruit purées can also serve as a replacement. Another option is to mix yogurt cheese (see the first tip above) with some fruit purée or cocoa powder and use that for frosting.

Low-Fat Desserts

Mele ripiene di albicocche e nocciole con salsa di amarena
Baked Apples with Dried Apricots, Hazelnuts and Bitter Cherry Sauce

Ciambella allo yogurt
Yogurt Pear Cake

Soufflés di pesche
Individual Peach Soufflés

Panettocini all'uvetta
Miniature Currant Panettones

Gelatine di limoncello al pepe verde
Citrus Gells with Limoncello and Green Peppercorns

Fragole al balsamico
Alpine Strawberries with Balsamic Vinegar

Semifreddo all'arancia
Orange Ginger Semifreddo

Bruschetta alle albicocche
Apricot Bruschettas

Low-Fat Tiramisù
Low-Fat Mascarpone Custard

Risotto di pere
Pear Risotto

Aranci al liquore
Oranges Marinated in Cointreau

Zuppa inglese alla fragole
Berry Trifle

Torta di polenta e albicocche
Polenta and Apricot Rum Cake

Mele ripiene di albicocche e nocciole con salsa di amarena

Baked Apples with Dried Apricots, Hazelnuts and Bitter Cherry Sauce

At Christmas, Tuscans eat twice as much as usual. It's a family holiday and no one has anywhere else to go so they can calmly sit at the table while lunch dissolves into dinner. At some point, however, everyone realizes that their pants are too tight, their jackets no longer buttoning properly. Then is when I bring out these simply delicious stuffed apples served on a pool of bitter cherry sauce. No one feels guilty for eating yet one more thing and the fluidity of the day's non-ending eating extravaganza can calmly continue. Amarena sauce can be found in specialty and gourmet food stores. It comes in a beautiful white porcelain jar painted with dark blue flowers. While Tuscany has a number of different manufacturers, the only one I have ever seen in the United States is "Amarena Fabbri."

MAKES 4 BAKED APPLES

TIME: 1 HOUR

LEVEL: MODERATE

4 large red apples, peeled and cored
2 tablespoons lemon juice
2 tablespoons finely chopped dried figs
10 dried apricots, finely chopped
1 tablespoon grated lemon zest
¼ cup finely ground hazelnuts
3 tablespoons cognac
1 cup apricot or other fruit juice
4 tablespoons *amarena**
Lemon zest, for garnish

1. Place the apples in a large bowl of water aciduated with the lemon juice. (The water should just cover the apples.)
2. Preheat the oven to 325°F. Combine the figs, apricots, lemon zest, hazelnuts and cognac in a large bowl.
3. Drain the apples and place in a medium-size baking dish. Fill the cavities with the fruit and nut mixture and pour the apricot juice over the top. Bake until tender (pierce with a knife), 40 to 50 minutes, basting frequently with the pan juices.
4. Place a tablespoonful of *amarena* on each serving plate. Using a

Low-Fat Desserts   283

skewer, fan the syrup into a spiral design. Top with an apple, sprinkle with lemon zest and serve.

* *Amarena* are bitter cherries packed in dark cherry syrup. They can be found in Italian specialty and gourmet stores.

VARIATIONS: Walnuts or almonds can be used in place of the hazelnuts.

Ciambella allo yogurt
Yogurt Pear Cake

MAKES
ONE 9-INCH
CAKE (8 SLICES)

TIME: 1 HOUR

LEVEL: EASY

The recipe for this delicious yogurt cake comes from Contessa Elena Pecchioli, owner of the Camporomano estate where our cooking school is located. "How healthy and light it is!" she said as she wrote down the ingredients. The Baron, her father (a real epicure, especially where desserts are concerned), scratched his brow. "Does the word 'cake' not, by its very nature, mean that sugar has been added?" he asked.

1 cup bread flour
1 egg, at room temperature
½ cup plain low-fat yogurt
1 teaspoon grated lemon zest
1 teaspoon vanilla extract
1 teaspoon baking powder
⅓ teaspoon baking soda
2 tablespoons extra-virgin olive oil
1 medium pear, peeled, cored and thinly sliced
4 tablespoons finely ground, lightly toasted almonds
1 cup mixed berries marinated for 1 hour in ½ cup orange juice and
   drained

1. Preheat the oven to 400°F. Line a 9-inch-round baking pan with parchment paper.
2. Place the flour, egg, yogurt, lemon zest, vanilla, baking powder, baking soda and olive oil in the bowl of a food processor and pulse until well blended.
3. Transfer the mixture to a medium bowl and stir in the sliced pears. Mix until well blended.

4. Pour the mixture into the prepared pan.
5. Bake until a tester inserted in the center comes out clean, about 40 minutes. Remove from oven and invert onto a rack. Let cool to room temperature and sprinkle with the ground almonds. Serve with the marinated berries.

VARIATIONS: Apples can be substituted for the pears.

Soufflés di pesche
Individual Peach Soufflés

"*Chi muore pace, e chi vive si da pace!*" *means something like "He who dies is dead but life goes on."*

Caterina Morelli is a 62-year-old widow who has, since her husband's death two years ago, turned to making delicious, low-fat desserts for the town's pastry shop. "I have very high cholesterol," she says, "and it wasn't much of an issue when Iacopo was alive, but now he is dead and I have a new fiancé to worry about."

MAKES SIX
4-OUNCE
SOUFFLÉS

TIME:
1¼ HOURS

LEVEL:
MODERATE

1 cup finely chopped dried peaches
½ cup hot apple juice
Cooking spray
½ teaspoon grated lemon zest
2 egg whites, at room temperature
¼ teaspoon salt
¼ teaspoon cream of tartar
Confectioners' sugar, for dusting
¼ cup frozen chocolate yogurt

1. Soak the peaches in the apple juice in a medium-size bowl for 30 minutes. Drain, reserving liquid.
2. Place reserved liquid, zest and all but 1 tablespoon chopped peaches into a food processor and purée until very smooth. Cool and stir in the reserved tablespoon of peaches. Transfer to a large bowl.
3. Preheat oven to 350°F and lightly coat six 4-ounce ramekins with the cooking spray.
4. Using an electric mixer or hand whisk, beat the egg whites and the salt in a large bowl until foamy. Add the cream of tartar and beat until stiff

peaks form. Gently fold about half the beaten whites into the peach purée, then fold in the rest and mix until just blended.

5. Spoon the mixture into the ramekins and arrange on a baking sheet.

6. Bake until puffed and golden, about 20 minutes. Dust with confectioners' sugar and, just before serving, slit open the tops of the souffés and fill each with 2 teaspoons frozen yogurt.

VARIATIONS: Dried apples, pears or prunes can be used in place of peaches.

MAKE AHEAD: The peach purée can be made up to 2 days in advance and stored, refrigerated, in a sealed container. Bring to room temperature when ready to use.

⋯⋯⋯⋯

Panettoncini all'uvetta
Miniature Currant Panettones

MAKES 10
PANETTONCINI

TIME:
3½ HOURS

LEVEL:
MODERATE

"Ma ti pare! Come fai a chiamare Panettone un panettone senza burro, me lo spieghi?" (*"How can you call it panettone if it's made without butter, can you explain it to me?"*)

½ tablespoon fresh yeast
6–7 tablespoons warm water
½ teaspoon sugar
1 cup bread flour
2 tablespoons warm skim milk
1 teaspoon grated lemon zest
1 egg white, at room temperature
2 teaspoons vanilla extract
3 tablespoons currants
1 tablespoon chopped candied citron

1. Dissolve the fresh yeast in 6 tablespoons warm water and stir in the sugar.

2. Place the flour, skim milk, lemon zest, egg white and vanilla in the bowl of a food processor and pulse until well blended. Pour in the water and yeast mixture and continue to pulse until incorporated. If the dough should be too hard, add 1 tablespoon warm water.

3. Transfer the dough to a medium-size bowl and cover with a cloth. Let sit until doubled in volume, approximately 1½ hours. Preheat the oven to 400°F.

4. Transfer the dough to a lightly floured work surface and knead for 5 minutes. Add the currants and citron and knead until well blended, about 2 minutes.

5. Divide the dough into 10 equal portions and place each in a 4-ounce paper baking cup. Arrange the paper cups on a 12 x 15-inch baking sheet, leaving about 1½ inches between each to compensate for the mushroomed caps that will top the cooked panettoni. Let sit until doubled in volume, about 30 minutes.

6. Bake until the tops are lightly golden, about 15 minutes. Remove from the oven and let cool on a rack. Serve the panettoncini with a glass of *Vin Santo*.

MAKE AHEAD: Baked panettoncini can be wrapped with plastic and stored at room temperature for up to 3 days.

⊰——⊰——⊰——⊰

Gelatine di limoncello al pepe verde
Citrus Gells with Limoncello and Green Peppercorns

Limoncello is an Italian liqueur made by marinating lemon rinds in sugar and spirits for anywhere from two weeks to two months, depending on who gives you the recipe. A relatively new drink, its popularity has swept the nation in the last few years, and it is virtually impossible to go to anyone's house, hotel or restaurant without someone offering you a small glass. Its combination of sweet-tart flavors comes especially alive when served over ice.

These simple yet elegant gels are served as small cup-shaped gelatin molds garnished with twists of fresh lemon and dusted with green peppercorns, which contributes a pleasant, surprising spiciness.

1 tablespoon (1 envelope plus ½ teaspoon) unflavored gelatin
¼ cup cold water
2 cups grapefruit juice, filtered
1 cup white grape juice

MAKES FOUR
½-CUP GELLS

TIME: 15
MINUTES PLUS
3 HOURS
REFRIGERATION

LEVEL: EASY

2 tablespoons Limoncello or other citrus liqueur
Green peppercorns, for dusting
Lemon twists or wedges, for garnish

1. In a small bowl, sprinkle the gelatin over the water. Let soften for 1 minute.
2. In a medium-size saucepan combine the grapefruit juice and grape juice and boil until reduced to 2 cups, about 15 minutes. Stir in the Limoncello. Stir in the gelatin mixture and continue stirring until the gelatin is completely dissolved and all the ingredients are well blended.
3. Pour into four ½-cup molds. Refrigerate until firm, about 3 hours.
4. To unmold, briefly dip the bottoms of the molds in hot water. Run a thin knife around the edges and invert onto individual dessert plates. Dust with freshly ground green peppercorns and garnish with lemon twists.

VARIATIONS: Experiment with different combinations of juice and spirits: white grape juice and framboise, apple juice and Calvados, apricot juice and peach brandy or pear juice and Pear Williams work well. When using thick juices such as pear or apricot, you might want to filter the boiled juices before gelling.

Fragole al balsamico
Alpine Strawberries with Balsamic Vinegar

SERVES 4

TIME:
20 MINUTES

LEVEL: EASY

Good balsamic vinegar is used for much more than salad dressings. As precious (and expensive) as white truffles, 10-year-old vintages are often served in liqueur glasses as digestives. The oldest balsamic vinegars are, in fact, not used for anything other than drizzling parsimoniously over foods such as grilled meats or vegetables and bowls of sliced fruit like this very simple dessert of wild alpine strawberries.

1 quart alpine strawberries or other berries, hulled
2 tablespoons aged balsamic vinegar
Sugar, for dusting

1. Marinate the berries in the vinegar in a medium-size bowl for 15 minutes, tossing occasionally.
2. Divide into 4 elegant serving goblets, dust with sugar and serve.

VARIATIONS: Other berries can be used instead of the strawberries.

Semifreddo all'arancia
Orange Ginger Semifreddo

The word semifreddo *means "half cold" and refers to the fact that this traditional mousselike dessert seems like ice cream but is actually only chilled. While the cup of heavy cream and half cup sugar might otherwise disqualify this dessert's inclusion in a low-fat chapter, it is a far cry from the large amount of cream and egg yolks often called for in similar recipes. I think you'll agree that the wonderful richness of this version warrants consideration for "special" occasions.*

SERVES 8

TIME:
50 MINUTES
PLUS 8 HOURS
REFRIGERATION

LEVEL:
ADVANCED

3 egg whites, at room temperature
¼ teaspoon salt
¼ teaspoon cream of tartar
½ cup plus 2 tablespoons sugar
¼ cup water
1 cup heavy cream
1 tablespoon grated orange zest
½ cup finely crushed low-fat ginger snaps

1. Line a 9 x 5 x 3-inch loaf pan with plastic wrap, leaving about a 4-inch overhang on all sides. Place in freezer.
2. Using an electric mixer, beat the egg whites and the salt in a large bowl until foamy. Add the cream of tartar and beat into very soft peaks. Cover and refrigerate.
3. Place the ½ cup sugar in a large saucepan along with the water and cook over low heat, stirring constantly until the sugar is completely dissolved. When the sugar reaches 240°F, add 1 tablespoon of the remaining 2 tablespoons sugar and beat until soft peaks form. Cool to 210°F. Gradually beat in the remaining 1 tablespoon sugar. With the beaters still beating, pour the sugar syrup into the egg whites and con-

tinue beating until the mixture has doubled in volume and cooled to room temperature, about 5 minutes. Beat in the zest.

4. Gently fold the cream, a little at a time, into the egg whites. Add ¼ cup cookie crumbs and fold in until just blended. Transfer the mixture to the prepared pan, leveling the surface with a spatula. Cover the top with the overhanging plastic and freeze until firm, 8 hours or overnight.

5. To unmold, remove the plastic wrap from the surface and invert onto a serving plate. Peel off the plastic, sprinkle with the remaining cookies, slice and serve immediately.

VARIATIONS: Any type of cookie crumbs can be used in place of ginger snaps.

Bruschetta alle albicocche
Apricot Bruschettas

MAKES 8 SLICES

TIME:
40 MINUTES

LEVEL: EASY

Fruit bruschettas have been a long-standing dessert in our cooking school. Students are always amazed when we suggest that this popular appetizer (often made with tomatoes or eggplant or puréed white beans) works just as well as a dessert with a minimal change of procedure.

16 very ripe apricots
1 cup white grape juice
8 ¾-inch-thick slices dry country-style bread
2 tablespoons extra-virgin (fruity) olive oil, slightly warmed
2 teaspoons brown sugar

1. Fill a 4-quart pot with water and bring to a boil. Drop the apricots into the water. Boil for 10 seconds. Remove with a slotted spoon, cool slightly and peel. Remove the pits and cut into ¾-inch-thick slices.

2. Heat the grape juice in a large skillet, and braise the apricots in the hot juice for 5 minutes, stirring often. Remove with a slotted spoon.

3. Baste the bread with the oil and arrange the apricot slices on the surface. Sprinkle with the sugar, and place on a baking sheet.

4. Bake until the edges of the bread are toasted, about 20 minutes. Serve immediately.

VARIATIONS: Butter can be used in place of oil; peaches or apples substituted for the apricots.

Low-Fat Tiramisù
Low-Fat Mascarpone Custard

Here is a low-fat version of this popular dessert with creamy pudding standing in as a satisfying substitute for high-fat mascarpone.

½ cup raspberries
1 tablespoon white grape juice
1½ cups low-fat (1%) milk
½ package (2 ounces) vanilla pudding mix
16 ladyfingers, halved
1 cup freshly brewed espresso
2 teaspoons cocoa powder

MAKES FOUR
4-OUNCE
PUDDINGS

TIME:
40 MINUTES

LEVEL: EASY

1. Place the berries and grape juice in a medium-size bowl, mash with a fork.
2. Using the low-fat milk, prepare the pudding according to package directions. Cool to room temperature.
3. Dip the ladyfingers briefly into the espresso, turning so that both sides are soaked. Drain on a plate.
4. To assemble the desserts, line four 4-ounce dessert cups with the soaked ladyfingers, pressing them against the bottoms and the sides. Divide the berries among the 4 cups and arrange on the bottom over the ladyfingers. Top with pudding, dust with cocoa and refrigerate for 3 hours before serving.

VARIATIONS: Pavesini biscuits, which are lighter than ladyfingers, can be substituted. The biscuits can be found in specialty stores.

Low-Fat Desserts   291

Risotto di pere
Pear Risotto

SERVES 4

TIME: 1 HOUR

LEVEL:
MODERATE

Dessert risottos are very common in Tuscany in the last few years. This version made with pears uses low-fat milk in place of stock and creates an elegant presentation when served on a pool of puréed berries.

2 ripe pears, peeled and finely diced
½ cup arborio rice
2–3 cups low-fat (1%) milk
½ cup white grape juice
¼ cup golden raisins
½ teaspoon ground cinnamon
Cooking spray
1 cup raspberries or blackberries
1 tablespoon sugar

1. Place the pears, rice and 1 cup milk in a large heavy-gauge skillet. Cook over medium heat until the milk has been almost completely absorbed, about 15 minutes. Add the grape juice and cook until almost dry, 3 to 5 minutes. Stir in the raisins and cinnamon. Add the remaining 2 cups milk, a ladleful at a time, until the rice is tender, 15 to 20 minutes. You may not use all the milk.
2. Preheat the oven to 350°F. Coat four 4-inch-diameter flan rings with cooking spray and place them on a baking sheet also prepared with cooking spray. Fill the rings with the risotto.
3. Bake until the rice is firm, about 20 minutes.
4. Meanwhile, purée the berries and the sugar in a food processor. Strain through a fine sieve to remove the seeds. Place 1 tablespoon purée on each of 4 plates.
5. Remove the risottos from the oven and let cool to room temperature. Remove the rings and center each risotto on the raspberries. Serve immediately.

VARIATIONS: Apples can be used in place of pears.

Aranci al liquore
Oranges Marinated in Cointreau

In Tuscany, this compote is made with blood oranges, which gives it a brilliant red color and slightly tart flavor. Any type of orange can be used in making this completely fat-free dessert.

SERVES 4

TIME:
30 MINUTES
PLUS 1 HOUR
REFRIGERATION

LEVEL: EASY

6 blood oranges, peeled and with pith removed
1 teaspoon honey
1 tablespoon water
¼ teaspoon ground cinnamon
2 (1 x ⅛-inch) strips lemon zest
1 tablespoon grated lemon zest
¼ cup Cointreau
Fresh mint leaves, for garnish

1. Using a sharp knife, separate the orange segments and peel them. Work over a bowl to catch any juice that drips and place each batch of segments into the bowl after peeling.
2. When all the oranges are prepared, pour off the juice, straining it into a small saucepan. Reserve the orange pieces. Add the honey, water, cinnamon, lemon zest strips and grated lemon zest to the juice, and bring to a boil over medium heat until the liquid is reduced by half and the consistency is thick and syrupy, about 3 minutes.
3. Remove the liquid from the heat and discard the lemon zest strips. Stir in the Cointreau and let cool to room temperature.
4. Pour the sauce over the oranges and toss to coat. Cover and chill for at least 1 hour (or up to 24). Return the fruit to room temperature before serving. Arrange on dessert plates and garnish with mint.

VARIATIONS: Any type of orange or mandarin can be used in place of the blood oranges.

Zuppa Inglese alla fragole

SERVES 6

TIME:
30 MINUTES
PLUS 3 HOURS
REFRIGERATION

LEVEL: EASY

Layered trifles are so much a part of Tuscan dessert lore that no one is any longer sure whether the English took the idea from us or we from them (I'm sure at this point I don't have to tell you what most Tuscans would say if asked their opinion on the matter). This delicious and colorful version is made with store-bought angel food cake, which is made with egg whites and, thus, a perfect choice for low-fat diets.

1½ cups fresh or frozen raspberries, stemmed
1½ cups hulled and finely diced strawberries,
½ cup water
½ cup white grape juice
1 tablespoon cornstarch
2 tablespoons light rum
4 cups prepared vanilla pudding, chilled*
1 (10 ounces) angel food cake

1. Reserve ¼ cup total mixed raspberries and strawberries. Place the remainder of the berries in a large, heavy-gauge saucepan along with the water and the grape juice and cook over low heat for 10 minutes, stirring constantly. Pour through a sieve, reserving the liquid. Do not press the fruit through the sieve. Transfer the fruit to a large bowl.
2. Transfer ¼ cup of the liquid to a small saucepan. Stir in the cornstarch until dissolved. Add the remaining liquid and bring to a boil, stirring constantly. Cook until the juice thickens and turns clear, about 5 minutes. Stir in the rum. Pour over the fruit. Toss to coat, cover and refrigerate for 1 hour. Reserve ½ cup fruit for topping.
3. Cut the cake into bite-sized pieces and place half in a straight-sided glass bowl. Spoon half the fruit over the cake. Cover with half the pudding. Repeat the layering, cake, fruit and pudding. Top with the reserved fruit, cover and refrigerate for 2 hours before serving.

* Vanilla pudding can be made with instant mix, regular mix, or it can be commercially prepared and purchased.

MAKE AHEAD: The entire dessert can be made up to 6 hours in advance and stored in a sealed container in the refrigerator until ready to serve.

Torta di polenta e albicocche
Polenta and Apricot Rum Cake

Like risotto, polenta is another of those Tuscan mainstays that are used for everything from appetizers to soups to first course to desserts. This delightful pudding can be made in individual portions using the flan-ring technique in the risotto recipe or in a cake pan as suggested in the following recipe.

3 cups low-fat (1%) milk

1 cup evaporated skim milk

½ cup medium-ground polenta

2 tablespoons acacia or other mild-flavored honey

2 teaspoons vanilla extract

½ cup finely diced dried apricots

¼ cup golden raisins soaked for 20 minutes in ¼ cup light rum

1. Place the milk and evaporated milk in a large, heavy-gauge saucepan and heat to boiling over low-medium heat. Gradually whisk in the polenta and continue whisking until the mixture thickens, 5 to 7 minutes. Add the honey, reduce heat to low and cook for 20 minutes, stirring frequently with a wooden spoon.

2. Remove from heat, stir in the vanilla, apricots, raisins and rum and pour into a 10-inch-diameter springform pan. Tap the pan against a countertop to level the surface of the polenta, and let cool to room temperature. Release the springform, slice and serve.

VARIATIONS: The cake can also be topped with a purée of fresh apricots or served on a pool of apricot purée.

MAKES
ONE 10-INCH
CAKE (10 TO 12
SLICES)

TIME:
40 MINUTES
PLUS COOLING
TIME

LEVEL:
MODERATE

Index

About the Authors

ANNE BIANCHI is a food writer and culinary educator who lives in New York and the Tuscan province of Lucca. She is the owner and Director of the Toscana Saporita Cooking School and Director of Toscana Saporita Food Imports. She has written a number of books, most recently *Solo Verdura: The Complete Guide to Cooking Tuscan Vegetables, Zuppa! Soups from the Italian Countryside* and *From the Tables of Tuscan Women,* all published by Ecco.

SANDRA LOTTI is the co-owner and Managing Director of the Toscana Saporita Cooking School as well as the Italian Director of Toscana Saporita Food Imports. Known throughout Italy for her cookbooks on Tuscan cuisine, Lotti frequently contributes to Italy's most prestigious cooking magazines and also conducts private cooking lessons.